Tombstones of the Irish Born

Cemetery of the Holy Cross
Flatbush, Brooklyn

Joseph M. Silinonte

HERITAGE BOOKS
2006

HERITAGE BOOKS
AN IMPRINT OF HERITAGE BOOKS, INC.

Books, CDs, and more—Worldwide

For our listing of thousands of titles see our website
at
www.HeritageBooks.com

Published 2006 by
HERITAGE BOOKS, INC.
Publishing Division
65 East Main Street
Westminster, Maryland 21157-5026

Copyright © 1994 Joseph M. Silinonte

All rights reserved. No part of this book may be reproduced or transmitted in any form or by any means, electronic or mechanical, including photocopying, recording or by any information storage and retrieval system without written permission from the author, except for the inclusion of brief quotations in a review.

International Standard Book Number: 978-0-7884-0077-0

DEDICATION

This book is dedicated to my parents
Carlo and Eileen O'Neil Silinonte

The tombstone of my great-great-great grandparents

CHARLES AND ANNE SCOTT O'NEIL.

TABLE OF CONTENTS

About the Author	2
Dedication and the O'Neil Tombstone	3
Table of Contents	4
Acknowledgements	5
Foreword	6
"READ THIS FIRST"	7
Map of the Cemetery of the Holy Cross, Brooklyn	8
Tombstone Inscriptions in Alphabetical Order	9
Some Photographs of Tombstones	55
Continuation of Tombstone Inscriptions	72
A Tabulation of Stones by Irish County	107
Deeds of Land Acquisitions	108
A History of the Cemetery	110
"Fight At Edge of Grave"	112

ACKNOWLEDGEMENTS

It would have been almost impossible for a work of this size to be successfully completed by one person. There are a number of people I must thank publicly. John T. Ridge, author and a man well versed in Irish and Irish-American history. B. Ann Moorhouse C. G., F.G.B.S., a genealogist's genealogist. Besides Miss Moorhouse's expertise in various aspects of the field, she is a leader in Irish-American genealogy.

Many thanks to the following: Norman Ringle, M.L.S., Leslie Ogan, M.L.S., Martin Orlian, Judith Walsh, M.L.S., Local History Librarian, Central Branch Grand Army Plaza, Brooklyn.

I must also thank Hiko Fukuda, Mario Valenti, Barry Donavan, Gallina Varon, Helen Adamczuk, Mike Esterov, the German Tourist Office and the waiters at Teresa's Restaurant, Brooklyn Heights, Joe Murphy and John Barton of The McManus Funeral Home, Brooklyn.

Special thanks to Maria McDade for processing the data. To John Becker of Becker Associates, Concord, Ontario for his work in helping me to understand the printing/publishing business. His generosity will always be remembered.

Finally to where it all began, Holy Cross Cemetery. Thanks to Amie, Betty, Eddie, Jimmy, Lillian and Walter. The biggest thank you goes to Susan Sciannameo Borek. Not only has she helped me during the past decade, she has also put up with me during this past year putting this book together.

Brooklyn, New York　　　　　　　　　　　　　　　　Joseph M. Silinonte
　　　　　　　　　　　　　　　　　　　　　　　　　August 1992

FOREWORD

Copying tombstone inscriptions is nothing new. However, except for smaller churchyards/graveyards, copying inscriptions has not been popular among genealogists in New York City. This book is the first large scale attempt. There are more than 500,000 people interred in Holy Cross Cemetery. We must remember, everything in New York City is big, including cemeteries. Calvary Cemetery which opened shortly before Holy Cross, has close to two and three-quarter million people interred there.

For Irish-Catholics the tombstones may be the only source where the place of origin in Ireland may be found. My decision to copy the inscriptions of the Irish-born was not made overnight. In 1981 I went to the cemetery to see if there was a stone over the graves of my great-great-great grandparents Charles and Anne Scott O'Neil. In section Plots, range 12 on the edge of the road I found the grave of Charles and Anne. (A photograph is reproduced on the Dedication page.) The plot was bought by Charles August 14, 1855 for $38.00. After reading the stone I felt a delirium only someone tracing their family tree could understand. Not only did the inscription give the county but also the parish in Ireland. I learned that Killeshandra was the only parish in county Cavan which still had its 1841 census returns available.

Using the 1841 census I discovered that Anne Scott O'Neil's parents were John and Catherine Scott. They lived in the Townland of Drumnawal. John had died in 1838 at the age of 44. A sister of Anne's, Elizabeth, died in 1840 aged 2. There was a brother, John and two sisters, Margaret and Sarah. After more research, I learned that Anne arrived alone in New York City, October 16, 1843. Her mother, Catherine and the remaining family, arrived May 27, 1844. As of Charles O'Neil, after eleven years of research I found through a different source, that he was born in county Leitrim, the son of John and Margaret Clark O'Neil.

    I hope that you too find your family among those listed here.

"READ THIS FIRST"

1. An inscription was copied when there was at least one name listed with an Irish birthplace. All the information pertaining to the other names on the stone was also copied.

2. Because the information is "written in stone" that does not mean that the information is accurate. Many stones were put up years after the first burial in the plot. When it came time for inscriptions, the surviving family member had to rely on their memory for vital statistics.

3. You may find information on a stone which will not be found on cemetery records. This is particularly true for early records. At the same time, there may be people interred in a plot but their name may not be inscribed on the stone. On early records, children were many times not listed under their own names. For instance, instead of two year old Catherine O'Neil being listed on the "plot card" with the date of her burial, the entry may read "child of Mr. O'Neil". The child's burial usually went under the name of the owner of the plot. What causes confusion is that if Mr. O'Neil's niece (i.e.) Maryanne Scott was buried in his plot, she would be listed as "child of Mr. O'Neil".

4. Since each stone had various pieces of information for each name, the same is true for the format of this book. Stones usually have name, date of death and birthplace in Ireland. Other stones may also give date of birth, relationships and age. The age is usually given after the date of death and immediately prior to the place of birth in Ireland, if the place is given.

5. The inscriptions were not copied word for word. If they had been copied word for word, this book would be as thick as "War and Peace". For example, many stones begin at the top "Erected by Charles O'Neill in memory of his beloved wife Anne O'Neill". In many instances, the name of the person who erected the stone appears twice. Once at the top (for what I call "billing") and then again when the information pertaining to the erector of the stone is inscribed. To eliminate the use of the same name twice, you will see "By". "By" is the name of the erector of the stone with usually a relationship to a person or persons above his or her name. Included on the same line with the erector's name will be the vital statistics for that person.

Instead of the above "Erected by Charles O'Neill ... it reads here:
    Anne O'Neill   3/25/1861   35-9-21   Killashandra, Cavan
    By husband Charles   3/29/1812 - 2/16/1887

6. Some monument dealers inscribed the place names in Ireland the way those names sounded. For instance "Teeholland, Cavan" is actually "Tehallan, Cavan". A number of books were consulted to solve such problems.

7. If a "?" appears after an entry, that usually means that there was a problem reading the inscription. Many stones are totally illegible due to age and pollution. Stone rubbings are not permitted in Holy Cross.

8. Concerning ages. After a date of death you may see for example 35-9-21. That means thirty-five years, nine months, twenty-one days. When you see an age ending in "0", or no days, that was usually placed by me. This was done to prevent me from having to go back to see if I missed the third set of digits (days).

9. Be cautious when reading relationships. For example the stone may read "Their Children" and then list a number of names. Sometimes it is difficult to know when the final child's name is given and when another relative or friend's name begins. The first three names may be those of the children. The fourth and fifth names may be cousins or nieces and nephews. Consider this carefully.

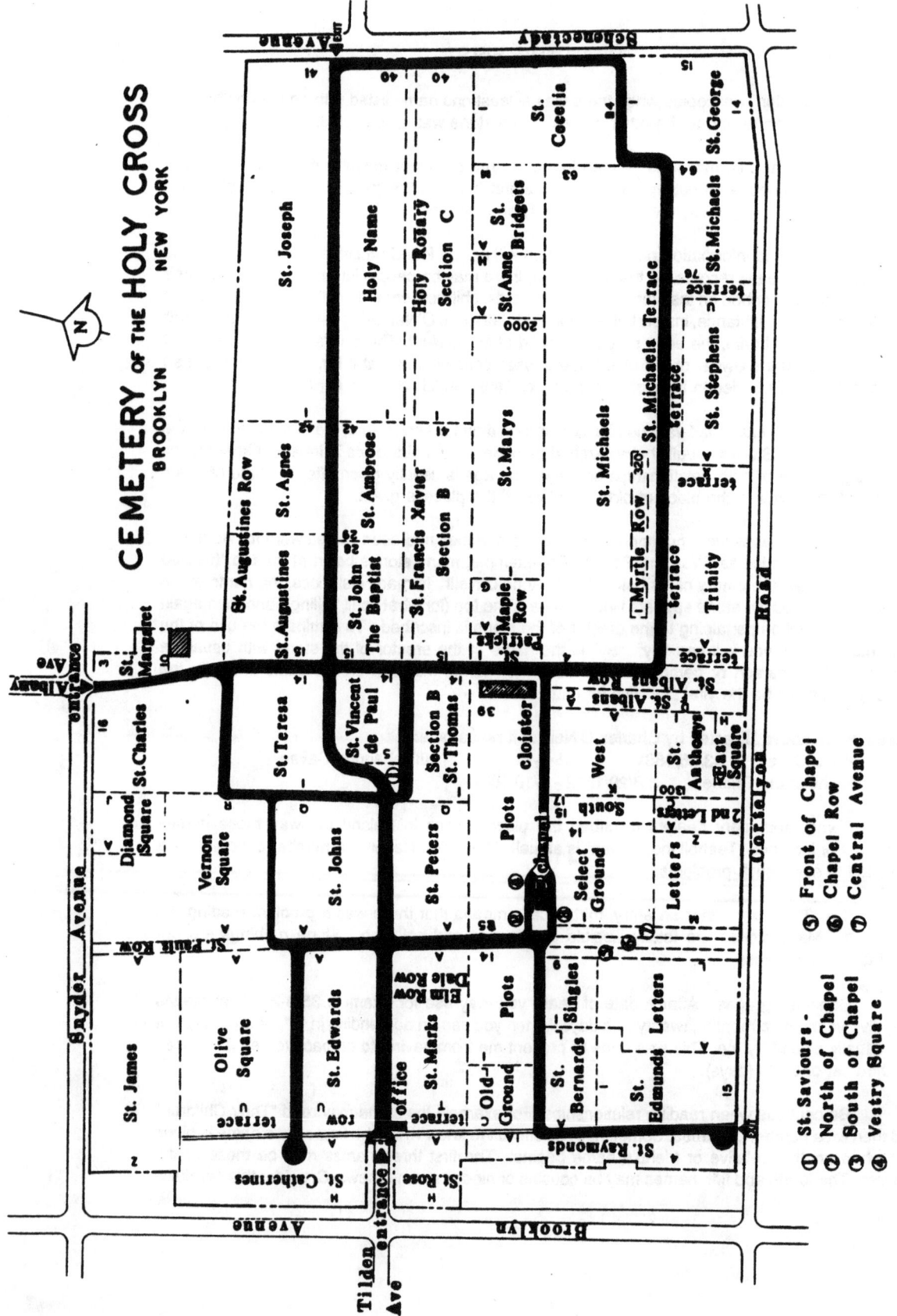

Adam
Hugh, 1869, 77?, Donegal

Ahearn
Mary, 1860-1/8/1922, Kildare
By husband Dennis, 7/8/1932

Ahearn
William, 12/27/1913, 41, Waterford
Catherine, 12/3/1945
Hannah Newell, 1876-1964

Ahearne
Mary, 4/7/1859, 23, Waterford
Patrick, 4/19/1904, Waterford

Allen
John T., 9/11/1989
See, Boland, Johanna, 2/1/1896, 53

Allen
Catherine, 2/5/1886, 46, Ballyhaunis, Mayo
By husband Patrick, 4/11/1893
Their children: Kate, Ellie, Thomas, Patrick died young

Allen
Frances, 1/31/1896, 72, Mayo
By husband Patrick

Anderson
Maria R.J., 11/11/1891, 55
Robert J., 11/16/1899, 57, Cookstown, Tyrone
See Rogers, Bridget, 4/15/1891, 65

Anderson
Matthew, 9/8/1873, 52, Meath
By wife Margaret, 11/14/1905, 83

Anglin
Redmond J., 4/14/1855-3/29/1912, Wexford

Archibold
Michael, 12/15/1919, 64 Dublin
See Ryan, Rose McDonnell 11/19/1916, 54

Armstrong
Ellen, 7/31/1881?, 50, Dublin
By husband James

Armstrong
Mary, 2/5/1892, Longford

Askin
William, 12/23/1891, 72, Derry
Wife Ellen, 11/21/1904, 71
Daughter-in-law Ella 10/11/1881, 29
Thomas F., 1904-1966
Clara, 1916
David J., 1943
William J., 1968

Attley
Margaret, 10/2/1879, 33-7-0, Dublin
By husband John, 11/24/1909, 65
Julia C., 1/26/1898, 6-7-25
John, 2/29/1885, 2

Autrop
Margaret, 2/20/1878, 69, Limerick
By husband John, 1/6/1882, 70, Copenhagen, Denmark

Bagley
Thomas, 10/10/1850
Joseph, 4/4/1861
Catherine, 1/5/1863
Michael P., 10/26/1867
Eugene, 3/7/1869
By parents William & Elizabeth both of Edenderry, Kings

O DEATH THAT WOULD NO LONGER SPARE
THE SONS THAT PARENTS LOVED SO DEAR
AND WHO IN CHRIST HAVE FALLEN ASLEEP
AND LET THEIR PARENTS HERE TO WEEP
MOURN NOT FOR US OUR PARENTS DEAR
WE ARE NOT DEAD BUT SLEEPING HERE

Bannahan
James, 11/12/1893, 38, Roscommon
By wife Mary A.

Bannen
Bridget, 4/5/1856, Ardagh, Longford

Bannon
Frank F., 1901-1955
Theresa V., 1903-1960
See Gallagher, Francis, 12/26/1901

Barclay
Margaret, 11/4/1908, 75, Newend?. Cork
By husband James, 10/31/1914, 80, Kildoagh, Templeport, Cavan
Their children: not inscribed
James, U.S.S., Quaker City, fireman, Civil War

Barr
James, 4/1879, 70
John, 3/1880, 38, File?, Donegal

Barrett
Charles W., 11/19/1899
Catherine Dalton Barrett, 2/11/1937
Charles H. Barrett, 5/18/1893 - 3/28/1955
Harriett Barrett, 2/2/1902-2/10/1983
See Dalton, Winifred 4/20/1883, 51

Barrett
Mary A., 7/13/1934
See Merrick, Mary C., 1/29/1899, 63

Barrett
Mary, 9/12/1926, Ballybunion, Kerry
Eileen Carey, 1921-1977
Tim McMahon, 1907-1953
Margaret, 1907-1963
Sgt. John, 1907-1983

Barrington
Patrick, 7/3/1901, 73, Ennistymon, Clare
By wife Mary, 9/10/1908, Glenmacoffer, Tyrone
Anna Kerrigan, 2/18/1972
John J., 4/30/1988

Barry
Ann, 2/21/1882, 82, Monaghan
See Boyle, Margaret

Barry
John, 2/25/1865, 59, Cork
Wife Margaret, 1/20/1890, 70, Carrickmacross, Monaghan

Barry
Maria, 9/15/1882, 48
By husband John W. 4/27/1897 65, Ballinvella, Lismore, Waterford
Their children Edward F., 10/3/1881, 25
Katie P., 6/4/1885, 19
James C, 11/5/1890, 22
Maria L., 4/21/1892, 26
John W. Jr., 3/3/1894, 35
Daniel P., 5/30/1860-10/15/1922
Catherine E. wife of Daniel P., 1/1/1859-8/19/1914
Timothy T., 5/29/1935

Basil
Theresa L., 7/1878-5/1961
See Grennan, Patrick, 2/13/1910, 46

Bates
Ellen Mahon, 7/6/1880
Her dau. Ellen
See Mahon, Patrick, 8/20/1860, 70

Battam
Jeremiah, 7/1/1894, 68, Newtown, Shandrum, Cork
By wife Ellen, 7/4/1896, 64

Behrend
Catherine E., 1886-1962
Emil, 1887-1971
See Leonard, John, 5/12/1888

Beirne
Ambrose, 3/6/1864, 30, Leitrim
By wife Catherine
Mary, 5/27/1861, 25

Bennett
Robert, 1/22/1874, Tallow, Waterford
Margaret, 7/12/1887, Tallow, Waterford
By Catherine Bennett

Bennett
Willie, died young
Johnnie, 12/20/1892, 6-8-11
See Mowen, John, 3/21/1891, 49

Benson
Ann V., 1/30/1982
See Conway, John, 12/29/1897, 35

Bergen
Bridget, 2/4/1894, 97, Galmory, Kilkenny
Fanny, 12/20/1907, 79
John J. McCue, 1875-1945
Pierre M. O'Connor, 1876-1956
Mary E. O'Connor, 1880-1976

Bermingham
Maria, 7/27/1903, 63, Philipstown, Kings
By sister Eliza Leslie
Joseph Leslie, 4/10/1893
John S. Leslie, 11/22/1927
John S. Leslie, Jr., 7/9/1937, 47
Eliza B., 12/8/1939
Myra McDonald
Thomas McDonald
Margaret McDonald

Berren
Mary, 7/5/1919, 73, Roscommon
Walter J. Collins, 6/12/1946
Ellen J., 9/9/1955
Marie E., 10/4/1962
Wm. H. Lindeman, 9/4/1964
Anna M., 12/6/1967
Bridget A. Carley, 1/15/1947

Bevans
Sgt. James, 1900-1948
Marie, 1903-1979
See Connell, Michael, 3/26/1895

Bierne
John, 6/26/1897, 61, Roscommon
Wife May, 5/12/1898, 63, Roscommon
By dau. Mary McGowan
Joseph Bierne, 12/12/1896, 17, Roscommon
Hanora Bierne, 7/26/1907, 28, Roscommon

Billish
Ann, 2/1855, Monaghan
By Margaret Billish

Birchall
Fanny, 8/23/1900, 45, Carrick-on-Shannon
By son Walter, 12/5/1934

Birmingham
Maryann, 7/11/1865, 52
Edward, 2/28/1859, 87
By husband Edward, Kings

Bittel
Mary, 3/25/1884-5/28/1928
Frank, 5/19/1884-1/23/1953
See McCarthy, Patrick, 7/28/1885, 50

Blackhahn
Mary, 9/10/1910, 27
See Gordon, Margaret, 3/19/1899, 41-10-0

Blackwell
Mary, 7/2/1901, Clare
By sister Catherine, 9/14/1924

Blake
Charles, 12/28/1850, 18
By parents William and May of, Main, Westmeath
William, 3/29/1884, 38
Ann, 2/25/1890, 51
Catherine, 8/26/1921, 87

Blake
James, 3/10/1885, 66, Dublin
By wife Catherine, 11/8/1892, 62, Roscommon
A. McDonnell, 1980

Bogan
Bridget, 5/18/1892, 57
By husband Walter, 9/15/1835-9/8/1902, Enniscorthy, Wexford
Edward J., 7/7/1950
Ella M., 5/12/1951
Walter, J., 2/18/1959

Boland
Johanna, 2/1/1896, 53, Doon, Limerick
Husband John, 7/8/1919, 77, Cappamore, Limerick
Son Johnney, 8/7/1891, 10
Johnnie & Rose Children of
James and Catherine Boland, 7/19/1893, 6 months
John T. Allen, 9/11/1989

Boland
John, 7/18/1898, 75, Glasson, Westmeath
By wife Bridget
James S., 2/12/1900, 39

Bonner
Hannah, 1892-1967
See McLaughlin, Neil, 10/25/1918

Bonner
Neil, 11/14/1958
See McCann, John, 6/19/1896, 35

Bourdy
Margaret
See Moore, Thomas & Mary

Bourke
Michael, 1878, Golden, Tipperary
By wife Ellen, 9/1893, 54
Bridget, 2/28/1881, 13-3-0
John, 7/15/1897, 30

Boylan
Bridget, 1/18/1892, Colrey, Westmeath
By husband John, 4/26/1913, 74

Boyle
Arthur, 2/28/1896, Carlingford, Louth
By wife Elizabeth, 12/23/1927
Son Francis H., 1/12/1898
Randolph, 9/6/1914
Arthur J., 7/13/1968
Mary F., 2/2/1985

Boyle
Margaret, 2/15/1871, Tedavnet, Monaghan
By husband Edward, 8/12/1881, 76
Ann Barry, 2/21/1882, 82, Monaghan

Boyle
Owen, 3/10/1904, 65
See Scully, Dennis, 12/10/1882, 69

Boyle
Rose, 5/14/1875, 61, Legan?, Longford

Boyle
Roseanne, 8/27/1890, 75, Moville, Donegal

Boyle
Sarah, 1879-1955
Joseph, 1924-1966
John, 1881-1966
Anna, 1921-1986
See McDavitt, Anne, 1/11/1885, 35

Boyle
Thomas, 12/7/1944, 70
Mary, 7/18/1946, 75
See Stack, John, 11/23/1907, 49

Bradley
James, 5/27/1881, 60, Meath
By dau. Margaret

Bradley
James, 8/21/1816-10/3/1892, Donegal
Ellen, 11/24/1898, 76
John J., 7/20/1908, 47

Bradley
Mary, 2/27/1883, 75, Redcastle, Donegal

Bradley
Patrick, 1/23/1927, Bardagh Glen, Moville, Donegal
By wife Jean, 2/12/1974, Moville, Donegal

Brady
Anne, 2/13/1898, 60, Cavan
Bridget, 2/22/1900, 62

Brady
Annie Smith, 3/25/1913, 23, Virginia, Cavan
By husband John

Brady
Bernard, Granard, Longford
Mary, Granard, Longford
dau. Annie, Granard, Longford
Margaret, 10/27/1922
Ellie Fallon, 1868-1937

Brady
Francis, Clonbroney, Longford
Other family not listed
Thomas J. Curran, 10/9/1939
Anna M. Curran, 12/8/1961

Brady
Hugh, 2/10/1914, Cavan
By wife Bridget
Their son John, 4/15/1926
Her brother Michael Bray, 10/30/1901

Brady
John, 5/7/1870, 34, Killan, Cavan
Dau. Mary, 4/15/1872
Catherine, 12/14/1874
Margaret A., 9/20/1884, 18

Brady
John, 1/14/1902, 80, Ballyatherland, Donegal
His cousin Ellen Furey, 3/13/1901, 61, Doorinpoint, Mount Charles, Donegal
Her granddau. Mamie Furey 1/23/1901 16

Brady
Kate, 6/26/1877, 32
See Barrett, John, 6/14/1895

Brady
Rose A., 2/28/1870, 19
See Reilly, Mary, 4/7/1886

Brady
Thomas, Longford
By Margaret

Braithwate
Kathryn P., 1889-1954
See Murphy, Sarah, 1/7/1910

Bray
John, 5/5/1858, 37, Kildare
By son John, 3/12/1898, 45
Margaret, 3/21/1899, 74

Bray
John, 7/29/1895, 66
By wife Ellen, 4/12/1901, 75
Son William, 9/1/1896, 33
John Jr. Eldest son of John & Ellen, 1/16/1901, 39-6-11, Cork
William Lynch, 11/1/1850-3/28/1918
John J. Lynch, 9/14/1883-3/8/1919
Elizabeth mother of John J. 6/28/1860-6/12/1927
Joseph Bray, 6/1/1870
Mary Bray, 5/24/1871, 4-4-0
Thomas G. Fleetwood, 2/18/1936
Josephine T. Lynch, 8/30/1942
Fred Goodwin, 5/1/1884-10/26/1959
Ellen Lynch Goodwin, 5/2/1894-7/4/1975
Walter G. Carlson, 2/17/1908-7/6/1986

Bray
Michael, 10/30/1901
See Brady, Hugh, 2/10/1914

Bree
Martin, 1852-1936
See Brown, Ellen, 9/27/1913, 70

Breen
Mary, 12/4/1895, 52, Grandford, Wexford
By sister Ann Graham

Breen
Thomas, 9/8/1898, 59, Wexford
Margaret, 12/27/1914, 82
James A. Murray, 1855-1923
Alice, 1860-1946
Thomas, 8/25/1876, 2-2-12
Frank J., 1898-1968
Joan M., 1903-1987

Brennan
Michael, 10/10/1874, 22-5-0, Roscommon
By sister Catherine Brennan, 12/25/1911
Her niece Mary Ellen Sarles

Brennan
Michael, 6/23/1891-12/15/1920, Ballinamuck, Longford
William P., 1/17/1943
Margaret, 1894-1980
See Coggy, Mary, 10/1/1917

Brennan
Thomas, 2/17/1887, 73, Coolmanagh, Carlow
By wife Anne Byrne, 12/19/1894, 79

Brennen
Bridget, 4/23/1881, 48, Longford
By husband Patrick, Longford
Children Mary and Josie who died young
James, 1893-1972
William V., 1897-1977

Brennen
Owen, 9/18/1871?, 54, Rathkenny, Meath
By wife Sarah

Breslin
Bridget, 3/19/1912
By husband Patrick
Her sister Anna Murray, 3/12/1917, 49, Ballyduffy, Roscommon

Breslin
Mary Jane, 6/28/1906, 71
By husband Patrick, 5/19/1914, 78, Moville, Donegal
Their children: Hannah, 5/8/1877, 2-5-0
George P., 4/23/1881, 3-6-0

Brett
Patrick, 4/3/1897, 25, City of Waterford
Maurice, 9/20/1906, 44, City of Waterford
By their sister Margaret Doyle
Maurice's children Irene and Walter died young
Margaret Geiger Doyle, 9/2/1948

Brew
Johanna, 7/31/1906, Tulla, Clare
By sister Annie A. Hartigan
Wife of Thomas Hartigan, 6/20/1912, Tulla, Clare

Bridgett
Anastasia, 3/20/1866 64-3-0, Paulstown, Kilkenny
By husband John, 3/7/1875
Son Nicholas, 3/18/1850 13-6-0
John Jr., 3/21/1891 42
William, 3/19/1892 65
Margaret, wife of William 11/6/1903 64

Briody
Johannah, 1/16/1884, 32
See Foohey, John, 12/15/1861, 35

Broderick
Margaret 11/1/1879, Tulla?, Clare
By husband John
Their son Joseph 12/22/1872

Broderick
Mary, 4/3/1918, Longford

Brolly
Mary, 1/10/1900, 75, Derry

Brophy
John, 12/1871, Kilkenny
Mary, 1/16/1881, Kilkenny
By dau. Julia Gerety
Mary E. Healy, 12/20/1896

Browers
William Died at sea, 1880, 42
Joseph F. Co.K. N.Y. Vol. 1870 - 1939
See Rossiters, Joseph, 4/1/1915, 71

Brown
Ann E., 4/13/1968
See McGreal, Michael, 12/15/1908, 47

Brown
Ellen, 12/21/1873 29, Whitechurch, Waterford
Joseph, 5/13/1868
Alice, 7/29/1869
Ellen, 8/24/1871
James

Brown
Ellen, 9/27/1913, 70
By husband Robert, 1/13/1918, Sligo
Martin Bree, 1852-1936

Brown
James, 10/31/1869-5/27/1891, 21-6-22
Patrick, 12/25/1899, 70, Tyrone

Brown
John, 5/25/1877, 22, Sligo

Brown
John, 3/21/1905, 77, Roundwood, Wicklow
Wife Elizabeth, 1/19/1889, 60, Roundwood, Wicklow
Dau. Mary McPartland, 9/29/1891, Roundwood, Wicklow
Her children Eddie and Mamie and cousin Katie Murray died young

Brown
Julia, 2/27/1899, 54, Bantry Bay, Cork
By husband Charles E., 5/17/1902
Josephine, 3/23/1900

Brown
Michael, 8/10/1893, 67, Youghal, Cork
By wife Margaret, 6/17/1915, Castlemartyr, Cork
Their son Maurice, 6/25/1888, 22

Brown
William, 7/4/1862, 53, Callan, Kilkenny
By wife Ellen, 5/18/1884, 70
Dau. Catherine, 6/1/1877, 21
Patrick Brown, husband of Elizabeth Brown Connors 2/28/1899, 48
Elizabeth Brown Connors, 9/25/1934

Bryson
Maria A., 3/19/1914, 58, Galway
By husband James, 1/24/1855-4/3/1920, Derry
George, 11/27/1914
Their children who died in infancy John and Agnes

Bulridge
Mary Fallon, 4/8/1929
See Fallon, Annie, 10/26/1895, 26

Bukouski
John J., 12/18/1892-11/8/1920
See McNamara, Bridget, 3/22/1882, 70

Bulger
Michael, 12/19/1886, 60, Wexford
Children: Dennis, 1/24/1869, 10 months
Daniel, 12/27/1862, 3-1-0
Wife Eleanor, 8/3/1911, 81

Burke
Celia, 3/21/1892, 39, Aughrim, Roscommon
By husband Peter

Burke
Celia, 12/13/1931, Mayo
Joseph F. Finnerty, 1886-1970
Mary N., 1905-1984

Burke
Deborah, 7/29/1885, 56, Kanturk, Cork
By niece Mary Daly
Peter Watters, 3/18/1888, 35, Castleblaney, Monaghan
His wife Mary Watters, 4/2/1891, 29, Kanturk, Cork

Burke
James, 1/23/1881, 70, Fethard, Tipperary
By wife Catherine

Burke
John, 6/1/1883, 47, Limerick
By wife Margaret, 5/28/1909, 67
Children: Mary, Annie, Johny
James F., 9/27/1912

Burke
John F., 5/15/1918
See Quinn, John, 3/15/1883, 64

Burke
Margaret, 1/3/1893, 8 years-28 days
By parents:
Thomas, 5/4/1893, 50, Mayo
Mary, 8/14/1939, 96
Also Esther Burke and her child Mary

Burke
Mary, 10/6/1873
Minnie, 9/3/1882
By their husband Thomas F., 1/1/1859 - 11/17/1889
Capt. James Burke, 10/12/1905, Limerick

Burke
Peter, 3/6/1904, Galway
By wife Anna, 1859-1932
Howard J., 1900-1942

Burke
Peter J., Carrickedmond, Longford
By wife Catherine E., 1/6/1958
Their son Corporal Luke P. Burke who died in the service
of his country at Spartanburg, South Carolina
Her sister Mary A. Campbell, 2/16/1904
Loretta K. Burke, 4/22/1984

Burke
William, 10/9/1888, 54, Tallow, Waterford

Burns
Andrew, 7/10/1905, 58, Wicklow
Laura B. Vasaturo, 1977-1979

Burns
Ellen, 1/18/1917, 74, Tipperary
By husband James, 4/30/1925, 76

Burns
Ellen, 9/12/1853, Monaghan
Lucy A. Byrne dau., 5/1899

Burns
James, 8/16/1894, 68, Stonehall, Limerick
By wife Catherine, 10/15/1900, 72, Rockhill, Limerick
Their son James J., 12/3/1898, 40

Burns
John, 3/23/1890, 55, Rathfarnham, Dublin

Burns
John, 5/25/1902, Wicklow
By wife Bridget

Burns
Luke, 4/7/1889, 34, Westmeath
Wife Catherine, 10/28/1912, Drumhand? Cavan
By their son James J.

Burns
Mary Agnes, 3/24/1878-4/9/1940
See Haire, Andrew J., 7/6/1910

Busby
James, 5/1/1840-3/12/1892, Enniskillen, Fermanagh
By wife Ellen
Her mother Ann Leonard, 2/10/1882, 66
Her brother Peter Leonard, 2/8/1892, 42
Her children: Annie, Catherine, John, Joseph, Elizabeth, Agnes
Mary and Gertrude died young

Bussinger
Marie C., 1/1/1918-4/1/1990
See McCarthy, Patrick, 7/28/1885, 50

Butler
Ann, 12/27/1883, 40-8-10, Ballymore, Westmeath
By husband John, 5/15/1897, 63

Butler
Catherine, 11/26/1903, 25
By mother Mary
Patrick, 12/3/1910, 63, Titcomb?, Kilkenny

Butler
James, 1864-12/31/1907, Dublin
2 babies Mary and Rose Ellen
Margaret J., 1862-3/15/1911, Meath
Brentwood L. Albertson, 4/12/1943
Agnes P. Albertson, 12/10/1953

Butler
James H., 7/17/1927, Clare
Wife Delia, 10/15/1929
See Connolly, John, 5/13/1885, 48

Butler
John, 7/16/1907, 48, New Ross, Wexford

Butler
Patrick Wm., 7/9/1908, City of Dublin
Wife Margaret, 9/26/1880
Their children, William, Annie, Richard
Bridget T., 2/22/1911
Ann Dalton, 6/1884

Butler
Thomas J.
Margaret M
See Ryan, Michael, 11/1/1918, 35

Byrne
Dominick, 3/24/1849, 45, Kiltullagh, Roscommon
Julia, 11/29/1863, 68, Kiltullagh, Roscommon
By daughter Bridget

Byrne
Edward, 9/1/1887, 55, Wexford
By wife Ann
John A. MacKinnon, 5/21/1964
Anne Byrne MacKinnon, 9/6/1986

Byrne
Edward J., 11/20/1939
Kathryn J., 6/19/1966
See Flynn, Catherine, 2/28/1907, 47

Byrne
Ellen, 6/8/1836-12/21/1899, Kingscourt, Cavan

Byrne
James, 7/18/1879, Wexford
By wife Bridget, 9/16/1828 - 3/26/1914, Wexford
Her father James O'Connor, 1/1852, Wexford
Her mother Margaret O'Connor, 11/1860, Wexford
Her dau. Mary Scallan, 9/1/1866, Wexford
Her brother John O'Connor, 11/22/1865, Wexford
Her sister Mary O'Connor, 3/11/1903, Wexford

Byrne
John T. 3rd, 1926-1971
See Merrick, Mary C., 1/29/1899, 63

Byrne
Margaret, 12/25/1907, 47, Dundalk, Louth
By husband Patrick, 1/14/1920
Mammie Engelhart, 9/7/1914

Byrne
Mary, 6/3/1917, 24, Bohola, Mayo
John, 4/5/1959
B. Roache Byrne, 1886-1988, Bohola

Byrne
Mary A., 4/18/1914, Cherrywood, Dublin
Our friend Nellie Noonan, 1/31/1915, Dublin

Byrne
Patrick, 3/24/1893, 48, Seven Churches, Wicklow
By wife Mary
His brother Dennis, 12/9/1888, 32

Byrne
Patrick J., 3/5/1901, 62, Wexford
By wife Julia, 9/7/1909, 75
Infant granddaughters: Margaret and Maria O'Neill

Byrne
Rose, 8/11/1885, 69, Inver, Donegal
By husband Martin, 5/20/1902, 83
Daniel J., 1850-1905
Mary C., 1874-1950
Rose M., 1877-1957
Rose Lantry, 1893-1962
Nellie A. wife of John H. Farrel, 7/20/1926, 69
Martin Farrel, 1920-1944
Grace, 1947
Helen, 1956
Joseph F., 1952
Martin B., 1955
Anna R., 1959
and the Cloonan Family

Byrne
Stephen, 5/11/1873, 60, Carlow
Wife Maryanne, 3/5/1891, 72, Dublin City

Eyrnes
Cathorine, 8/7/1868, 50, Roscommon
By sister Elizabeth

Byrns
Mary, 10/18/1883, 53, Ballinakill, Queens
By husband Patrick
Grandchild, Mary Gallagher, 4 months

Caffrey
John J., 5/28/1915, Ardleny, Cavan
By brother James and sister Catherine

Cahill
Catherine, 3/30/1885, 59, Thurles, Tipperary
By husband Patrick, 1/10/1887, 64

Cahill
Daniel, 10/2/1896, 57
Wife Ellen, 3/30/1922
Margaret, 9/25/1876-2/2/1945
See Hanley, Thomas, 2/10/1889

Caldwell
Thomas, 3/28/1883, 49, Mayo
Catherine, 10/12/1902, 58, Roscommon
By son William J.

Callaghan
Bridget, 8/9/1892, 70, O'Callaghan's Mills, Clare
By dau. Bridget Callaghan
Her niece Bridget, 6/10/1893, 3
Maggie, 6/11/1895, 10 months
Cornelius, 11/7/1896, 33, O'Callaghan's Mills, Clare

Callaghan
Patrick, 2/6/1892, 68
His wife Mary, 2/3/1887, 60, Tralee, Kerry

Callahan
Mary, Westmeath
James, Westmeath
Mary's sister Ann Flaherty, Westmeath
Edward Flaherty, Westmeath

Callahan
Michael, 1/20/1888, 61, Lismore, Waterford
By wife mary, 8/28/1897, 62

Campbell
Bridget, 6/29/1882, 63, Ballyshannon, Donegal
By husband John

Campbell
J.J., 1873-1938
See Noonan, John, 3/5/1895, 65

Campbell
Margaret, 2/1/1862, 34, Louth
By husband Michael

Campbell
Margaret, 5/12/1944, 54
See Dunleavy, Thomas L., 5/7/1907, 38

Campbell
Mary A., 2/16/1904
See Burke, Peter J.

Campbell
Robert, 1861, Granard, Longford
By wife Ann, 8/27/1880
Also his mother Ellen, 74

Campbell
Robert, 1/10/1864, 56, Fermanagh
Margaret, 10/10/1875, 65, Cavan
Robert Jr., 1/19/1882, 46, Fermanagh
By son and brother Thomas Campbell

Campbell
Thomas, 1/31/1898, 63, Clonsilla, Dublin

Campbell
Thomas F., 4/21/1890, 32
By wife Kate, 11/16/1890, Louth
John Coulson, 4/9/1912
Katherine Campbell Coulson, wife of John, 7/1/1914

Campbell
Thomas Francis, 4/11/1918, 74
See Ward, Peter, 1/17/1886, 78

Canning
Robert, 3/3/1893, 25, Donegal
Bernard, 7/6/1893, 27, Donegal
By brother Patrick, 6/12/1907, 50
His wife Catherine, 3/7/1906, 48, Donegal

Canning
Samuel, 3/1/1891, 69, Donegal
By wife Isabella, 5/23/1905
Dau. Bella Campbell, 5/7/1892, 32
Son S.J. Canning, 6/15/1899, 34
Rose, 7/13/1911
Rev. Francis J., 5/16/1935

Cantwell
John, 5/16/1918, 71, Tully, Kings
Elizabeth, 10/12/1923
Frank P., 2/15/1924

Canwan
Mary Maxwell 10/21/1870, 50, Tipperary
Wife of John, 12/22/1885, 69
Mother of John H., 12/12/1876, 34
Sister of Thomas, James and John

Carberry
James, 7/9/1876, 45, Kill, Westmeath
By son John
Sister of John, Ellen, 3/27/1883, 31
Brother of John, Patrick 10/25/1886, 23-8-0
Brother of John, Michael 12/22/1888, 23

Carberry
Julia, 6/8/1867, Westmeath
By husband John

Carberry
Rose, 5/28/1896, 26, Westmeath
By sisters Bridget and Mary

Carboy
Ellen, 1848 -, 10/23/1892, Dunkerrin/Duncoarn, Tipperary
John, 1836 -, 1/15/1901, Kings
Dau. Julia, 7/19/1900
2 children died young

Carey
Bridget, 1874-1922
William A., 1870-1958
See Feeney, Ann, 9/19/1862, 48-7-0

Carey
Eileen, 1921-1977
See Barrett, Mary, 9/2/1926

Carey
Margaret O'Hara, 9/1/1964
Harry W. O'Hara, 11/15/1954
Harriett, 2/14/1972
See O'Hara, wife of James, 4/1872

Carley
Bridget A., 1/15/1947
See Berren, Mary, 7/5/1919, 73

Carlin
Alice, 5/13/1920, Mullaghoran, Cavan
By sister Bridget Maguire, 6/7/1925, 81

Carlis
Catherine, 6/22/1928, 79
See Coen, Patrick, 8/6/1924, 85?

Carlon
Charles, 5/1885, 88, Mullagh, Cavan
Mary, 1/1880, 78, Mullagh, Cavan
By dau. Rose Carlon,
Her sister Bridget, 11/1912, 84, Mullagh, Cavan
Her niece Mary Sommers, 4/16/1890, 31, Mullagh, Cavan
Her nephew Patrick Geary, 4/25/1917, 38, Glenfin, Donegal

Carlson
Gustave, 4/19/1926, 39
Irene V., 4/6/1976, 84
See McNeely, Anthony Roe, 10/24/1891

Carlson
Walter G., 2/17/1908-7/6/1986
See Bray, John, 7/29/1895, 66

Carmody
Hanora, 4/20/1904, Kilkee, Clare
See Turner, Peter E., 12/5/1908

Carney
Elizabeth, 3/14/1939, Tyrone
For parents and brother Henry
Catherine Raymond, 10/13/1939
James H. Raymond, 3/9/1952

Carney
Joseph B., 1910-1952
See Dunlap, Alice, 7/22/1886, 63

Carney
Margaret, 10/22/1881, 74, Donegal
By son Edward, 85
His wife Catherine, 10/17/889
Margaret
Ellen, 2/9/1930, 62

Carney
Margaret, 6/6/1911, 43, Roscommon
By husband Michael, 5/11/1939

Carney
Mary, 2/22/1888, 77, Drumkeerin, Leitim
By dau. Ann
Ann's brother Patrick, 10/20/1890, Drumkeerin, Leitrim

Carney
Patrick, 9/17/1876, 63, Ballymore, Westmeath
By wife Rosie E. Carney

Carolan
Edward, 1/2/1902, 58, Waterloo, Cavan
By wife Annie
Son Edward died young

Carraghar
Ellen, 1/23/1890, 53, Cootehill, Cavan
By husband Patrick, 10/3/1893, 55

Carring
Mary, 4/18/1893, City of Dublin
By dau. Catherine Claffey, 11/18/1910, City of Dublin
Her sister Dorothy Carring 10/24/1886, City of Dublin
Her brother Thomas Carring 2/19/1903, City of Dublin

Carroll
Alice F., 4/20/1916, 27, Dungarvan, Waterford
By husband John

Carroll
Annie, 2/7/1916
By husband John
Children: James and William died in infancy
Patrick, 12/13/1916, Kings
Marie C. Zwick, 1923-1980
Members of the Ryan family

Carroll
Hannah C., 2/10/1913
Ellen Hansin Carroll, 8/19/1919, Twomileborris, Tipperary
William, 1/7/1944
See Hansin, Peter, 7/5/1909, 61

Carroll
James, 7/26/1854, 35, Cork

Carroll
James 1869?, Tipperary

Carroll
John T., 1/28/1887, 24
By parents:
Ellen, 2/15/1892, 70, Queens
Maurice, 3/12/1910, Kerry
Mary Carroll, 1/5/1982, 89

Carroll
Michael, 11/20/1902, 76, Cork
By dau. Ellen O'Reilly

Carscaden
Mary M., 10/12/1901, Ballincor, Donaghmore, Donegal
By sister Sarah Marley Duffy
Authur Carscaden, 12/8/1910

Casey
Ellen, 4/14/1882, 64, Killashee, Longford
By husband John, 2/20/1883, 70

Casey
Hanora, 1/14/1888
James, 2/10/1898
Ida, 6/29/1923
David F., 4/10/1924
See Duffy, Maria, 10/30/1884

Casey
James, 3/29/1875, Bruff, Limerick
By wife Margaret, 12/2/1905, 84, Bruff, Limerick
Their dau. Mary, 1/11/1890, Bruff, Limerick
Ellen Halloran, 1/28/1911, 70
Patrick J. Halloran, 6/8/1929
Mary Agnes, 5/18/1936
Abie, 12/27/1946
John, 11/30/1956

Casey
John P., 11/15/1874-11/20/1921, Longford
Dau. Catherine, 2/18/1907 -4/25/1928
Mary and Elizabeth who died young

Casey
Margaret, 3/24/1886, 75, Killashee, Longford
By niece Catherine Casey 5/12/1915, Longford

Casey
Mary A., 3/30/1912, 45
John F., 3/4/1989, 64
See Kirby, James, 12/7/1880, 52

Casey
Patrick, 2/26/1899, 43, Cashel, Longford
Wife Mary Skelly, 9/24/1937, 76

Casey
Peter, 8/6/1856, 62, Clontuskert, Galway

Casey
Peter
See Farrell, John, 11/21/1871

Cashman
James J., 1/20/1909, 47, City of Cork
By wife Ellen

Cassidy
Bridget, 10/20/1881, 48, Ballymore, Westmeath
By husband Patrick

Cassidy
Bridget, 8/31/1885, 38, Drumraney, Westmeath
By brother Michael

Cassidy
Mary, 1895-1984
See Devaney, John J., 7/3/1890, 44

Cassidy
Neil, 12/17/1899, 68, Greencastle, Moville, Donegal

Cassidy
Patrick 2/1882?, Donegal

Cassidy
Patrick, 11/6/1898, 37
See Ryan, Mary, 5/1/1885, 78

Cassidy
Patrick, 10/12/1901, 46, Roscommon
By wife Mary, 7/20/1919, 65, Roscommon
Annie, 12/8/1889, 50, Longford
James Kellesey, 4/1/1873, 23, Longford
Mary's brother Peter Hopkins 5/21/1905, 43, Longford
Patrick Cassidy, son of Patrick and Mary Cassidy
4/7/1905, 16
Joseph T. Malone, 1889-1965

Cassidy
Rosa, 11/5/1890, 57, Kinawley, Cavan
By husband Michael, 3/9/1903
Son Rev. Hugh Cassidy, 2/9/1886, 24, Templeport, Cavan
Peter M., 1/9/1895, 35

Caufield
Michael, 1/9/1872, 78, Galway
Children: Martin and Bridget

Caufield
Bridget, 7/23/1925, 79
See Seery, Julia, 2/19/1887, 34

Cavanagh
Hugh, 3/11/1877-2/17/1921, Ballymacarthur, Greencastle, Donegal
Mary Reid dau. of James and Mary Reid, 9/27/1908 - 3/1/1919
Mary Reid, 11/22/1927
Michael Cavanagh, husband of Jennie Nixon, 2/4/1936
James Reid, 6/3/1939
Jennie Reid wife of Martin Reid, 8/30/1941

Cavigan
John A., 2/25/1872, 50, Longford
By wife Julia
Their dau. Margaret, 11/1/1878, 23

Cavley
Bridget, 6/13/1898, 84, City of Waterford
By husband William

Celsh
John, 5/13/1882, 41, Meath
By sister Ann Stanton, 10/14/1890, 54
His children, Daniel, Harry, Eddie
Her husband Patrick Stanton, 5/6/1888, 57, Galway

Christy
Mary A., 3/8/1908, 39, Leitrim
Anna May, 5/5/1915, 9
James, 2/1/1939, 75, Antrim
Elizabeth M., 7/10/1950
Margaret Fullerton, 1912-1964
Thomas Fullerton Sr., 1911-1981
Our nephew Patrick Finegen, 8/14/1925, 24

Claffey
Catherine, 11/18/1910
See Carring, Mary, 4/18/1893

Clancey
Thomas A. 11/21/1926, 33
Catherine 2/10/1936, 63
See Kane, Thomas 4/11/1894, Leitrim

Clancy
Charles, 6/28/1909, 58, Leitrim
By sister Bridget, 5/22/1919, 82

Clancy
Lacky, 8/16/1896, 49, Leitrim
By wife Annie
Alex "Mamas Pet", 6/17/1896, 9

Clark
Edward, 7/13/1868, 41, Roscommon
By wife Bridget

Clark
John, 4/24/1896, 55, Longford
By wife Ellen
Children Henry and John died young

Clark
Mary, 1/16/1871, 62, Mourne, Down
Charles, 9/26/1881, Mourne, Down
Dau. Catherine, 4/4/1871, 24-8-0, Mourne, Down

Clark
Michael, 5/31/1897, 37, Mayo
By wife Mary, 9/27/1943, Sligo
Michael J., 1/23/1957, 67

Clark
Patrick, 11/7/1871, 66, Drumsnat, Monaghan
By wife Ellen

Clark
Patrick, 11/1/1872, 37, Cavan
By wife Ann, 4/18/1910, 79
Charles S., 5/16/1894
Thomas F., 7/8/1895

Clark
Susan, 4/19/1883, Ballyduff, Dromard, Longford
Mary Kiernan, 10/30/1884

Clark
Thomas, 7/29/1903, 52, Dublin
By wife Theresa
Grandson Stephen, 2/2/1896, 7

Clark
Thomas Jr., 5/6/1872-2/22/1873
By parents Thomas C. and Ann F.
Catherine Fitzpatrick, 10/16/1884, 55, Monaghan, Monaghan
Mary E. Lindley, 3/18/1920

Clark
Timothy, 9/16/1882, 51, Westmeath
Wife Ellen, 5/24/1910, 78
Dau. Susan L., 3/12/1904, 35

Clarke
James, 11/2/1942
Elizabeth, 7/3/1955
Thomas F., 9/2/1982
See Tynan, Lucy M., 7/6/1911

Clarke
Thomas, 1/22/1893, 47, Kingscourt, Cavan
His sisters:, Mary A., 3/2/1908
Rose M., 5/25/1916
Ellen, 4/21/1933
John Dooling, 1/12/1981
His wife Dorothea, 5/31/1983

Clavin
James, 3/29/1897, 55, Westmeath
By wife Delia, 2/7/1907, 60
Catherine T. McNally wife of William Clavin, 11/7/1937

Clay
Charles, 11/27/1889, 92, Donegal
Ann, 1/9/1890, 78, Donegal
Their dau. Kate Clay, 12/31/1874, 34
Mary Shields Parters, 3/15/1874-4/7/1957

Cleary
John A., 10/1/1968
See Mangan, Annie, 2/17/1912, 45

Cleary
Mary, 10/13/1867, Castletown, Westmeath
By son Peter, 11/6/1913, 72

Cleary
Owen, 2/10/1894, 63, Ballyshannon, Donegal
By wife Bridget, 7/29/1910, 74

Cleary
Thomas, 10/18/1864, 45, Bornough, Tipperary
By wife Margaret
Son Patrick, 9/12/1870, 20-10-0

Clifford
William E., 2/7/1877-8/15/1930, Ballina, Mayo
Mary, 9/28/1882-10/17/1944

Clifton
Mary, 1/21/1921, Meath
By husband Henry, 5/19/1945, 90
Marian, 7/21/1912, 11

Clinane
Mabel, 1903-1979
See Halpin, William, 8/1/1878, 68

Cline
Catherine, 1876, Mullingar, Westmeath

Cline
James, 5/4/1890, 84
Bridget, 10/8/1900, 77, Cashel, Longford
By son James, 4/23/1919, 68, Newtown, Cashel, Longford

Clynn
Timothy J., 10/9/1894, 32, Kilrush, Clare
Michael, 12/9/1895, 47
Maria Driscoll, 10/3/1905, 37
Her son Timothy, 7/21/1904, 4-5-0

Code
Gen. Patrick H., 1776 - 2/2/1851, Wexford
Anne, wife of Thomas, 9/28/1885, 27-11-0
Their son John, 11/7/1852, 2
Thomas' uncle P. Code, 2/2/1852, 75
Annie F. MacAlpine, 6/13/1932

Cody
Michael, 2/1/1885, 57, Roscommon
By wife Ann, 12/1/1892, 65
Peter, 3/21/1884
Gertrude Elting Cody, 9/5/1912

Cody
Patrick, 7/17/1914, 49, Waterford
Wife Catherine, 10/21/1915, 41, Limerick
Son Edward, 2 months
James, 1901-1942
Kathleen, 1906-1959

Coen
Patrick, 8/6/1924, 85?, Kildare
By children Catherine Carlis and James J. Coen
Catherine Carlis, 6/22/1928, 79

Coffey
Joseph, 4/6/1886, 47
See Graham, Michael, 1/12/1882, 28

Coffey
Patrick, 3/4/1909, Westmeath
Catherine, 1/7/1906, Westmeath
William P., 3/12/1892
Robert Watt, 1885-1935

Coffield
Mary A., 4/21/1882, 15-7-0, Balla, Mayo
By father James, 9/29/1913, 70
Mary Spellman, 4/12/1918, 79
Mary Spellman, 1/30/1929

Coffin
Ellen Dowd, 12/8/1934, 30
See Scully, Dennis, 12/10/1882, 69

Coggy
Mary, 10/1/1917, Lagan, Longford
Michael Brennan, 6/23/1891-12/15/1920, Ballinamuck, Longford
William P., 1/17/1943
Margaret, 1894-1980

Coleman
James, 11/30/1873, 35, Ardagh, Longford
By wife Mary

Coleman
Margaret, 5/21/1888, 63
By husband Thomas, 11/14/1906, 81, Tallanstown, Louth
Their children: Maria, 9/14/1874, 17
Thomas, 1/7/1898, 34
James, 1/2/1902
Margaret Kallmeyer, 6/23/1949
Andrew
Charles, 8/5/1938
Mary, 1/16/1942
Christian Moldenhauer, 10/16/1953
Mary J. Moldenhauer, 10/3/1971

Coll
Edward, 1/6/1872 - 7/26/1914, Roscommon
By wife and children

Collins
Alice, 9/16/1875, 66, Droghera, Louth
By husband Philip
Thomas F., 8/1/1903, 56
Margaret, 1/21/1919, 76

Collins
Ann, 7/7/1883, 38
See Golden, Michael, 3/18/1878

Collins
George, 5/7/1887, Clonard, Meath
By wife Lettitia
Their son Michael J., 1/22/1890, 26

Collins
John, 4/20/1900, Mahona, Cork
By dau. Hannah Collins, Mahona, Cork
Her brother Daniel, Mahona, Cork
Her sister Minnie, Mahona, Cork

Collins
John F., 1852-1914, Bessbrook, Armagh
Wife Ellen, 1854-1924
Children:, Francis Joseph, 1880-1882
Francis Joseph 2nd, 1887-1892
John Stephen, 1889-1891
Gertrude Loretta, 1892-1896
Mary Josephine, 1882-1913

Collins
Mary, 6/28/1897, Golden, Tipperary
By husband Michael, 12/16/1901, 58
Dau. Mary Mahady, 3/3/1902, 33

Collins
Maureen A., 1/26/1966
Timothy J., 11/22/1967
Loretta, 7/9/1975
See Lyons, Michael, 11/24/1901, 65

Collins
Patrick, 9/27/1871, 32, Doon, Limerick
By father Timothy, 9/8/1889, 75
Patrick, 7/28/1875, 8 months
Mary, 10/30/1894, 80
Timothy, 5/5/1897
Michael, 9/14/1915

Collins
Walter J., 6/12/1946
Ellen J., 9/9/1955
Marie E., 10/14/1962
See Berren, Mary, 7/5/1919, 73

Collopy
Patrick, 8/10/1896, Fedamore, Limerick
Children: Annie and Bridget and mother Margaret
Son Patrick, 5/2/1959
Wife Mary, 8/21/1966

Colton
Thomas J., 10/12/1894, Tyrone
Wife Mary A., 9/1/1910, Tyrone
Dau. Sarah E., 11/9/1895

Columby
Anna M., 1889-1967
See Graham, Mary, 7/1/1879

Comerford
Mary Theresa, 9/30/1856-6/1/1893, Dublin
Dau. of the late Joseph and Mary Hart
By husband Philip, 9/23/1916, 64
Mary T. (Mollie), 2/19/1878-6/20/1902
Patrick J. Joe, 8/11/1870-4/16/1905
William, 1886-1952
Philip H., 1884-1955
Ellen, 1879-1956
Philip, 1915-1977

Comeringer
Leo, 2/8/1897, 74, Baden, Germany
Ceceila, 6/25/1890, 45, Galway
Their children: Philip, 3/10/1872, 5
Mary, 12/1/1871, 6
Margaret Frazer, 5/17/1933
John M. Frazer, 10/30/1937
Thomas Frazer, 1/10/1938
Joseph Frazer, 9/21/1944, 74
His wife Mary C., 1892-1957

Conboy
Ann, 3/18/1886, 65, Mohill, Leitrim
By son Thomas, 8/19/1890, 43
His children:, Thomas, James B., Joseph P., George L. died young

Condren
Daniel, 7/2/1901, 66, Wexford
Wife Margaret, 9/30/1923, 77
Elizabeth, 1948, 65

Conkin
William 1805-1876 died Brooklyn, Longford
Ellen 1810-1888 died Brooklyn, Westmeath
Eddie 1867-1871 died Brooklyn, Missouri
John, James, Amy died young
Edward H., 2/18/1874-1/8/1934

Conklin
James, 7/6/1907
William, 12/17/1916
By parents: Thomas, 8/14/1858-2/27/1921, Rathmore, Longford
Maryann, 11/29/1936

Conlon
James, 7/31/1870, 26
Lizzie, 2/1/1852, 1 yr. 7 mos.
Mary, 60
By Patrick, father and husband, Moydow, Longford

Conlon
Joseph M., 1905-1958
Ethel G., 1910-1969
See Murphy, Hannah, 3/16/1910, 49

Connaughton
John, 1/24/1884, 30, Roscommon
By wife Maria Gavin, 1/17/1916
Son John P., 6/25/1884, 5 months

Connaughton
Sarah
See Lamb, Catherine 1865 St. John's?, Roscommon

Connell
Michael, 3/26/1895, 55, Glassan, Westmeath
By wife Ellen
Children: Sgt. James Bevans, 1900-1948
Marie, 1903-1979

Connelly
Annie, 9/5/1875, 31, Donegal
Alice, 4/2/1900, 50, Lisnaskea, Fermanagh

Connelly
James, Carrickmacross, Monaghan

Connelly
Margaret, 1871, 68, Cashel, Longford
By husband James
Son John

Connelly
Mary, 59, Mullaghoran, Cavan
Matthew, 5/11/1864, 65, Mullaghoran, Cavan
By daughter Ann Gaffney
Her sister Catherine Connelly, 6/17/1879, 43, Mullaghoran, Cavan

Connolly
Ann, 3/10/1887, 54, Westmeath
By sister Bridget

Connolly
Belinda, 4/23/1987
See Maloney, Bessie, 3/16/1930

Connolly
Bridget Morrisey, 1/20/1913, Glennamaddy, Galway
By husband John Connolly, 1/13/1929
Michael, 12/16/1912, Glennamaddy, Galway
Wife May, 11/21/1937

Connolly
Catherine, 8/15/1900, 70, Skerrick Scots House, Monaghan
Parents:, Philip and Margaret

Connolly
Catherine, 2/15/1899, 69, Cloughrinkoe, Kildare
Her children:
Susan, 5/27/1887
Michael, 9/22/1889

Connolly
John, 5/13/1885, 48
By wife Ann
Cousin James H. Butler, 7/17/1927, Clare
His wife Delia, 10/15/1929
Patrick Flannery, 5/3/1954

Connor
Ellen, 10/8/1903, 60, Leitrim
By husband Peter, 1834-1929
His mother Ann, 3/28/1887, Tarman?, Roscommon
James J., 1906-1972
Ambrose P., 9/8/1914, 37
Mary Jane, 13 months

Connor
Mary C., 3/16/1880-1/22/1910
By parents:
John, 10/30/1845-4/4/1924, Longford
Catherine, 10/6/1929

Connor
Mary, 7/6/1883, Kerry
By husband Michael, 2/10/1919, 80
Julia, 10/4/1907, 26
Thomas, 3/6/1939

Connors
Herbert F., 1883-1968
Martha, 1885-1978
See Farrell, Hugh, 9/2/1894, 54

Connors
John, 11/1/1907, 33, Galway
By wife Bridget A., 1/30/1954

Connors
John, 8/27/1897, 36, Easky, Sligo
By sister Bessie Connors
Her brother-in-law Patrick Stanton, 2/25/1895, 36
Alice Stanton, 12/27/1890, 3
Mary E. Stanton, 3/5/1918
Agnes L. Kiers, 6/12/1967

Connors
Thomas, 7/14/1895, 33
Francis W. Little, 7/11/1904, 4 months
Agnes J. Little, 4/5/1912, 9
Annie Connors, 11/15/1914, 53, Longford

Conrahn
Ellen
William
See Ryan, Mary, 5/1/1885

Conroy
Bridget, 2/6/1888, 60, Westmeath
By husband Patrick, 5/22/1890, 65, Arlas, Queens

Conroy
John, 8/21/1858, 56, Lagan, Longford
By wife Ann, 4/3/1874, 65

Conroy
Mary A. Phillips, 1/12/1914, Drumsnat, Kilmore, Monaghan
By husband and daus.

Conway
Dennis, 11/13/1897, Tipperary
By wife Ellen, 1/5/1931,
Dau. Jane, 8 months

Conway
Elizabeth, 12/20/1896, 78, Feakle, Clare
By daus.:
Bridget, 11/21/1926
Elizabeth, 2/5/1949
Thomas, 10/27/1908
Nora O'Beirne, 9/25/1973
Joseph O'Beirne, 2/6/1976

Conway
James, 12/4/1885, 70, Stonepark, Tipperary
Wife Johanna, 4/17/1900, 80
James Cummings husband of Mary Conway, 5/18/1865-7/18/1903
Mary A. Cummings, 10/14/1947
Catherine M. Hanley, 8/23/1935

Conway
John, 12/29/1897, 35, Feakle, Clare
By wife Bridget, 12/19/1945, 85
Son James, 8/12/1892, 8 months
Elizabeth Nee, 11/1/1976
Ann V. Benson, 1/30/1982

Coolan
Catherine, 4/1886 Tipperary

Cooley
Elizabeth, 6/6/1923, 58, Kings
Mary Sagendork, 10/15/1933, 40
Matthew Cooley, 12/23/1944, 86
Margaret Cooley died in infancy

Cooney
Rose, 6/30/1939
James, 10/29/1940
See Cox, Mary, 8/19/1902, 18

Cooney
William, 10/10/1917, 68, Kildare
By wife Mary, 10/23/1925, 65
Emil Joseph Sanger, 3/19/1942, 69

Cooper
Edward, 3/12/1882, 42, Carrick-on-Shannon, Leitrim
By wife Winifred Rovers 3/29/1900, 50
Their children:, Edward, Annie, Kattie, Winifred
John, 1877-1948
Delia, 1881-1961
Catherine V.

Cooper
John, 1/12/1884, 50
Mary, 4/22/1888, 52
Both of, Kiltoghert, Leitrim

Corbett
Delia, 1/4/1928, Ballycushion, Donegal
By sister Sarah Hyland

Corbitt
Mary, 6/5/1868, 44, Clifden, Omey, Galway
By husband Luke

Corcoran
Catherine, 10/28/1895, 73, Lorra, Tipperary
Husband John, 10/7/1898, 70
Son James F., 11/3/1895, 32

Corcoran
James 4/1865?, Ardagh, Longford
By wife Ann
Thomas

Corcoran
John, Tipperary
Wife Mary/Nancy, 6/20/1856, 72

Corcoran
John, 1/31/187C, 76, County Dublin
By son Alexander
Elizabeth, 4/6/1885, 84
Katie, 1/22/1887, 4
Andrew Joseph, 5/21/1891

Corcoran
Peter, 9/16/1881, 50, Longford
Son Peter, 10/5/1869, 6-6-0
By wife/mother Mary A., 8/3/1912, 80
Patrick F., 2/22/1917, 52

Cornell
Anna Nerney, 4/16/1952
See Nerney, Bridget Fitzsimmons, 1/3/1866

Corr
Margaret, 5/22/1869, Longford
By husband Owen

Corrigan
Mary, 8/19/1895, 79, Westmeath
Peter McLaren, born 9/25/1805, Blairdrummond, Scotland
Margaret McLaren born 6/25/1818

Cors
Elmer J., 1/18/1957
Margaret M., 12/25/1980
See Coyne, James, 4/12/1906, 61

Cosgrove
Katie, 3/11/1893, 26
Her baby Alice
See Hopkins, Catherine, 3/17/1912

Costello
Bernard P., 12/14/1908, 51
Margaret M, 12/17/1915, 51, Portarlington, Cushina, Queens
By dau. Mary Watson, 9/12/1929, 42
Her husband Foster B. Watson

Costello
Mary, 10/25/1882, 62, Loughkeen, Tipperary
By husband Michael, 8/27/1902, 78

Costello
Thomas, 12/10/1877, 48, Longford
By wife Mary

Cotter
Mary, Kilbrittain, Cork

Coughlin
Daniel, 10/31/1863, 77
Mary, 3/29/1872, 75, City of Cork
John E. Lynch, 1/21/1868, 4
Julia A. Lynch, 10/28/1879, 22

Coughlin
Thomas Sr., Roscommon
Thomas Jr., Roscommon
See Logan, Mary, 5/1/1907, 39

Coulson
John, 4/9/1912
Katherine Campbell, Wife of John, 7/1/1914
See Campbell, Thomas F., 4/21/1890, 32

Courtney
Elizabeth, 11/7/1917
See Rawl, Thomas, 4/16/1882, 67

Cowan
Ann, 10/24/1909, 82, Longford
By son John E. Sr., 5/29/1933, 68
Wife May, 7/1/1911, 34
Ann, 4/15/1880, 24
Bridget, 1/11/1895, 24
Arnold, 11/27/1925, 10
James, 2/18/1948, 12
Robert, 2/8/1953, 15

Cowley
Margaret, 6/30/1940
See Turnbell, Maryann, 12/23/1904, 68

Cox
Ann, 5/27/1861, Rathaspick?, Westmeath
Dau. Margaret, 6/9/1863, 39-6-0
Thomas

Cox
Ann, 10/12/1880, 80, Ballymore, Westmeath
By son William, 2/19/1895, 62, Ballymore, Westmeath
George Martin Jacob, husband of Annie C. Jacob, 9/17/1914, 71-6-0
Annie Cox Jacob, 11/9/1915

Cox
Mary, 8/19/1902, 18, Fermanagh
Rose Cooney, 6/30/1939
James, 10/29/1940

Coyle
Mary, 10/20/1884, 54, Cavan
Husband Owen, 12/1/1892, 72

Coyle
Margaret M., 3/16/1932, 68
See Greene, Peter, 3/4/1915, 34

Coyle
Patrick, 2/18/1947
Margaret M., 9/17/1962
See Murray, Henry, 1/3/1885

Coyne
James, 4/12/1906, 61, Ballinabrackey, Meath
Wife Mary E., 5/20/1927
Dau. Mary E., 7/22/1939
Elmer J. Cors, 1/18/1957
Margaret M. Cors, 12/25/1980
Joseph P. Higgins, 9/11/1901, Loughrea, Galway
Wife Sarah Higgins, 9/21/1936, 75
Son John J.

Coyne
John, 6/15/1839-11/13/1895, 56, Roscommon
Wife Catherine Connelly 7/4/1848- 10/14/1898
Kate, 11/14/1891, 2 yrs. 9 days
James J. O'Connor, 1/9/1876-1/18/1902
Wife Helen, 1/25/1878-4/10/1912
Their son James J., 3/10/1902-8/1/1902

Coyne
Martin, 8/31/1878, 76, Sligo

Crawley
Patrick, 12/7/1883, 50, Tallanstown, Louth
By wife Margaret

Creeley
Margaret, 12/27/1889, Shrule, Longford
By husband Dennis, 1913
Son Frank, 9/27/1881
James, 3/18/1916

Creighton
Rev. Patrick, born, 4/2/1817, Howth
Ordained, 3/25/1861, died, 7/12/1904, Riverhead, N.Y.
Elizabeth Leavy, 9/10/1919, Meath

Croak
Bridget, 11/9/1902, 53, Dunnemaggan, Kilkenny
By husband Thomas, 3/27/1920, 78, Dunnemaggan, Kilkenny
Children:, Martin and Michael died young
Gertrude Rhaesa, 6/7/1909-1/28/1910

Croak
James, 5/21/1891, 37, Tullagher, Kilkenny
By brothers Martin and Patrick both of, Tullagher, Kilkenny
Mary J. dau. of Martin and Bridget Croak, 3/11/1891, 6 months

Crogan
Margaret, 3/26/1863, 33, Mullingar, Westmeath
Bridget, 12/9/1897, 68, Mullingar, Westmeath
By sister Mary Murphy

Cronin
Edna M., 1885-1943
John J., 1876-1945
Edna M., 1913-1984
See Quirk, Andrew, 1/31/1892, 44

Cronin
Timothy, 12/18/1893, 71, Clogheen, Tipperary
Wife Bridget, 2/4/1888, 72, Clogheen, Tipperary
Son Michael, 5/7/1892, 49, Clogheen, Tipperary
Son Thomas F., 9/13/1899, 37
William, 7/19/1910, 58
Ellen, 6/28/1928
Johanna, 12/15/1900

Crowe
Catherine Burke wife of Morgan Crowe
12/25/1912, 72, Wexford
Their son Patrick, 11/17/1897, 36
His wife Mary, 3/23/1906, 37
Their son Morgan, member of Co. A 1st Engs. A.E.F.,
8/11/1921, 27
Margaret, Nellie, Katharine

Crowley
Dennis, 10/13/1907
See McDonald, Mary Crowley, 12/20/1908

Crowley
Dennis J., 7/11/1914
His wife Mary E., 8/29/1959
Richard A., 1/23/1981
See Murphy, Jeremiah, 1/18/1876, 77

Crowley
James, 1801-9/17/1875, Tralee, Kerry
Cornelius, 3/3/1883, 45

Cuff
Peter, 9/2/1883, 56, Belturret, Drumlane, Cavan
By sister Jane
Ellen Sheehan, 6/10/1957
Michael J. Sheehan, 7/18/1961

Cuffe
Mary, 7/16/1904, 56
Ellen McNerney Dorsey, 9/1/1905
By Ann and Martin Cuffe of, Roscommon

Cullen
Annie, 9/1/1892, 28, Mullaghoran, Cavan
Rose, 5/15/1894, 22, Mullaghoran, Cavan
Edward, 11/24/1894, 29, Mullaghoran, Cavan
By their sister Mary Cullen

Cullen
Patrick, 5/27/1881, 49, Crookstown, Kildare
By wife Bridget, 11/20/1908, 72
Her brother William Stanley, 10/2/1871, 43, New Abbey,
Kildare

Cullen
Patrick E., 1917
Joseph F., 1945
Annie F., 1946
Vincent de P., 1980
See Flynn, Michael, 10/27/1887, 75

Cullen
Terrence, 6/6/1861, 46, Drumhome, Donegal
By wife Ann

Culley
John J., 4/5/1907, 56
By wife Margaret, 5/25/1927, 78, Ardfallen Terrace, Cork

Cummings
James, 5/18/1865-7/18/1903
Mary A., 10/14/1947
See Conway, James, 12/4/1885

Cummings
Mary C., 7/13/1903, 33
See Curtin, John, 6/17/1870

Cummings
Mary, 7/16/1861, 65
Dau. Hannorah Ryan, 8/4/1858, 34, Tipperary
Johanna Leonard, 12/2/1853, 26, Tipperary
Anthony Figuerira, 6/12/1861, 9 months
Thomas Armstrong, 8/29/1864, 54
Wife Mary, 4/23/1887, 63

Cummings
Michael, 3/14/1860-6/25/1912, Toomevara, Tipperary
By sister, Nora Cummings for oldest brother, Michael, 1866-1950

Cummings
Michael, 12/20/1884, 50
James J., 5/30/1945
Philomena, 1952
See Feeley, Patrick, 10/25/1887, 56

Cummins
James, 9/6/1880-9/18/1913, Glennamaddy, Galway
His brother Thomas J., 1907 ? - 1935

Cunning
Elizabeth, 2/1/1876, Longwood, Meath
By dau. Mary, 10/15/1904
Her brother Hugh, 7/14/1882
Bridget, 9/24/1908, 73

Cunningham
Anna A.
See Egan, Bridget 12/12/1932, Longford

Cunningham
Hugh, 7/25/1900, 62, Donegal
Children died young
By wife Mary
Martha J. Smith, 1/30/1941, 78

Cunningham
Maggie, 5/3/1907, 32, Sligo
Catherine, 1/20/1930, 72

Cunningham
Margaret, 4/18/1888, 39
By sisters Mary and Bridget Reilly
Margaret's husband Peter, 2/25/1890, 45, Drumraney, Westmeath
Their son Bernard died young
Edward, 11/28/1899, 33
Mary, 11/14/1917, 75

Cunningham
Michael P., 1/14/1949
Mary Mee, 5/11/1965
See Mee, John J., 3/28/1904

Cunningham
Robert, 3/1/1853-8/21/1868, Cork
John J., 4/15/1855-8/25/1876, 21-4-0, Cork

Cunningham
Winifred, 10/14/1853, 20, Killashee, Longford
By sister Bridget
Patrick Casey, 9/30/1882, 19
Mary Burns, 10/21/1900, 60
Loretta Sullivan, 11/26/1947, 49
Marilyn Ryan, 4/6/1943, 15
Henrietta Ryan, 2/7/1974, 71
John J. Ryan, 9/22/1976, 77

Cunnion
John J., 1/9/1879, 34
Anna, 5/13/1925
See Weldon, Hugh, 12/23/1887, 64

Cunnion
John, 3/25/1852, 34, Edgeworthstown, Longford
By wife Ellen, 5/12/1890, 80

Curley
Catherine, 9/21/1896, 61
See Waldron, Mary, 7/22/1887

Curley
Malachy, 12/11/1836 ?, 50, Clontuskert, Galway
Margaret, 8/10/1876, 75
Michael, 3/1852, 23
Malachy, 6/11/1852
Frank, 2/28/1854, 21
Maria, 10/15/1872, 40
Maggie, 1/1837 ?, 13 months
By dau. of Malachy and Margaret, Bridget Curley

Curley
Michael, 4/28/1870, 43, Athlone, Roscommon
By wife Rose

Curran
Johanna 1/21/1886, 56, Listowel, Kerry
By husband Timothy 7/5/1886, 57
His mother Mary 11/23/1886, 72, Castle Island, Kerry

Curran
John, Frank, Margaret, Edward
See Gill, Bridget, 11/19/1895, 65

Curran
Michael, 11/26/1856, Monaghan

Curran
Rev. Michael 11/26/1856, Errigal Trough, Monaghan

Currey
Alton F., 12/31/1911-2/1/1913
See Mulcahy, Catherine, 7/16/1890, 54

Curtin
James J., 4/26/1911, 24, Mitchelstown, Cork
Anna Thompson Hennessy, 1883-1952
Thomas Curtin, 1876-1966
Margaret Sullivan Curtin, 1880-1960
Daniel, 1883
Christina Thompson Curtin, 1885

Curtin
John, 6/17/1870, 60, Cork
By wife Mary, 1/27/1898, 87, Cork
Daniel, 5/2/1879, 26, Cork
John, 8/3/1880, 30, Cork
Fannie O'Shaughnessy, 11/24/1886, 66, Cork
Cornelius Curtin, 12/22/1886, 45, Cork
Catherine A. Murphy, 3/8/1892, 30
Mary C. Cummings, 7/13/1903, 33
John T. Murphy, 1/12/1912, 63

Curtin
Timothy, 9/5/1866, Doon, Limerick

Curtis
John, 7/9/1909, 31, Louth
By sister Katie Curtis

Cusack
Bridget Hassett, 12/5/1909, 30, Doonass, Clare
By husband Thomas, 4/5/1946
Francis M., 1/19/1951
Thomas, 1909-1974

Cusack
Thomas, 11/26/1909, England
By wife Elizabeth, 7/5/1921, Longford
Her sister Ann O'Neil, 11/5/1914
Her brother Patrick Rhatigan, 3/15/1916, Longford

Cutler
Helen V., 9/4/1918
Ellen J., 7/9/1930
See Fegan, Michael, 10/16/1882

Dailey
Mary, 1/16/1904, 69, Westmeath
By dau. Agnes Grieve
Husband Thomas Grieve, 9/27/1925
Son John T., 2/20/1928

Dalton
Ann
See Butler, Patrick Wm., 7/9/1908

Dalton
John, 2/13/1864, 47, Golden, Tipperary
By wife Bridget
Also grandchildren Johnny and Tommy Dalton

Dalton
Michael, 9/29/1892, 61, Clooneen, Longford
Bridget, 2/9/1894
Their only child Regina, 7/2/1875-4/13/1878

Dalton
Thomas and Rose of, Legan, Longford
Thomas, 7/1/1914
Catherine McCormick wife of Thomas Dalton
8/30/1913, Westmeath
Joseph P. O'Connor, 1875 - 1946
Josephine D. O'Connor, 1875 - 1947

Dalton
Winifred, 4/20/1883, 51, Ballymahon, Longford
By husband Patrick, 10/4/1902, 64,
Dau. Elizabeth, 7/19/1882, 14-2-0
Mary A., 9/23/1905, 47
Charles W. Barrett, 11/19/1899
Catherine Dalton Barrett, 2/11/1937
Charles H. Barrett, 5/18/1893 - 3/28/1955
Harriett Barrett, 2/12/1902 - 2/10/1983

Daley
Catherine, 4/1875
See McLaughlin, Patrick, 1/30/1869

Daly
Ann, wife of Thomas, 12/6/1886, 67, Rathcline, Longford
By dau. Mary
Children of Ann and Patrick:
Thomas, 3
Annie, 8
Mary, 1/21/1900, 59
John T., 5/12/1907, 28
Ann Farrell Daly, 1/13/1914, 62

Daly
Dennis, 1866, 67, Cork

Daly
Elizabeth, 3/25/1901, 69, Wexford
By son James, 1/14/1944
By dau. Mary, 5/2/1944
Katherine, 6/17/1959

Daly
Hanorah, 8/19/1889, 56, Kilarney, Kerry
By husband John

Daly
Margaret, 4/18/1872, 45
Thomas, 12/2/1913, 79
See Hickey, Mary, 3/13/1872

Daly
Mary, 2/14/1895, 53, Columbkille, Longford
By husband Thomas
Son James, 2/4/1894, 25
Marion E. Reynolds, 1901 - 1968

Daly
Michael, 6/16/1864, 65, Roscommon
Dau. Bridget Healy, 4/1867, 27, Roscommon
Her son Patrick, 7/18/1864

Daly
Michael, 9/7/1888, 55, Kill, Westmeath
By wife Bridget, 10/16/1904, 62
Their dau. Katie, 9/26/1887, 5
Michael, 12/29/1935, 59
Elizabeth, 8/23/1949, 70
Dora, 3/31/1952, 77

Daly
Patrick, 8/10/1912, Clara, Kings
By wife Margaret

Daly
Thomas, 5/13/1893, 48, Roscommon
By wife Annie, 4/24/1914
Granddau. Maddine A. Daly, 1/3/1910 - 10/11/1911
Patrick Mullins, 8/10/1912, Tipperary
Mary J. Heitkamp, 12/6/1933
Henry Heitkamp, 1870 - 1937
Ann V. Mullins, 1861 - 1953

Danaher
Ann, 1/22/1878, 51
Annie, 1/15/1871, 13
Mary, 2/1/1891, 38
By sister Kate of Clare

Darcy
Michael, 1/22/1871, 40, Westmeath
By brother Richard

Davin
Anthony, 5/20/1865, Galway
Mary, 4/29/1865

Davis
Geoffrey, 8/29/1959, 1
See Harden, Edward, 5/25/1889, 76

Davis
Patrick F., 11/30/1887, 43, Claremorris, Mayo
Wife Bridget, 11/6/1911, 70, Claremorris, Mayo
Julia M., 1/10/1890, 33, Claremorris, Mayo
Thomas B. Davis husband of Julia, 9/2/1926, 73

Dayton
John, 6/7/1898, Kerry
By wife Johanna, 7/13/1925
Margaret L., 12/16/1954
William J., 7/8/1955

Dawkins
Sarah F., 4/20/1882 - 12/1/1966
Eleanor V., 1/21/1899 - 8/9/1983
See Howley, Richard, 3/7/1885, 75

Deady
Frank P., 10/21/1963
Gertrude, 5/3/1967
See Doyle, Dennis, 1/18/1907

Deegan
Michael, 9/21/1911
By sister Annie Deegan Donohue, 1865 - 1950, Baltinglass, Wicklow
Sister Elizabeth Deegan Sampson, 4/25/1916
James Sampson, 5/30/1937
Edward Deegan
Bernard G. Griffin, 11/13/1969

Deely
Mary, 9/15/1914, Kings

Deery
Margaret, 4/18/1892, 48, Tyrone
By sister Catherine

Degnan
Mary Dixon, 3/7/1848 - 7/21/1883
By husband James, 5/24/1928
Children:, Maryanne, 1/6/1875 - 10/19/1876
Annie, 7/13/1877 - 8/14/1878
Lawrence, 7/17/1873 - 9/8/1897
Anne Donnelly Degnan wife of James, 10/26/1916, Timpo, Fermanagh

DeGroat
Walter, 1879 - 1944
Margaret Kennelly, 1873 - 1955
See Kennelly, Dominick, 1802 - 9/28/1884

Deighan
Maryann, 8/1/1876, Enniskillen, Fermanagh
By husband James
James' mother, Rose, 5/25/1876, 55
Francis, 3/3/1875, 8 months
Sarah, 6/30/1876, 1-1-19

Delahanty
Patrick ?/29/1878?, Westmeath
By wife Ann
Mary O'Neill

Delahanty
William, 2/23/1891, 25, Granard, Longford
By the trackmen of the Kings Co., E.L.R.R.

Delaney
Joseph P., 1/28/1894, Kings
By sister Mary Delaney
Sister Anna D. Hurley, 4/23/1915, Kings
James T. Delaney, 7/19/1920

Delaney
Martin, 5/6/1902, 63, Queens
By wife Maria C., 11/1/1910, 68

Delaney
Mary, 9/2/1885, 54, Kilkenny
By husband John, 10/1/1895, 66
Dau. Catherine, 9/11/1874, 3
Sons Frank and William

Delaney
Thomas, 4/24/1867, 33, Parkavilla, Queens
By sister Ann

Delany
James, 5/19/1871, 57, Johnstown, Kilkenny

Delany
Joseph, 6/15/1856, 58, Roscrea, Tipperary
Maria, 5/21/1859

Delehanty
Catherine McElhern, 1/29/1879, 68, Antrim
Conner, 4/21/1889, Tulla, Clare

Delehanty
Patrick, 3/28/1889, 37, Feakle, Clare
John, 7/12/1889, 30, Feakle, Clare
By sisters Mary and Catherine
Margaret, 11/11/1904, 42
Thomas C. Keenan, 11/14/1964, 74
Rita A. Maher, 12/27/1988, 54

Delehanty
Sarah, 7/28/1865, 36, Sharavogue, Kings
Also sister Jane, 3/30/1891, 57
Norah, 8/15/1896, 70
Sarah, 5/4/1916

Dempsey
Elizabeth, 1855 ?, Westmeath
Wife of John

Dempsey
Michael, 2/15/1881, 77, Maryborough ?, Queens

Dempsey
Patrick, 7/22/1848, 65, Wexford
Mary, 2/15/1858, 73
Hanora, 1/26/1887, 60
Mary McDonald, 11/10/1881, 67, Wexford
Her husband Christopher, 11/20/1854, 40, Dublin

Dennedy
Mary
Ann
Sisters of James O'Hara
See O'Hara, wife of Jas., 4/1872

Dennigan
Patrick, 5/27/1942
Mary C., 6/17/1961
See Goldrick, Annie, 7/7/1924, 79

Dennin
John, 8/3/1909
His mother, sister Mary and brothers:, Jeremiah, Thomas, Patrick
All of, Ballinacargy, Westmeath
His wife Rosemarie, 10/8/1928, 68, Westmeath

Dennington
John, 9/12/1885, 52, Derry
By wife Margaret, 1/14/1913, 77
Their children:, Robert T., 5/20/1880, 15-11-8
Mary E., 5/5/1880
John S., 2/11/1878, 2-1-0
John T., 8/28/1872, 1-1-0
Grandchild May Reilly, 8/1/1888, 1-6-0
Augusta Dennington Reilly, 1/19/1918
Peter F. Reilly, 5/2/1862 - 1/18/1936
Margaret D. Reilly, 12/21/1947
Peter F. Reilly Jr., 9/15/1960
Augusta Reilly Randolph, 5/10/1977

Derrin
Catherine, ?/20/1877, Ballinasloe ?, Galway
See Kelly, Fergus, 11/27/1859

Derwin
Michael, Cashel, Longford

Derwin
Michael, 1/15/1910, 48,
See Dowd, Ann, 8/16/1890, 82

Desmond
Ellen, 6/1/1899, 75, Midleton, Cork
See Henebry, Thomas, 7/6/1888, 19

Devane
Rev. Joseph A., 6/21/1884 - 2/15/1920, Nenagh, Tipperary
Ordained St. Patrick's College Maynooth, 6/21/1909

Devaney
John J., 7/3/1890, 44, Meanus, Bruff, Limerick
By wife Julia, 4/14/1891, 47, Ballgrennan, Croom, Limerick
Henry A ., 4/9/1907
Bridget L., 10/2/1928
Thomas F., 3/18/1936, 63
Ellen T. Gannon, 3/30/1927
Daniel Moloney, 4/6/1926
Mary J., 5/29/1927
James J. Gannon, 11/14/1945
Geraldine Sheehan, 1903-1974
Mary Cassidy, 1895-1984

Devereaux
Mary, 1/1/1864 - 5/15/1922, Wexford
By husband Martin, 6/10/1928, 67
John, 1887 - 1971
Mary C., 1897 - 1986

Devine
John, 8/23/1908
Kate, 3/5/1911
See Murphy, John, 6/29/1895, 30

Devitt
Michael, 8/6/1864, 38, Durnware, Leitrim
James, 1/29/1876, 46, Durnware, Leitrim
By their wives
Abbey, 2/9/1897, 66
Mary, 5/20/1906, 78

Diffeely
Catherine, 7/15/1868, Longford
Bridget Gill, 12/20/1870, 44, Killashe, Longford
Wife of John Gill, 1/4/1894, 56, Longford

Dillon
Christopher, 4/30/1898, 60
Wife Hanora, 1/20/1914, 76, Athy, Kildare
His brother Patrick, 3/26/1864, Athy, Kildare
Their children: Jennie, 4/20/1868, 4
Denis, 5/3/1875, 5-5-0
Their grandson Christie, 2/23/1892, 17 months-15 days
Only son of Patrick and Mary Dillon

Dillon
Edward, 4/14/1867, 56-6-0, Mohill, Longford
By brother George
John Thomas, 9/6/1868, 1 yr.

Dillon
John, 4/7/1885, 84, Ballynahown, Westmeath
Mary, 9/30/1852, 40, Ballynahown, Westmeath
By daus. Bridget and Mary

Dillon
John, 6/27/1857, 72, Westmeath
Mary, 9/6/1865, 73
Son James, 5/12/1910, 67

Dillon
John, 4/24/1899, 63, Kerry
By wife Jane
Their son John F., 7/4/1894, 38

Dillon
Michael, 10/28/1885, 42, Ballinabrackey, Meath
Margaret, 4/5/1917, 72, Ballinabrackey, Meath
Mary, sister of the above, 2/6/1922, 89, Ballinabrackey, Meath

Dixon
Mary Nee Green, 9/4/1877, 56
Her sister Ann, 4/12/1875, 47, Roscommon
Husband Thomas, 1852

Dixon
Richard 1847-3/1923
Wife Matilda 6/3/1856 - 10/29/1919
Children: Richard, Hilda, Cyril
Kate A., wife of Richard 11/2/1888, 38
Their children:
Richard 4/5/1886 - 9/12/1886
Thomas Coran 7/1887 - 11/11/1887
See Lamb, Catherine 1865, St. John's?, Roscommon

Doherty
George, 9/8/1897, 60, Donegal
Willie J., 1/27/1876, 2-10-0
Margaret, 11/15/1900, 63

Doherty
Thomas G., 1926 - 1964
See Donovan, Peter, 1/15/1890, 65

Doherty
William, 6/28/1872, 46, Culdaff, Donegal
Wife Grace, 2/27/1899
and 4 children, (No names)
Grandson, John Hunter, 9/16/1903

Dolan
Patrick, 12/21/1915, Elphin, Roscommon

Dolan
Sarah, 8/31/1896, 34
Svea L., 1905 - 1985
Francis J., 1901 - 1987
See Keeren, Thomas, 9/26/1888, 51

Dolan
Timothy, 5/25/1887, 84, Lagan, Longford
Mary, 10/28/1858, 50, Lagan, Longford
By daus.:
Anne, 11/21/1909, 81
Bridget, 12/9/1912, 69
Other children Elizabeth and Margaret

Donahoue
Andrew, 5/1877, 20, Taughboy, Donegal
Thomas, 7/28/1886, 73
Elizabeth, 2/6/1888, 72
Hugh

Donlon
Ellen 4?/10/1865, 55, Moydow, Longford

Donlon
Patrick F., 6/19/1932
Delia, 9/12/1961
John J. M.D., 6/18/1965
See Thorton, Mary, 6/30/1907

Donlon
Peter, 9/21/1863, 24, Longford
By Peter and Ellen

Donnell
Mary, 3/13/1893, 1-3-0
John, 9/25/1933, 76
Rose, 4/23/1932, 74
Willie F., 2/2/1908, 21
See Dunn, Bridget, 4/4/1899, 70

Donnellan
James, 10/10/1888, 44, Westmeath
By wife Catherine, 1/26/1930, 81
Their son Peter F., husband of Matilda, 5/7/1918
Mary E., 7/6/1933

Donnellan
Mary, 5/19/1883, 26
See Glynn, Thomas, 7/28/1926, 70

Donnellon
Patrick, 11/14/1892, 45, Clare
By wife Ann, 2/5/1926, 82
Niece Bridget O'Connor, 1/27/1885, 23

Donnelly
Christopher C., 3/10/1885, 47, Longford
Died in California

Donnelly
Winifred Griffin, 12/26/1923
See Griffin, Michael J., 7/8/1907

Donoher
Daniel F., 11/7/1937
Wife Agnes J. Leahon, 12/5/1938
See Leahon, Margaret, 6/1/1886, 53

Donohue
Annie Deegan, 1865 - 1950, Baltinglass, Wicklow
See Deegan, Michael, 9/21/1911

Donohue
Eliza, 8/15/1893, 57-4-0, Doneraile, Cork
By husband Michael, 5/3/1907, 65
Children:, Mary and Annie
Bartholemew, 10/23/1893, 23-10-0
Michael Jr., 3/10/1895, 21
Maggie, 5/21/1895, 19
Mary A., 1/24/1898
Catherine, 10/19/1917

Donohue
Margaret, 3/12/1877, 33, Clonegall, Carlow
By sister Maria Donohue

Donohue
Margaret, 12/13/1877, 38, Milltown, Galway
By father Patrick Murphy
Her son William
Also:, Hanah, John and William Murphy

Donohue
Mary, 12/10/1861, Leck, Donegal
By husband B. Donohue

Donohue
Matthew, 4/14/1891, 48, Queens
By wife Bridget, 8/14/1913, 61
Children Maggie and Elizabeth died young
Esther, 1/21/1893, 15
Daniel L., 4/28/1948
Catherine C., 10/2/1953
Ellen A., 6/19/1957

Donohue
Thomas, 11/2/1877, Shrule, Longford; By wife Catherine

Donovan
Peter, 1/15/1890, 65, Ross, Cork
His brother Daniel, 9/10/1887, 50, Ross, Cork
Ellen, wife of Daniel, 1/21/1906, 57
Their granddau. Nellie Wilkins, 5/11/1902, 2-5-0
Peter, 1880 - 1960
Thomas G. Doherty, 1926 - 1964

Donovan
Richard, 3/4/1861, 90, Cork
Mary, 8/31/1868, Cork
Grandson John Murry

Dooley
Ellen, 1/2/1846?, 20, Carrickedmond, Longford
Margaret, 1/23/1857, 24, Carrickedmond, Longford
By sister Catherine, 9/17/1897, 80

Dooley
Margaret, 2/11/1936
See Mullery, Edward, 5/16/1897

Dooley
Patrick, 2/27/1899, 60, Longford
By wife Ann

Dooling
John, 1/12/1981
Dorothea, 5/31/1983
See Clarke, Thomas, 1/22/1893

Doonan
Francis J., 12/20/1907, Blackbog, Fermanagh
By brother Daniel, 1/11/1946
Mary E., 5/22/1944

Doorly
Mary, 4/17/1886, 57, Glenavo, Bracken, Kings

Doran
Michael, 1/4/1881, 50
See Fitzpatrick, Mary, 8/31/1871

Doran
Sarah (O'Donnell), 12/15/1851, 52, Killybegs, Donegal
By husband Leslie, 2/17/1861, 72, Killybegs, Donegal
Their children:
Jane, 1824 - 1899, Killybegs, Donegal
Ann, 1828 - 1886, Killybegs, Donegal
Sarah, 1832 - 1898, Killybegs, Donegal
Francis P., 1842 - 1908, Killybegs, Donegal
Margaret, 1836 - 1911, Killybegs, Donegal
Ellen B., 1826 - 1907, Killybegs, Donegal
Mary, 1830 - 1869, Killybegs, Donegal
Joseph, 1834 - 1904, Killybegs, Donegal
Catherine, 1839 - 1880, Killybegs, Donegal

Dorney
James, 6/5/1885, Thurles, Tipperary
By wife Julia, 12/21/1892, 62, Comer/Cummer/Commoge, Kilkenny

Dorr
Edward J., 11/19/1961
Mary D., 6/20/1962
See Dunn, Mary Theresa, 9/9/1890 - 8/6/1892

Dorsey
Ellen McNerney, 9/1/1905
See Cuffe, Mary, 7/16/1904, 56

Dorsey
John, 7/3/1884, 41, Wexford
Wife Catherine
John

Dougherty
Edward, 1870, 41, Culduff, Donegal
By sister Ann Gleason, dau. of Michael and Bridget
Dougherty
1/5/1895, 65, Culduff, Donegal

Dougherty
Ellen, 3/28/1884, 45, Lower Moville, Shrove, Donegal
Ceceila A., 3/13/1890, 35
Patrick, 2/4/1909, 96

Dougherty
By George
Richard 1866?
Peter 1/1871, Cumber, Derry
George
Ellen, wife of George

Dougherty
John, 1/9/1910, 50, Derry
By wife Mary, 2/27/1921, 58
Son John Jr., 10/3/1896, 11
Catherine Ronnerberg, 2/5/1943

Dougherty
John, 5/17/1920, 60, Ennistimon, Clare
Capt. Edward A., Engine Co. 202 N.Y.F.D., 12/1/1881 - 10/4/1930
Mary, 1861 - 5/18/1942, Feakle, Clare
George J., 8/31/1889 - 7/21/1964

Dougherty
Mary, 12/1872, 92, Rye ?, Donegal

Dougherty
Mary, 2/1879, 72, Galway
By son Thomas
Bridget, 3/23/1917
Catherine Regan Flannery, 8/13/1885 - 11/6/1922

Dougherty
Mary, 2/5/1890, 62, Culdaff, Donegal
By husband Patrick, 4/19/1904, 74
Children:, Mary, Bernard, Michael, Annie and Mamie
Patrick J., 10/11/1893, 27
John F., 12/3/1906, 38
Catherine, 5/31/1927

Dougherty
Timothy, 10/10/1898, 49, Tipperary
By wife Delia, 3/11/1913, 68

Dowd
Ann, 8/16/1890, 82, Moydow, Longford
By dau. Ellen Dowd, 12/23/1909, 66
Michael Derwin, 1/15/1910, 48

Dowd
Michael, 11/21/1906, 85, Monasterevin, Kildare

Dowd
Thomas
Dennis, 6 months
See Scully, Dennis, 12/10/1882, 69

Dowdall
Maria, 2/2/1935
See Finneran, Catherine, 6/16/1907, 74

Dowling
John, 4/7/1834 - 7/10/1896, Queens
By wife Mary, 2/11/1918, 72, Queens
Their children died young, James, Daniel, Mary, Daniel J., Julia
Thomas, 7/25/1928
Elizabeth, 10/6/1929

Downey
Ann
Mary
Erected 1863 by parents John and Mary, Ballybacon, Tipperary

Downey
Bridget, 4/15/1876, 74
By Jeremiah and Eliza Griffin., Eliza dau. of Bridget Downey
Michael Price, uncle of Eliza Griffin
5/4/1866, 62, Shellumsrath, Kilkenny

Downing
Michael, 6/15/1908, 40, Cork
By wife Catherine, 8/26/1945
Her brother Timothy Riordan, 3/31/1909, 40
Eleanor, 4/8/1934
Frank J., 6/4/1969
Michael J., 8/22/1970

Doyle
C., 2/19/1952
See Quinn, James, 1/2/1879, 52

Doyle
Dennis, 1/18/1907, 63, Killorglin, Kerry
By wife Mary, 11/21/1908, 70
Frank P. Deady, 10/21/1963
Gertrude Deady, 5/3/1967

Doyle
James, 8/23/1877, 44, Drogheda
By wife Margaret
Son William J., 11/11/1900, 31
His wife Laura, 7/24/1907, 38
William F. Mullins, 8/31/1917
Mary A., 8/17/1939
James J., 10/13/1955

Doyle
John, 12/4/1870 - 12/22/1930, Rathvilly, Carlow

Doyle
Maggie, 3/10/1873, 1
Mary, 4/9/1877, 7
By parents Peter and Ann both of, Milltown, Westmeath
Ann wife of Peter, 1/18/1898, 52

Doyle
Mary, 2/13/1922, 74
See Harrington, Michael, 11/9/1910, 37

Doyle
Michael, 5/6/1893, 58, Dublin
By wife Mary, 3/8/1905, 75
Their children: John, Mary, Michael died young
James, 3/22/1893, 31
His children: Mary, Natalia and Jerome
Mary Doyle's sister, Anastasia Sullivan, 12/8/1885, 53

Doyle
Thomas, 4/21/1880, 50, Kilanieran, Wexford
By wife Bridget Carey, 11/29/1892, 76
Thomas' brother James, 3/4/1885, 70

Drew
Henry, 12/15/1958
See Madigan, Bridget, 2/13/1909, 34

Driscoll
James, 1/16/1882, 46, Cork City
His mother Ellen, 7/13/1876, 74
By wife Mary A., 8/22/1892, 50/56

Driscoll
Maria, 10/3/1905, 37
Her son Timothy, 7/21/1904, 4-5-0
See Clynn, Timothy, 10/9/1894, 32

Dudley
Mary, 12/15/1872, 65, Doneraile, Cork
By son Richard, 4/1/1908, 68
His children Robert and Hannah died young
Andrew, 7/22/1898, 61
Mary, 2/3/1924, 80
Mary Hanning, 1867 - 1957

Duff
Mary
See Golden, Michael, 3/18/1878

Duffy
Anthony 5/27?/1904
See Dunn, Julia 18??, Roscrea, Tipperary

Duffy
Francis, 4/22/1858, Monaghan
Also wife Margaret and children Thomas, Margaret, Lizzie

Duffy
John, 10/26/1893, 60, Dromard, Longford
By wife Catherine

Duffy
John, 11/12/1892, 65, Roscommon
By wife Eliza

Duffy
Maria, 10/20/1884, Tallow, Waterford
Her sister Hanora, wife of James Casey, 1/14/1888
James Casey, 2/10/1898
Ida Casey, wife of David F., 6/29/1923
David F. Casey, 4/10/1924

Dugey
Patrick, 10/19/1908, 36, Waterford
By wife Nellie

Duncan
John, 1/4/1900, 61, City of Dublin
By wife Catherine

Duncan
Maud C. Mulledy wife of P.F. Mulledy, 4/5/1899, 26
See Mulledy, Patrick, 12/27/1891, 73

Dungan
William, Kells, Kilkenny
By Hanora

Dunlap
Alice, 7/22/1886, 63, Fermanagh
By husband William
His grandchildren:, Willie J. Harris, 3
John, 11 months
Josie, 10 months
Joseph B. Carney, 1910 - 1952

Dunleavy
Bridget, 4/21/1900, 35, Mayo
By husband Thomas, 8/17/1947, 83
Winifred, 1868 - 1954
Anna, 1909 - 1959
Andrew J., 1905 - 1984

Dunleavy
Rose, 1/29/1888, 37, Donegal
Bridget, 12/19/1899
Rose, 2/29/1904, 84

Dunleavy
Thomas L., 5/7/1907, 38, Mayo
By wife Margaret M., 7/23/1931
Their daus.
Helen V. McCarthy, 6/10/1930
Mary E. Dunleavy, 7/15/1900, 15
Margaret Campbell, 5/12/1944, 55

Dunn
Bridget, 4/4/1899, 70, Viper, Kilkenny
Mary Donnell, 3/13/1893, 1-3-0, dau. of
John, 9/25/1933, 76
Rose, 4/25/1932, 74
Their grandson S/Sgt. William J. Loughrey, U.S.A.F. killed in action, 4/6/1945
Willie F. Donnell, 2/2/1908, 21

Dunn
Christopher, 11/2/1892
By wife Mary, 7/20/1923
Her sister Ellen, 3/15/1909
Ellen's husband Bernard, 7/9/1880, Kings
Annie Halloran, 2/26/1943

Dunn
James, 11/30/1895, 60, Drum, Roscommon

Dunn
James, 1/27/1927, 63, Mount Mellick, Leix
Rose M., 1/9/1955, 51
James F., 7/7/1956, 27
David J., 10/17/1964, 70

Dunn
Julia 18??, Roscrea, Tipperary
By Mary Reardon 1/20?/1889
Anthony Duffy 5/27?/1904
Walter Hayes 2/10/1945

Dunn
Maria, 12/30/1852, 24, Kildare
James Gallagher, 11/19/1856, 33
By Rosa Dunn, sister of Maria, 4/8/1897, 64

Dunn
Mary, 2/23/1918, 55, Dungarvan, Waterford
By husband Daniel, 3/20/1927, 74, Cloncannon, Mount Mellick, Leix
Anna, 1889 - 1971
James F., 1850 - 1976

Dunn
Mary Theresa, 9/9/1890 - 8/6/1892
By parents:
Christopher, 11/15/1910, 48, Kildare
Mary, 7/4/1925, 62
Edward J. Dorr, 11/19/1961
Mary D. Dorr, 6/20/1962

Dunne
Anne 30?, Tipperary
By Thomas

Dunne
Dennis, 10/5/1915, 72, Phillipstown, Kings
By brother Patrick, 12/26/1916
Eliza, 1/28/1925

Dunne
Dennis, 10/4/1887, 64, Kildare
Wife Margaret, 11/19/1897, 69
Their daus.:
Mary F. Leddy, 4/4/1924
Margaret Shanley, 3/27/1936

Dunne
Michael, 12/14/1869, 64, Edenderry, Kings
By wife Bridget, 7/11/1881, 75
Catherine Dunn Victory, 4/29/1892
Also children: Mary, 9/30/1835, 1
John, 8/18/1837, 10 months
Arthur, 7/3/1839, 1-4-0
James, 9/10/1854, 3

Dunne
Patrick, Stradbally, Queens
By wife Elizabeth

Dunne
Patrick, 8/14/1898, Sligo
By wife Julia, 1/30/1903

Durgo
Catherine L., 10/31/1871 - 6/7/1941
See McCarthy, Charles, 6/8/1873 - 4/12/1916

During
Carl Heinrich, 1/14/1852 - 12/30/1914, Frankfurt, A/Main, Germany
By wife Julia, 12/1/1862 - 6/21/1926, Killorglin, Kerry

Durkan
Daniel, 12/3/1897, 22, Mayo
By brother William

Durning
Ann, 8/1/1877, 68, Fermanagh
Bernard, 8/17/1877, 70, Fermanagh

Dwyer
Cornelius H., 8/15/1843 - 3/15/1914, Tipperary
By wife Catherine Butler, 4/15/1916, 65
Their sons:
James J., 2/6/1870 - 1/11/1891
Matthew P., 1/31/1924
Dau. Margaret Fitzgerald, 5/12/1908

Dwyer
Mary, 3/17/1839 - 7/22/1886, Tipperary
By husband Patrick, 8/7/1895, 56, Limerick
James, 7/14/1870 - 4/9/1871
Emily, 7/2/1872 - 10/2/1874
Lucy Dwyer Smith, 1/18/1917
Nan Dwyer, 6/4/1938
Fred Weaver, 1888 - 1969
Eulalie Weaver, 1899 - 1976

Eagan
Mary, 3/20/1885, 68, Clogh, Longford
By son Owen
Ellen, 8/4/1901
Thomas, 8/11/1901
Ann, 8/18/1901
Owen, 9/14/1901

Early
John, 5/11/1894, 64, Edenderry, Kings
By wife Catherine

Early
Julia, 6/16/1906, Meath
By husband John, 12/28/1915, Streete, Westmeath
Bernard J., 3/13/1941

Eckman
Catherine M., 9/1/1904, 11 months
Mary Stevens O'Gorman, 4/30/1930, 76, Clare
Catherine Fitzgerald Eckman, 8/12/1933, 53

Edgerton
Frank, 7/16/1913, 48, City of Dublin
By wife Ellen
Laurence Redican, 1908 - 1975
Kevin T., 1938 - 1981

Edmunds
Thomas, 4/17/1881, 37, Tipperary
John, 5/21/1885, 35, Tipperary
By sister Mary Edmunds
Celeste M. Johnson, 1916 - 1972
Celeste M. Johnson, 1950 - 1973

Egan
Bridget 12/12/1932, Longford
By husband James F. 8/20/1955
Andrew
Anna A. Cunningham
Mary Gray
Patrick Gray

Egan
Elizabeth, 4/23/1939
See Glavin, John, 3/4/1885, 54

Egan
Mary, 6/20/1910, 70, Clare
See Murphy, Hanora, 8/11/1899, 55

Egan
Mary, 1/22/1906, Galway
By husband James, 11/29/1910, 72

Egan
Mary, 1/1/1887, 44, Castlecomer, Kilkenny
Anne, 2/15/1912, 65
Mary F. Glennon, 12/4/1929, 34
Walter J. Six, 5/2/1947, 30
Walter A. Six, 1894 - 1952
Margaret A., 1890 - 1981

Elliott
Patrick, 11/27/1878, 40, Tubberclare, Westmeath
Formerly of Ulster County, New York
By sister Mary Elliott
Also Vesey family

Engelhart
Mammie, 9/7/1914
See Byrne, Margaret, 12/25/1907, 47

Ennis
Mary, 8/18/1895, 56, Meath
By husband Hugh
Marie Heyser, 10/4/1971

Enright
Mary, 8/27/1884, 73, Londonderry
Daniel, 6/9/1888, 42

Evans
Bertha, 3/7/1965
See Reilly, Rose, 3/8/1915

Evans
Edith May Clifton, 11/14/1863 - 12/10/1915, Cork

Fagan
Catherine B., 4/3/1891, 68, Castlematyr, Cork
Her sister Abagail Barry, 3/28/1897, 72

Fallon
Annie, 10/26/1895, 26, Leitrim
By sister Margaret Fallon Buiridge, 4/8/1929

Fallon
Ellie, 1868 - 1937
See Brady, Bernard

Fallon
Thomas, 6/15/1860, Mount Prospect, Roscommon

Famalette
Majorie M., 12/23/1967, 62
See Grant, Michael, 3/5/1884, 60

Farley
Elizabeth M., 7/21/1904 - 1/31/1929
See Fitzgerald, Edward, 11/12/1923

Farrell
Ann, 5/5/1880, 69, Carrickedmond, Longford
Joseph, 10/31/1882, 29
Peter, 4/6/1896, 51
Anna, 4/18/1901, 90
Elizabeth Connell, 8/19/1907, 45
Annie M. Leich, 12/2/1914, 65
Charles More, 2/18/1959, 69
Dates of burial

Farrell
Catherine, 3/3/1887, 53, Ardagh, Longford
By husband James, 4/21/1894, 50
Their children:, James, Mamie, Katie died young
Their grandchildren: Johnnie, Katie Hatton, James Farrell
Edward Farrell, 1907
Roseanna, 1917
Leo Hatton, 1897
Anna Maria, 1901
Mary Farrell Hatton, 1866 - 1929
John A. Farrell, 1934
John F., 1859 - 1942
John M. Lloyd, 1886 - 1945
Esther C. Hatton, 1886 - 1956
Mary F. Hatton, 1896 - 1964

Farrell
Christopher, 7/20/1896, 47, Naas, Kildare
By wife Kate

Farrell
Hugh, 9/2/1894, 54, Carlow
By wife Maria, 6/26/1900, 56
Their children Kate and Joseph died young
Lena, 22
Hebert F. Connors, 1883 - 1968
Martha Connors, 1885 - 1978

Farrell
James, 10/19/1947, 76
See McGrath, Mary

Farrell
John, 5/13/1870, 62, Longford
By wife Ellen

Farrell
John, 11/21/1871, 51, Clongesh, Longford
By wife Mary
Her brother Peter Casey

Farrell
John, 11/3/1904, 56, Longford
By wife Catherine

Farrell
John, 2/11/1917, Longford
Thomas, 1934
Anne, 10/20/1950
Michael, 11/30/1953

Farrell
Mary, 2/23/1891, 93, Longford
By son James, 11/14/1901, 57

Farrell
Mary, 86, Moydow, Longford
By dau. Catherine Farrell
Bridget, 7/29/1852/1862
Thomas, 28

Farrell
Nellie A., 7/20/1926, 69
Martin, 1920 - 1940
Grace, 1947
Helen, 1956
Joseph F., 1952
Martin B., 1955
Anna R., 1959
See Byrne, Rose, 8/11/1885

Farrell
Patrick, 3/11/1875, Edgeworthstown, Longford
Ellen, 2/2/1882, 60
Anna M., 3/13/1935

Farrell
Peter, 3/4/1892, 76, Cashel, Longford
By wife Mary, 12/7/1904, 75
Joseph, 5/25/1915
Anne, 1/1/1933
Julia, 8/10/1937

Farrell
Roger, 4/10/1820 - 4/15/1891, Ardagh, Longford
By wife Bridget

Farrelly
Joseph, 2/1/1870, 33, Cavan
By wife Ann, 7/29/1882, 42, Aughmullen, Monaghan

Farrelly
Margaret, 2/12/1878, 38, Ballinacargy, Westmeath
By husband Patrick J., 3/10/1918
Their children:
Catherine, 9/17/1868, 2-2-0
James, 2/1/1870, 10 days
Catherine, 8/23/1871, 0-1-17

Farren
Denis, 7/17/1857, 52, Donegal
Wife Frances, 3/29/1866, 52
John H., 12/19/1858, 21
Dennis Jr., 7/3/1857, 9
Mary Farren, wife of George Hegerty, 10/2/1894
Frances, 7/28/1847, 4
Patrick Henry McMahon, 1929
Annie A. McMahon, dau. of Denis Farren, 1846 - 1922

Farrington
Patrick, 3/12/1887, 86, Mayo
By son John, 12/6/1905, 69

Fay
Catherine, 3/16/1861, Culdaff, Donegal
By husband John, 1/28/1881, 68

Fayne
Winifred, 12/24/1916, 29
See Leonard, Frank, 6/24/1906, 39

Feehan
Patrick, 5/10/1887, 62, Kilkenny
Wife Mary, 5/30/1883, 63

Feeley
Ambrose, 9/1869, Monaghan

Feeley
John, 2/8/1866 - 4/4/1914, Kerry
By wife Nora, 7/24/1916, 50
Margaret, 2/23/1922, 20

Feeley
By Patrick for brothers and sister
John, 7/11/1853, 25, Legan, Longford
William, 12/2/1880, 52, Legan, Longford
Mary Larkin, 12/2/1882, 55, Legan, Longford
Her dau. Mary, 12/20/1894, 17, Legan, Longford

Feeley
Patrick, 10/25/1887, 56, Legan, Longford
Margaret, wife of Michael, 2/27/1902, 71
Michael Cummings, 12/20/1884, 50
James J., 5/30/1945
Philomena, 1952

Feely
Mary, 8/20/1890, Longford
By husband Peter

Feely
Mary, 4/18/1902, 70, Longford
See Mallon, John, 1834 - 6/4/1890

Feeney
Ann, 9/19/1862, 48-7-0, Garristown, Co. Dublin
By son Thomas Sherlock
Bridget Carey, 1874 - 1922
William A. Carey, 1870 - 1958

Feeney
Catherine, 11/2/1859, 62, Waterford City
By daughter Maria Neff
William Neff, 5/6/1889, 65, Kilkenny

Feeney
Joseph P., 11/30/1910, Loughrea, Galway
By wife Ellen, 10/24/1935
Her sisters Mary Ward, 4/20/1901
Catherine Noone, 7/6/1926
Her brother John, 8/23/1932

Feeny
Michael, 2/26/1889, 49, Tipperary
Wife Margaret, 12/22/1896, 55
Son William

Fegan
Michael, 10/16/1882, 52, Dublin
Michael J. Nolen, 8/8/1910, 41
Elizabeth Hedden, 12/28/1912, 50
Helen V. Cutler, 9/4/1918
Ellen J. Cutler, 7/9/1930

Fennesey
Daniel, 12/4/1917, 72, Tipperary
By wife Mary, 11/15/1924
John S. Regan, 10/23/1958

Fernie
Catherine A., 9/6/1902, 33-7-0
See Lyons, Michael, 11/24/1901, 65

Figueirra
Anthony, 6/12/1861, 9 months
See Cummings, Mary, 7/16/1861, 65

Finegen
Patrick, 8/14/1925, 24
See Christy, Mary A., 3/8/1908, 39

Finerty
John J., 3/6/1904, 45, Ballinrobe, Mayo
Mary A., 7/5/1916, 53, Ballinrobe, Mayo
By sisters Margaret and Mary, Ballinrobe, Mayo

Finn
Michael P., 4/18/1916, 45, Kilconnell, Galway
By wife Mary A., 9/28/1932
Norah A., 11/15/1925
George H. McCarthy, 5/16/1954
Ann M. McCarthy, 9/29/1963

Finn
Thomas F., 10/25/1888 - 10/7/1942
Mary, 1885 - 1906
See McCann, John, 6/8/1906, 46

Finnan
Margaret, 6/14/1845, died shipboard, Killashee, Longford
Bernard, 2/9/1856, 72, Killashee, Longford
By dau. Ann Finnan
Her sister Julia, 1/4/1892, 60, Killashee, Longford

Finnan
Michael, 12/22/1862, 35, Moydow, Longford
Son Thomas M., 7/2/1879, 17-10-10
Ellen M., 12/9/1889, 30

Finnegan
Annie, 5/11/1893, 34, Sligo
By husband John
Her mother Jane Rouse, 4/24/1876, 62
Mary McGrath, 1/29/1908, 60

Finnegan
Mary, 10/13/1918, 35
See Fitzgerald, Thomas, 7/8/1891, 49

Finneran
Catherine, 6/16/1907, 74, Newtown, Cashel, Longford
Dau. Margaret, 2/23/1895, 36, Newtown, Cashel, Longford
Dau. Ann Mahon Finneran 11/17/1901, 47, Newtown, Cashel, Longford
John J., 1/6/1931
Kathryn, 9/24/1934
Maria Dowdall, 2/2/1935
Edward Finneran, 1/27/1945
John G., 3/31/1946
Catherine, 10/15/1947
Maria B., 9/3/1965
Kathleen Finneran Ryan, 1971

Finley
Mary 1878?, 65, Aughmullen, Monaghan

Finnerty
Joseph F., 1886 - 1970
Mary N., 1905 - 1984
See Burke, Celia, 12/13/1931

Fitzgerald
Edward J., 1901 - 1969
See Kennedy, John J., 5/6/1914, 70

Fitzgerald
Edward, 11/12/1923, Cork
Dau. Elizabeth M. Farley, 7/21/1904 - 1/31/1929
Mary Fitzgerald, 1/2/1935

Fitzgerald
John J., 3/22/1926, 64
See Leonard, Frank, 6/24/1906, 39

Fitzgerald
Margaret, 5/12/1908
See Dwyer, Cornelius H., 8/15/1843 - 3/15/1914

Fitzgerald
Mary, 10/31/1914, 54, Emly, Tipperary
By husband Patrick, 6/13/1933, 90
James, 10/10/1924, 31
Helen, 10/20/1986, 74

Fitzgerald
Thomas, 7/8/1891, 49, Croom, Limerick
By wife Mary, 3/18/1919, 75
Son Richard, 12/25/1916, 39
Dau. Mary Finnegan, 10/13/1918, 35
Edward Fitzgerald, 2/23/1937

Fitzpatrick
Catherine, 10/16/1884, 55, Monaghan, Monaghan
See Clark, Thomas Jr., 2/22/1873

Fitzpatrick
Catherine, 10/16/1868, Edenderry, Kings
Michael, 12/20/1857, 58, Edenderry, Kings
By Mary Fitzpatrick dau. and sister

Fitzpatrick
Dorothy, 12/28/1863, 48, Edenderry, Kings
By husband John and 6 children

Fitzpatrick
Mary, 8/31/1871, 88, Donaghmore, Tyrone
Michael Doran, 1/4/1881, 50

Fitzpatrick
Patrick, 1878, 79, Carrickedmond, Longford
By wife Bridget

Fitzpatrick
Patrick, 7/8/1883, 64, Kilkenny
Wife Bridget, 4/9/1899, 60, Roscommon
Their children:
James, 7/27/1892, 24
Ceila, 2 years

Fitzpatrick
Richard, 7/26/1877, 55, Longford
By Rose Lewis
Rose Fitzpatrick, 10/2/1889
Rose Sweeney, 8/21/1907, 90 ?

Fitzpatrick
Timothy, 7/5/1878, New Hall, Kilone, Clare
By wife Johanna

Fitzsimons
Francis, 2/23/1870, Bundoran, Donegal
By brother John

Flaherty
James, 11/17/1911, 45, Menlough, Galway
By wife Catherine, 2/16/1925, 56

Flaherty
John, 1860, Granard, Longford
By father Michael

Flaherty
John F., 7/18/1909, Dunmore, Galway
By sister Bridget, Dunmore, Galway
Nephew Frank Flaherty, 7/4/1908, Dunmore, Galway

Flanagan
Ellen, 12/5/1924
See Murray, John, 3/4/1885, 47

Flanagan
John J. 6/14/1910, 63, Ardare, Limerick
By wife Mary nee Canty
Their children:
Hanna 1/15/1890, 20
John J., Teresa, Ellen and John
Mary Flanagan 10/6/1935
Mary C. 8/3/1953
Lillian F. 5/29/1967

Flannery
Catherine Regan, 8/13/1885 - 11/6/1922
See Dougherty, Mary, 2/1879, 72

Flannery
Mary, 5/12/1881, 56, Galway

Flannery
Patrick, 5/3/1954
See Connolly, John, 5/13/1885, 48

Flattery
James, 2/27/1909, Kilcommuck, Longford
By wife Mary C., 12/23/1925
Children: Catherine, Michael, James, Kilcommuck, Longford
His parents Michael and Catherine Flattery, Kilcommuck, Longford
Nephew James Sarsfield Flattery, Kilcommuck, Longford

Flattery
Timothy, 3/4/1860 - 10/24/1892, Longford
By wife Margaret

Fleetwood
Thomas G., 2/18/1936
See Bray, John, 7/29/1895, 66

Fleming
Mary, 2/27/1897, 53, Islandeady, Mayo
By husband Matthew
John, 2/15/1868 - 6/29/1878
James J., 1/6/1871 - 1/28/1893
Thomas F., 1/27/1873 - 8/20/1895
Martin, William, Annie, Mary, Margaret and Francis died in infancy

Fleming
Patrick, 12/23/1871, 33, Cavan
By wife Eliza

Fletcher
Anna Fogarty, 2/5/1958
See Barrett, John, 6/14/1898

Fletcher
John Y., 7/12/1960
See Rawl, Thomas, 4/16/1882, 67

Fletcher
Susan, 4/22/1880, 39, Killama, Donegal
By husband John, 12/8/1915
Also 7 children

Flood
John, 6/15/1886, 60, Cavan
By wife Ann, 11/10/1889, 52

Flood
Robert, 9/27/1886, 53
By wife Ann, 5/18/1906, 72
Her mother and sisters
Natives of Longford and Westmeath

Flynn
Catherine, 2/28/1907 47, Ballingar, Roscommon
By husband Michael J., 8/15/1857 - 3/19/1919
Rathmore, Strokestown, Roscommon
Walter E. Whitehead V.F.M., 5/30/1895 - 3/10/1936
Edward J. Byrne, 11/20/1939
Mary E. Flynn, 2/1/1884 - 6/19/1954
Thomas F., 7/7/1958
Kathryn J. Byrne, 6/19/1966
Susan Whitehead, 8/23/1969

Flynn
Christania, 4/10/1859, 35, Kings
Catherine, 12/6/1899, 77
By husband Edward, 10/13/1901, 78
His mother Mary, 3/1885
Ann Flynn, 4/20/1903, 73

Flynn
Edwin J., 3/7/1915, 41, Mayo
By wife Mary

Flynn
James, 7/25/1896, 67, Moate, Westmeath
By wife Mary, 6/23/1910, 70

Flynn
John, 1/24/1889, 43, Rathaspic, Westmeath
By wife Bridget

Flynn
Michael, 10/27/1887, 75, Leitrim
Wife, 2/7/1903, 90, Leitrim
Patrick E. Cullen, 1917
Joseph F., 1945
Annie F., 1946
Vincent de.P., 1980

Fogarty
John J., 2/4/1919, 70, Tipperary
By wife Mary, 4/1940, 73, Tipperary
Their dau. Mary McCormack, 6/18/1918, 33
Her infant Dau. Veronica, grandchild of Mary Fogarty
Mary Ritter died in infancy 1927
Son William Fogarty, 9/11/1941, 58
John Jr. Fogarty, 10/4//1891 - 11/22/1961

Fogarty
John Joseph, 2/28/1898, 3
See Barrett, John, 6/14/1895

Fogarty
Margaret, 8/8/1905, Kilkenny

Folan
Thomas, 3/29/1902, 55, Galway
Wife Sarah A., 1/8/1916, 76
Children: Rosie, 3/29/1879, 2-3-7;
Maria, 3/3/1879, 4-3-0

Foley
Thomas, 4/9/1909, Headford, Galway
By wife Mary, 1876 - 1917
Twin children John and Julia
Mary Ellen, 1901 - 1915
Julia McDonough, 1889 - 1953

Foohey
John, 12/15/1861, 35, Carrigtwohill, Cork
Mary, 9/17/1873, 52, Carrigtwohill, Cork
Catherine, 9/15/1867, 12, Carrigtwohill, Cork
Johannah Briody, 1/16/1884, 32, Carrigtwohill, Cork
By children Johannah and Matthew

Ford
Bridgid, 10/16/1860, 64, Dorduff, Monaghan
Margaret, 4/28/1858, 20, Dorduff, Monaghan

Ford
Lawrence, 1/5/1895, 36, Mayo
By brother Anthony
Anthony's wife Mary, 8/8/1894, 31, Mayo

Ford
Martin, 1/6/1918, 40, Galway
By wife Celia, 5/9/1943
Son John P., 10/13/1922, 19
Mary, 6/16/1943

Forrest
John, 6/10/1869, 77, City of Cork
By wife Ellen, 4/26/1887, 88, Armagh
Thomas Freeman, 11/10/1900
Son Arthur J. Freeman, 8/8/1911, 24
Wife of Thomas, Sarah Donnelly Freeman, 1849 - 8/11/1911, Armagh
James Donnelly, nephew of Sarah Freeman, 2/20/1872 - 1/8/1926, Milltown, Armagh on the banks of Loughreagh

Forrester
Margaret, 1884 - 1967
See Tuite, Matthew, 3/26/1909, 22

Fox
Delia Mullery, 5/12/1914
James C., 5/15/1901
See Mullery, Edward, 5/16/1897

Fox
James, Westmeath
By wife Ann
Children: John, Timothy, Thomas

Fox
Margaret, 6/15/1897, 76, Legan, Longford
By husband Thomas

Fox
Michael, 9/8/1871, Doon, Limerick

Foy
Emily M., 1/3/1946
See McPadden, John, 6/23/1877

Frawley
Bridget, 5/21/1888, 63, Clare
By dau. Mary

Frawley
Michael, 12/29/1929, , Limerick City
Son Gerard
Christopher V., 5/15/1932
Margaret, 8/28/1949
Catherine, 6/26/1979

Frazer
Margaret, 5/17/1933
John M., 10/30/1937
Thomas, 1/10/1938
Joseph, 9/21/1944, 74
His wife Mary C., 1892 - 1957
See Cominger, Leo, 2/8/1897

Freeman
Bernard, 4/16/1888, 60, Pesth, Hungary
Wife Maria Brady, 10/4/1883, 52, Ballinalea, Wicklow
Agnes Niemann, 12/19/1965
Margaret Freeman
Alfred F. Freeman
Alfred P. Freeman
Margaret Stern

Frewen
Mary, wife of the late John, 6/17/1904, Tipperary
Her son Jeremiah J., , 3/29/1904
Her dau. Annie M., , 4/21/1892
Granddau. Mary J.B. O'Sullivan, 8/28/1905
William A. Frewen, 10/12/1912
Margaret, 5/7/1925
Lillian

Fruin
John, 9/11/1861 ?, 60, Tipperary
Catherine, 9/26/1863 ?, 44, Tipperary

Fullerton
Margaret, 1912 - 1964
Thomas Sr., 1911 - 1981
See Christy, Mary A., 3/8/1908, 39

Furey
Margaret, 7/8/1880, Legan, Longford
Thomas, Longford
MaryAnn, Longford
Matthew, Longford
Edward H., 2/17/1923

Furlong
James, 8/31/1891, 55, Wexford

Gaffney
Martin, 4/12/1905, , Longford
Margaret Carroll, 3/7/1926, Longford
By their children

Gallagher
Annie, 2/14/1921
See McLaughlin, Neil, 10/25/1918

Gallagher
Anne M., 1/3/1896 - 4/25/1960
Helen R., 1882 - 1969
See Henry, Thomas D., 1852 - 7/12/1914

Gallagher
Catherine, 5/13/1921, 63
See Nelson, Rose, 12/25/1913, 52

Gallagher
Elizabeth, 2/18/1882, 48, Templemore, Tipperary
By husband James, 3/11/1895, 87

Gallagher
Francis, 12/26/1901, 62, Leitrim
Catherine, 3/7/1908, 59, Donegal
By son Francis, 1879 - 1941
Mary A., 1883 - 1930
Frank F. Bannon, 1901 - 1955
Theresa V. Bannon, 1903 - 1960

Gallagher
James, 11/19/1856, 33
See Dunn, Maria, 12/30/1852, 24

Gallagher
Margaret, 1/23/1899, 67
See Moran, Roger, 7/7/1854, 26

Gallagher
Mary, 4 months
See Byrns, Mary, 10/18/1883, 53

Gallagher
Mary L., 7/19/1955
See McCallig, Edward, 12/6/1895, 62

Gallagher
Patrick, 3/7/1887, 49, Belmullet, Mayo

Gallagher
William H. Sr., 12/27/1882 - 7/16/1867, 84
Agnes E., 2/15/1882 - 1/18/1969, 86
See McDonough, Margaret, 9/1866

Galligher
Charles, 8/2/1862, 2-3-0
Hannah, 5/12/1869, 7-1-25
Sarah, 5/24/1869, 5-2-17
Margaret, 6/6/1867, 1-6-6
By parents:
Catherine, 10/17/1898, Raphoe, Donegal
Charles, 1/2/1899, Raphoe, Donegal

Galvin
Donald A., No date
See Ryan, Michael, 11/1/1918, 35

Galway
James, 1/27/1888, 71, Wexford
By wife Margaret, 6/30/1895, 84
Mary, mother of James, 8/15/1860, 77
Margaret, sister of James, 3/31/1884, 63
James Jr., 3/24/1887, 46

Gammell
Ned, 3/17/1865 - 1/9/1894, Limerick
Ned Jr., 10/23/1893 - 5/8/1918
Mother, 1/5/1865 - 1/8/1928

Ganley
Daniel J., 11/4/1917, 38, Moate, Westmeath
See Hanley, Elizabeth, 4/8/1902, 64

Gannon
Bridget, 11/15/1867, 70, Ardagh, Longford
By son John

Gannon
Ellen T., 3/30/1927
James J., 11/14/1945
See Devaney, John J., 7/3/1890, 44

Gannon
Jane, 1870, Rathcline, Longford
By sister Catherine

Gannon
Maria, 4/27/1913, Elphin, Roscommon
Dau. of Edward and Mary Gannon
Annie, 5/24/1929

Garrahan
Michael, 12/16/1907, Longford
Mary, 3/1/1910, Longford

Garvey
James, son of the late Thomas and Bridget, Aughrim, Roscommon
By sister Jennie

Garvey
Rose
See Leonard, John, 5/12/1888

Garvin
John, 8/2/1893, 31, Newport, Mayo
By mother Anne
Edward, 12/5/1893, 27
Bridget Macklin, 4/25/1910, 46

Gavin
John, 4/16/1880, 35, Mayo
By wife Annie

Garwin
Ellen, 10/16/1878, 44, Kilbridge, Roscommon
By sisters Mary and Bridget

Gaynor
Ellen, 1858, Mullingar, Westmeath
By husband Michael
Son Joseph
Edward Urell

Geary
John, 3/25/1879, 80, Queenstown, Cork
Ellen, 7/26/1889, 80

Geary
Patrick, 4/25/1917, 38, Glenfin, Donegal
By aunt Rose Carlon
See Carlon, Charles, 5/1885

Geoghegan
John died young
See Hamilton, James, 1/11/1886, 60

Gerrarty
William, 8/9/1877, 30, Westmeath
By wife Bridget, 7/6/1899, 54
Son Willie, 6/19/1874

Gianella
John, 1/14/1838 - 5/16/1914, Switzerland
Marguerite Higgins, 2/22/1857 - 3/12/1942
John, 8/14/1885 - 3/15/1973
See Higgins, Dennis, , 1/12/1863

Gibbons
Catherine, 5/20/1898, Kilmeena, Mayo
By sister Bridget, Kilmeena, Mayo

Gibbons
John, 3/28/1914, 38, Mayo
By wife Margaret, 1875 - 1966
Son Michael, 1909 - 1935
John J., 1904 - 1952

Gibbons
Michael F., 9/23/1913, Limerick
Wife Josephine, 3/29/1919, 46
See Stanton, John, 5/23/1902, 63

Gibbons
Patrick, 7/31/1915, 38, Mayo
By wife Nora Gibbons Glennon, 8/3/1879 - 8/25/1958
John J. Hourihan, 1904 - 1976
Mary Ellen, 2/16/1912 - 3/21/1989

Giger
Helen Phillips, 1905 -
Simon F.X., 1898 - 1970
See Phillips, Charles J., 12/10/1925, 23

Gilbride
Catherine, 7/10/1871, 40, Templemore, Tipperary
By husband William, Templemore, Tipperary

Gill
Bridget, 12/20/1870
Wife of John, 1/4/1894
See Diffeely, Catherine, 7/15/1868

Gill
Bridget, 11/19/1895, 65, Lanesboro, Rathcline, Longford
Catherine Curran Williams, 11/24/1927, 28
John, Frank, Margaret, Edward Curran

Gill
Michael, 3/20/1899, 42, Mayo
By wife Margaret, 5/30/1959
Her sister Annie Reilly, 11/9/1954
Patrick Reilly, 7/5/1955

Gillen
Maryann, 2/1/1883, 40, Monaghan
By husband John
Daus. Katie and Winifred Gillen

Gillen
Mary V., 11/2/1879 - 10/31/1965
See McCarthy, Charles, 6/8/1873 - 4/12/1916

Gillen
Michael, 3/17/1867, 50, Westmeath
By wife Mary
Ellen, 11/21/1889, 77, Westmeath

Gillen
Michael J., 7/31/1908, 3
By father Michael, 8/13/1862 - 8/16/1935, Glebe, Derry
Genevieve Walsh, 2/10/1895 - 11/9/1940
Mary Gillen, 3/20/1862 - 3/7/1946
James J. Walsh, 11/11/1889 - 1/23/1954

Gillin
Daniel, 7/20/1851, Emper, Kilmacnevin, Westmeath

Gillon
Katie, 8/15/1860 - 8/9/1904
Sister Mary Mullins, 4/3/1883, Clare
By John husband of Katie
Also niece baby Norah Sheehan, 11/19/1869
John Sheehan, 12/11/1911

Gilroy
Eliza, 3/12/1876
By niece Bessie Gilroy, 12/9/1919, Leitrim
Ellen, 12/20/1926, Leitrim
Cousins John Travers, 12/20/1902
Margaret Travers, 10/23/1911

Giovannoli
Senerino, 1885 - 1967
See Judge, Jane, 11/6/1897, 60

Glander
Husband of Margaret, 5/23/1884, 50-3-0
See Scanlon, Timothy, 9/7/1879, 50

Glavin
John, 3/4/1885, 54, Tallow, Waterford
By wife Bridget, 4/12/1901, 69, Castle ?, Waterford
Elizabeth Egan, 4/23/1939

Gleason
Ann daughter of Michael and Bridget Dougherty, 1/5/1895, 65
See Dougherty, Edward, 1870, 41

Gleason
Johanna, Rockhill, Limerick
Kathryn C. Harrington

Glenn
Elizabeth, 5/13/1937, 65
See Gray, William, 8/7/1904, 64

Glennon
Bridget, 7/28/1872, 37, Tipperary
By husband James

Glennon
Mary F., 12/4/1929, 34
See Egan, Mary, 1/1/1887, 44

Glennon
Mary, 9/28/1891, 70, Ballinabrackey, Meath
Her dau. Lizzie, 4/9/1912, 60
Anne Cooney Glennon, 1/27/1953, wife of Philip Glennon, 5/31/1924
Thomas, 11/15/1897

Glennon
Nora Gibbons, 8/3/1879 - 8/25/1958
See Gibbons, Patrick, 7/31/1915, 38

Glynn
Sabina, 1/6/1896, Galway
See Heverin, Alice M., 2/22/1901

Glynn
Thomas, 7/28/1926, 70, Ballinasloe, Galway
Wife Delia A., 10/3/1934, 83, Claremorris, Mayo
Mary Donnellan, 5/19/1883, 26
Ellen Glynn, 1/22/1886, 11 months
Thomas Glynn Jr., 6/30/1888, 3 months

Goggin
Maria, wife of James, 10/29/1938
See Plunkett, John, 9/24/1890, 35

Goggins
Bridget, 5/23/1881, 36, Partry ?, Mayo
By husband Thomas
Dau. Mary
Thomas, 11/30/1894, 57
Ellen C., 4/10/1933, 92

Goggins
Patrick, 4/29/1887, 75, Mayo
By dau. Bridget Reilly, 1/24/1914, 76
Her husband John Reilly, 11/30/1917, 79

Golden
Michael, 3/18/1878
Mary Duff, Mayo
Ann Collins, 7/7/1883, 38

Goldenberg
Irene A., 10/25/1910 - 7/7/1980
See McDonough, Margaret, 9/1866

Goldrick
Annie, 7/7/1924, 79, Longford
By nephew Patrick Dennigan, 5/27/1942
Mary C. Dennigan, 6/17/1961

Goodwin
Fred, 5/1/1884 - 10/26/1959
Ellen Lynch, 5/2/1894 - 7/4/1975
See Bray, John, 7/29/1895, 66

Gordon
Margaret, 5/19/1847 - 3/19/1899, 41-10-0, Down
By husband James, 2/13/1917, 71
Mary C., 1876 - 1931
James F., 1873 - 1955
Mary Blackhahn, 9/10/1910, 27

Gorevin
Ellen, Sligo
By husband Thomas, 9/11/1938, Town of Sligo

Gorham
Bartholemew, 4/21/1900, Galway
Mary, 4/4/1909, Galway
By daus. Mary and Delia Gorham
Their sister Annie, 6/13/1901, Galway
Peggy, 5/1/1936

Gorman
Ann, 10/29/1903, Buncrana, Donegal
By husband John, 5/24/1910, 78

Gorman
James, 7/11/1911, Queens
By sister Mary J., Queens

Gorman
Martin H., 10/23/1913, 56, Clare
Son Fergus
By wife Annie nee Baker, 10/6/1943

Gormen
Margaret, 2/18/1885, 74, Ardagh, Longford

Gormley
Family
See McManus, Annie, 5/2/1898, 52

Gough
Edward, 7/17/1876, 53, Dungarvan, Waterford
By wife Mary
Their children:
Maggie, 8/25/1866, 4
Ambrose, 1/26/1871, 4
Lillie, 2/10/1871, 6

Gouldsbury
Bridget, 1/3/1916, 34, Longford
Anna M., 1911 - 1959

Grace
Julia, 2/1879, Limerick
By dau. Bridget Carey

Grady
Daniel G., 3/8/1886 - 9/27/1938
Catherine N., 1897 - 1970
See Powers, James, 3/19/1892, 9-4-0

Grady
James, 2/12/1912, 36, Clarina ?, Limerick
By wife Margaret
Their dau. Mary M., 5/2/1910, 3
James J., 10/16/1965, 55

Graham
Ann
See Breen, Mary, 12/4/1895, 52

Graham
Ann, 11/3/1913, Boyle, Roscommon
Veronica A. Sanguinetti, 12/3/1894 - 8/13/1960

Graham
Mary, 8/21/1888, 58, Down
Her son John E., 1/10/1896, 37

Graham
Mary, 7/1/1879, Westmeath
By husband Michael
David
Mary, 1867 - 1953
Anna M. Columby, 1889 - 1967

Graham
Michael, 1/12/1882, 28, Castletown, Westmeath
By brother Joseph Graham
Joseph Coffey, 4/6/1886, 47

Grant
Michael, 3/5/1884, 60, Fofanny, Kilcoo, Down
Patrick, 5/3/1887, 52, Fofanny, Kilcoo, Down
By sister Mary Grant, 4/19/1901, 85
Majorie M. Famalette, 12/23/1967, 62
Anna M. Maguire, 1/7/1973, 73

Gray
Bartholomew, 9/30/1858, 42, Granard, Longford
Jane, 9/13/1882, 66, Granard, Longford

Gray
Mary
Patrick
See Egan, Bridget 12/12/1932, Longford

Gray
William, 8/7/1904, 64, Drumlish, Longford
By wife Ann, 10/30/1914
Elizabeth Glenn, 5/13/1937, 65

Greany
William, 10/30/1883, 61, Cork City
By wife Margaret, 1/11/1903, 79

Greeley
Michael F., 5/1/1836 - 3/14/1911, Shrule, Longford
Margaret, 11/3/1911 64
James Greeley, 10/2/1918 21
By his son William F. Greeley

Green
Ann, 4/12/1875, 47, Roscommon
See Dixon, Thomas

Green
Patrick, 5/2/1887, 63, Lagan, Longford
By wife Ann, 1/27/1902

Greenan
James, 11/1869, Westmeath
Mary, 4/18/1882, 80
Son Bernard F., 9/26/1886, 56

Greene
Peter, 3/4/1915, 34, Gweedore, Donegal
John son of Patrick and Sarah, 5/11/1915 21
Margaret M. Coyle, 3/16/1932 68
Margaret M. Greene, 3/6/193, 25 months
Anthony Greene, 1978
Brigid

Grennan
Patrick, 2/13/1910, 46, Westmeath
By sister Margaret Grennan
His wife and children
Theresa L. Basil, 7/1878 - 5/1961

Greenan
Thomas, 9/30/1916, Monaghan
By wife Bridget, 3/25/1938
Dau. Mary A., 9/21/1926

Gribbin
Patrick, 9/11/1884, 43, Belfast
By wife Mary

Grieve
Thomas, 9/27/1925
John T., 2/20/1928
See Dailey, Mary, 1/16/1904, 69

Griffin
Ann, 1880, 50, Clare

Griffin
Bernard G., 11/13/1969
See Deegan, Michael, 9/21/1911

Griffin
Ellen, 7/24/1896, 78, Donegal
By son James

Griffin
Jeremiah
Eliza
See Downey, Bridget, 4/15/1876, 74

Griffin
Margaret Anne, 6/16/1849 - 4/28/1918, Galway
Wife of Dr. John Griffin, 8/26/1846 - 9/4/1927, Clifden, Galway
Mary K., 4/1/1938
Claire A., 3/8/1945

Griffin
Mary, 1860?, Edgeworthstown, Longford

Griffin
Michael J., 7/8/1907
His sister Mary, 12/12/1888, Claremorris, Mayo
Mother Nora, 3/17/1920
Winifred Griffin Donnelly, 12/26/1923

Grosson
Edward and Family, Culdaff, Donegal
By Bridget O'Donnelly

Guerin
Michael, 6/29/1877, 64, Carerline ?, Limerick
By dau. Bridget Guerin

Guerin
William F., 4/27/1904, 26, Limerick
By mother Bridget

Guerra
Mary O'Connor, 1914 - 1956
See Kennelly, Dominick, 1802 - 9/28/1884

Guerrin
Jerome J.
See Ragan, Owen, 8/3/1969, 42

Guinan
Frank, 2/11/1894, 54, Five Alley, Eglish, Kings

Guinane
William, 3/30/1890, 45, Kilrush, Clare
By wife Mary, 11/19/1911, Kilrush, Clare
His sister Mary, 10/11/1884, 65, Kilrush, Clare
Her mother Mary Stamar, wife of John, 11/4/1890, 69, Ennis, Clare

Guiry
Johanna, 11/2/1885, 34, Dulles, Croom, Limerick
By sister Hanora, 3/5/1922

Guy
Margaret, 11/2/1927
See Rogers, Michael J., 7/4/1932

Hackett
James retired U.S.A., 2/21/1917, 70
By wife Bridgie
His nephew Joseph Ryan, 10/2/1916, 28, Waterford

Hackett
Patrick, 10/17/1894, 29, Edenderry, Kings
Wife Tessie
Annie, 9/21/1895, 4-6-0
James, 7/11/1893, 11 months
Ellen, 7/1/1895, 9 months

Hagan
Bridget, 2/14/1901, 82, Killoe, Longford
Her brother Denis, 5/2/1890, 63
His wife Rose, 11/23/1890, 46
Peter J., 3/3/1903

Hagerty
Michael, 10/10/1891, 75, Cork
By wife Jane, Cork

Haggerty
John, 8/30/1863, 37, Clanmire, Cork
Hannah wife of John, 4/11/1824 - 7/19/12
Their children:
John, 13 months
Hannah, 11 months
Michael, 4 years 10 months

Haire
Andrew J., 7/6/1910, Clare
By wife Maria G., 9/27/1850 - 1/11/1922
Son Edward J., 11/20/1874 - 12/8/1911
Harriet J., 3/2/1880 - 2/4/1920
Alphonsus P., 8/1/1883 - 3/4/1924
Mary Agnes Burns, 3/24/1878 - 4/9/1940

Haley
James, 4/18/1913, 85
Wife Sarah, 11/27/1913, 84
See Scanlan, Mary Teresa, 12/20/1908

Hallinan
Thomas, 3/18/1910, 68, Ennis, Clare
By wife Elizabeth, 7/26/1913, 68, Newry, Down

Halloran
Annie, 2/26/1943
See, Dunn, Christopher, 11/2/1892

Halloran
Catherine, 2/10/1914
Michael E., 2/9/1919
Lydia C., 3/8/1929
Patrick F., 2/22/1942
By Catherine Halloran
See Lyons, Patrick, 11/24/1901

Halloran
Ellen, 1/28/1911, 70
Patrick J., 6/8/1929
Mary Agnes, 5/18/1936
Abie, 12/27/1946
John, 11/30/1956
See Casey, James, 3/29/1875

Halpin
William, 8/1/1878, 68, Arthurstown, Louth
By wife Catherine, 12/16/1920, 86, Louth
Dau. Mary died young
Jane Quinn, 1873 - 1955
Mabel Clinane, 1903 - 1979

Hamilton
James, 1/11/1886, 60, Mayo
By wife Kate
John Geoghegan died young
Julia Shortell, wife of Richard 1/1888, Galway

Hand
Catherine, 4/20/1900, 52, Tipperary
By husband Michael J.

Hand
Rev. Hugh, 1845 - 1908
See Murtaugh, John, 4/21/1899

Hanigan
Ellen, 12/5/1920
See Purcell, John, 3/19/1876

Hanihan
Francis M., 1921 - 1982
See Madigan, John, 3/2/1896, 54

Hanley
Catherine M., 8/23/1935
See Conway, James, 12/4/1885

Hanley
Eleanor, 7/3/1860, 40, Easky, Sligo
By husband Dudley

Hanley
Elizabeth, 4/8/1902 64, Moate, Westmeath
By husband John, 9/1/1904 67, Derry ?, Longford
Nephew Daniel J. Ganley, 11/4/1917 38, Moate, Westmeath

Hanley
John, 4/3/1891, 71, Ruskie, Roscommon
His mother Bridget, 6/22/1855
By his wife Eliza

Hanley
Mary Teresa Flood, 8/15/1883 - 8/15/1905, Longford
By husband Michael P.J.
Dennis Hickey, 1899 - 1969
Marcella, 1905 - 1983

Hanley
Patrick, 1/19/1915, 53, Claremorris, Mayo
By wife Helen, 3/19/1940
His brother John, 4/4/1914, 44

Hanley
Thomas, 2/10/1889, 50, Carrickedmond, Longford
Catherine, 8/25/1894
By their sister Mary, 6/22/1896, 76
Daniel Cahill, 10/2/1896, 57
His wife Ellen, 3/30/1922
Margaret, 9/25/1876 - 2/2/1945
William E. McDermott, 1908 - 1965

Hanly
Patrick R., 5/12/1912, 74, Galway
His wife Mary, 8/18/1919, 73, Kerry

Hanning
Mary, 1867 - 1957
See Dudly, Mary, 2/15/1872

Hannon
Margaret, 8/23/1882, 60, Limerick
By sister Bridget Donevan

Hansin
Peter, 7/5/1909, 61, Hamburg, Germany
Hannah C. Carrol, 2/10/1913
Ellen Hansin Carrol, 8/19/1919, Twomileborris, Tipperary
William, 1/7/1944
Amalie Louise Recht, 4/15/1951

Hardcastle
Mary, 4/16/1914, 43
James, 7/22/1953
See Skelly, Catherine, 12/24/1872, 29

Harden
Edward, 5/25/1889, 76, Granard, Longford
Wife Catherine, 12/11/1869, 51
Their children:
Edward, 11/8/1876, 24
Elizabeth Metcalf, 10/4/1881, 31
Geoffrey Davis, 8/29/1959, 1
Claire Indrizzo Roe, 2/18/1976, 46
Catherine McBride, 7/24/1894, 47 wife of
Francis J., 1/9/1908, 63
William F., 6/29/1916, 30
Francis, 11/17/1932, 48
Claire Rodney, 5/11/1940
Dorothy Belle Indrizzo, 11/4/1988, 86
James McBrien, 7/28/1869, 2
Edward, 4/15/1875, 6
Thomas F., 4/28/1875, 4
Mary C., 8/6/1876, 2
Joseph, 8/14/1883, 5

Harkin
Charles, Donegal
Ceceila, Donegal
Ellen, Donegal
Michael, Donegal
Catherine, Donegal
By Mary

Harkins
Daniel, 1/7/1895, 30, Moville, Donegal
By wife Delia, 4/24/1936
Their son Joseph, 2/17/1896, 3-5-10
Their nephews and niece: Joseph, John and Helen Harkins

Harkins
James, 7/15/1887, 36, Leitrim
By sister Bridget Harkins
Margaret Harkins Edelman, 1880 - 1933
Cornelius J. Edelman, 1903 - 1939
Theodore J. Edelman, 1872 - 1948
James C. Edelman, 1900 - 1981

Harnett
Lawrence, 8/10/1910, 49, Moroe, Limerick
By wife Margaret Harnett Kane, 11/26/1913
Her father James Ryan, 11/1/1908, Pallas, Limerick
Her brother Matthew K., Ryan, 3/3/1911, Pallas, Limerick
Her brother John Ryan, 3/1/1913, Pallas, Limerick

Harney
John, 4/8/1875, Crannaghmore, Athlone, Roscommon

Harper
William, 5/13/1868, 63, Wexford
Died at Florence, Italy

Harrigan
Maurice, 4/4/1884 50, Askeaton, Limerick
Ellen, 11/17/1894 61 Askeaton, Limerick
By dau. Kate Harrigan
Kate's brother Patrick, 4/3/1883 27, Askeaton, Limerick
Kate's brother Maurice F., 2/16/1897 31 Askeaton, Limerick
Kathleen wife of Maurice Jr. 4/15/1857 - 3/15/1909
Kate M., 4/27/1954
Hugh V. McHugh, 1918 - 1974

Harrington
James, 6/12/1915, Fedamore, Limerick
Margaret, 1/12/1927
Mary F., 7/6/1982

Harrington
John, 11/17/1888, 54, Chareville, Cork
By wife Mary, 7/18/1896, 70

Harrington
Kathryn C.
See Gleason, Johanna, Rockhill, Limerick

Harrington
Michael, 11/9/1910, 37, Kerry
By wife Margaret, 1/28/1958
Their dau. Mary Ellen, 6/16/1897 - 7/25/1897
Margaret's mother Mary Doyle, 1/13/1922 74

Harrington
Patrick, 2/5/1913, 45, Newtown, Sands, Kerry
By wife Johanna, 1/21/1958
Six children
Son Patrick J., 3/24/1958

Hart
Bridget, 6/23/1885, 62, Sligo
Patrick, 4/14/1895, 70, Sligo
By dau. Mary Hart

Hart
Margaret
Mamie, 8/5/1885
John, 1895, 65, Cork

Hartigan
Annie A., 6/20/1912
See Brew, Johanna, 7/31/1906

Hartz
Bridget, 12/15/1929
See Lynch, Michael, 5/12/1838 - 5/28/1916

Harvey
Bridget, 1/27/1910, 48, Tyrone
By sister Annie Kelly
John Lynch, 2/22/1916, 26

Harvey
Ellen, 36, Armagh
By husband Patrick, 6/1889, Armagh
Owen Murphy, 1/18/1878
His dau. Ellen C., 4/27/1877

Harvey
Samuel, 3/10/ no year
Alice, 6/11/1906, Armagh
Margaret, 9/24/1936
Annie, 2/15/1940
Edward Kells, 9/16/1982
Gertrude

Hatton
Johnnie
Katie
Leo, 1897
Anna Maria, 1901
Mary Farrell Hatton, 1866 - 1929
Esther C., 1886 - 1956
Mary F., 1896 - 1964
See Farrell, Catherine, 3/3/1887, 53

Haughey
Husband died in Dromore, Letterkenny, Donegal
His wife Sarah
No dates

Haughton
Thomas, 8/15/1862, 26, Edenderry, Kings
Wife Anne, 9/24/1904, 66
See Powers, James, 3/19/1892, 9-4-0

Hawkins
Winifred A., 1885 - 1960, Mayo
John, 1884 - 1962, Mayo

Hayden
Thomas, 5/28/1905 44-5-0, Strokestown, Roscommon
By wife Maria, 11/28/1955

Hayes
Margaret, 7/14/1795 - 3/8/1859, Wexford
Captain John Sullivan, 8/16/1862, 46
90 Regt. U.S. Vol. died Key West Florida
Margaret Josephine Hayes, 1/23/1829, 15

Hayes
Michael, 2/1/1897, 46, Tipperary
By wife Ellen

Hayes
Patrick S., 1/13/1899, 34, Dublin
By wife Mary T.
Sons William and Francis died young in infancy

Hayes
Rose A. 10/16/1908
See Lowery, John, Monaghan

Hayes
Thomas, 1/9/1900, 60, Feakle, Clare
By wife Ann, 6/21/1911, 69
Dau. Norah, 11/20/1910
Anne Marie Parks, 1914 - 1984

Healey
Ellen, 91, Killevan, Monaghan
By dau. Anne Jane Healey

Healey
James, 2/13/1907, 60, Carry Cloyne, Blarney, Cork
By wife Jane 6/26/1914, 65
Their children: William and Timothy died young

Healy
Bridget, 4/1867, 27
Her son Patrick, 7/18/1864
See Daly, Michael, 6/16/1864, 65

Healy
Mary E., 12/20/1896
See Brophy, John, 12/1871

Healy
Mary, 4/30/1902, 53, Dublin
Husband John
Dau. Mary, 4-6-0

Healy
Patrick, 3/7/1899, 57, Tipperary
Children: Mary and Josephine
By wife and mother Bridget

Heaney
Mary Ellen Pohlman, 6/24/1891
By parents Bernard and Ellen Heaney
Bernard, 7/19/1891, Armagh

Hedden
Elizabeth, 12/28/1912, 50
See Feegan, Michael, 10/16/1882, 52

Hegarty
Margaret, 4/11/1891, 83, City of Cork
Ellen, 5/18/1909, 84, City of Cork

Heitkamp
Mary J., 12/6/1933
Henry, 1870 - 1937
See Daly, Thomas, 5/13/1893, 48

Henebry
Thomas, 7/6/1888, 19, Midleton, Cork
By mother Ellen Desmond, 6/1/1899, 75, Midleton, Cork
William Henebry, 3/15/1944, 75

Henery
John, 1/12/1861, 63
Mary, 11/13/1876, 75, Ballynascreen, Derry
Their children:
James, 1/14/1858, 28
Rosie, 1/25/1857, 13
Bridget, 1/26/1875, 40
Mary H. Johnson, 7/19/1915, 76
Mary E. Lynch, 2/28/1918, 43
By daus. of John and Mary Henery
Mary E. Johnson and Margaret Henery

Hennessy
Anna Thompson, 1883 - 1952
See Curtin, James J., 4/26/1911, 24

Hennessy
James, 12/29/1884, 51, Westmeath
Wife Ann, 10/5/1901, 75, Westmeath
Their son James Jr., 11/14/1887, 29
James F. Private Co. B 106 Inf. A.E.F. served in France
and Belgium with 27 Div., 11/3/1923
Andrew J., 1856 - 1927
Lillian, 12/27/1961
Thomas E., 8/8/1963

Hennessey
Mary, 9/5/1884, 58, Ballymona, Cork
By husband John
Catherine Wade, 3/27/1871, 15-4-0
Dau. of James and Ellen Wade

Hennessey
Richard 1?/1881?, Tipperary
Catherine 12/27/1880, 56, Tipperary
By dau. Hanora, Mortibly
Katie Hennessey 11/15/1858 - 10/28/1879
Mary Londrigan 1/24?/1873
Catherine Londigran 2/25?/1873, 2 months
John Londigran 3/17?/1899, 45

Henry
Thomas D., 1852 - 7/12/1914, Tyrone
By wife Bridget M., 1856 - 1/9/1924, Mayo
Paul A., 1/27/1898 - 3/18/1929
Charles V. Kirk, 7/26/1935
Anne M. Gallagher, 1/3/1896 - 4/25/1960
Helen R. Gallagher, 1882 - 1969

Heslan
Mary, wife of Thomas J., 6/15/1908, Athlone, Westmeath
By son Michael J.
Her dau. Annie J., 5/3/1923
Capt. Michael J., 4/24/1937
Catherine Savage, 5/24/1941
Elizabeth M. Savage, 4/4/1948

Hester
Mary, 10/12/1937, Clooncah, Castlereagh, Roscommon
Dau. of late Thomas and Ellen Kelly Hester

Heverin
Alice M., 2/22/1901
Timothy, 3/7/1898
Sabina Glynn, 1/6/1896, Galway
William A. Heverin, 3/12/1931
John, 4/10/1952

Heyser
Marie, 10/4/1971
See Ennis, Mary, 8/18/1895, 56

Hickey
Darby, 8/20/1866, 78, Tipperary
By son John, 3/1/1916, 90
Catherine, 1/2/1897, 60
Sarah, 12/7/1930
William F., 9/22/1897, 37
Maggie, 1/1/1892, 1-4-0

Hickey
Dennis, 1899 - 1969
Marcella, 1905 - 1983
See Hanley, Mary Teresa Flood 8/15/1883 - 8/15/1905

Hickey
John, 1/31/1896, 67
See Kiely, Margaret, 7/8/1892, 23

Hickey
John J., 8/12/1896, 32, Cork
By brothers Cornelius and Patrick

Hickey
Laurence, 5/13/1890, 63, Golden Abbey, Tipperary
Wife Julia, 4/6/1904, 76
John J., 12/24/1903, 42

Hickey
Mary, 8/12/1906, 77, Kerry

Hickey
Mary, 3/13/1872, 50, Westmeath
Margaret Daly, 4/18/1872, 45
Thomas Daly, 12/2/1913, 79

Hickey
Mary, wife of the late Morris, 9/20/1869, 88-8-0, Golden Abbey, Tipperary
Her son Morris, 2/6/1852
Dau. of the above Mary, 10/8/1876, 52
Stephen, 12/17/1895, 60
Margaret, 1/3/1902

Hickey
Thomas, 6/2/1897, 55, Tullassa, Clare
Ellen, 8/4/1902, 62, Tulla, Clare
By children

Hielderbrand
Henry, 6/22/1835 - 3/24/1912, Westport, Mayo
George, 1889 - 1946

Higgins
Dennis, son of Hugh of Mohill, 1/12/1863
Dennis' wife, Rachel Elizabeth dau of Charles Flan Tracy, 12/16/1813 - 10/12/1901, Athlone
John Gianella, husband of Marguerite Higgins, 1/14/1838-5/16/1914, Switzerland
Marguerite, 2/22/1857 - 3/12/1942
John, 8/14/1885 - 3/15/1973

Higgins
James
Margaret, 1869, Killarney, Kerry
By son Daniels

Higgins
James, 10/13/1893, 22-8-0, Belleville, Westmeath
By sister Mary Higgins
Patrick, 6/11/1899, 49
Mary, 11/11/1901, 45

Higgins
Joseph P., 9/11/1901, Loughrea, Galway
Sarah, 9/2/1936, 75
John J., --
See Coyne, James, 4/12/1906, 61

Higgins
Thomas, 7/8/1901, 42, Bellemill, Westmeath

Hill
Mary, 5/9/1913, 44, Bantry, Cork
Son David B., 3/27/1917, 14
By husband and father, 4/29/1911, 54

Hoar
Patrick, 4/18/1872, St. Johns, Roscommon
Catherine, 9/14/1916, St. Johns, Roscommon
By their sister Margaret, 4/10/1918, St. Johns, Roscommon

Hogan
John, 3/30/1891, 77, Clare
Hannah, 4/24/1891, 64, Donegal
By nephew Patrick, 1/16/1905, 64
John H., 9/30/1909, 37
Wife Mary A.

Holland
Margaret, 8/28/1870, 36, St. Johns, Roscommon
By husband Thomas

Holland
Sarah, 9/22/1905, Derry
By sister Mary A., 11/8/1934
Bessie Murphy, 7/31/1904 - 10/22/1918

Holmes
Patrick, 9/11/1888, 21-6-0, Kilargue, Leitrim
By parents Daniel and Ellen
Alice Rose, 4/3/1952

Honen
Ann, 11/29/1891, 52, Waterford
Children: Mary, Annie, James, Katie died young

Hopkins
Catherine, 3/17/1912, Cahirciveen, Kerry
By son Joseph T., 12/20/1859 - 6/27/1926
His sister Katie Cosgrove, 3/11/1893 26
Her baby Alice

Hopkins
Elizabeth, 8/15/1882, 87, Turlaugh, Mayo
By dau. Bridget Hopkins

Hopkins
James, 7/25/1888, 68, Tyrone
By wife Margaret

Hopkins
Peter, 5/21/1905, 43, Longford
See Cassidy, Patrick, 10/13/1901, 46

Hopkins
Thomas 1/6?/1868, Borrisoleigh?, Tipperary
By son Philip 5/12/1913

Horan
Margaret, 12/17/1886, 75, Cappabane, Clare
See McCawley, Eugene, 9/27/1886, 35-3-20

Horan
Michael, No dates, Queens
By wife Ellen

Hore
Bridget, 6/21/1840 - 10/2/1940, St. Johns, Roscommon
See Kane, Patrick, 1/23/1900

Horn
Francis J., 1915 - 1981
See Ryan, Michael, 11/1/1918, 35

Horrigan
Patrick
James
Mary
See Ryder, Patrick, 8/9/1871

Hosey
Edward, 1/24/1888, 51, Canard, Meath
By wife Ann, 7/17/1900, 64
Dau. Annie, 1/20/1876, 8
John J., 1/26/1905, 43

Houlihan
Catherine, wife of the late Cornelius, 1/1/1895, 72, Mallow, Cork
Their dau. Catherine, 6/27/1915, 22

Hourigan
Mary, 4/12/1904, 76, Doon, Limerick
By children:
Edward, 12/25/1927
Michael, 8/8/1928

Hourihan
John J., 1904 - 1976
Mary Ellen, 2/16/1912 - 3/21/1989
See Gibbons, Patrick, 7/31/1915, 38

Houston
Frank S., 10/28/1973
See Ward, Thomas, 8/21/1874 - 3/21/1914

Howley
Richard, 3/7/1885, 75, Kilkenny
By wife Mary, 7/4/1919, 95
Mary F. Wylie, 6/8/1870 - 10/28/1958
Devoted friends:
Sarah F. Dawkins, 4/20/1882 - 12/1/1966
Eleanor V. Dawkins, 1/21/1899 - 8/9/1983

Hoye
Thomas, 8/3/1871
His mother Anne, 1/15/1885, 57, Kings
James McGuire, 7/25/1918, 57

Hoynes
Margaret M. 7/21/1847 - 3/3/1911, Borrisoleich, Tipperary
Patrick, 12/21/1920
Sons:
Michael J., 4/20/1877 - 1/23/1914
Joseph P., 2/10/1888 - 3/21/1932
His son Daniel C., 12/8/1919 - 7/14/1933
Mary E., 5/8/1889 - 2/5/1936
Joseph P., 8/13/1915 - 7/29/1959
Richard R., 7/22/1921 - 4/21/1984
Donald P., 10/10/1949 - 1/21/1985
Kathleen Burns Hoynes, 5/25/1924 - 8/2/1988

Hughes
Bernard, 4/13/1871, Caledon, Tyrone
Bridget, 3/17/1906

Hughes
David, 2/12/1863, Tipperary
By Ann

Hughes
James, 2/17/1881, 45, Tehallan, Monaghan
By wife Mary

Hughes
James, 3/8/1868, 30
William, 3/18/1861, 29, Kilkenny
By mother Mary
Ann O'Neill, 3/1/1869, 29
Edward Hughes, 6/4/1873, 28

Hughes
John, 1/8/1839 - 1/12/1907, Doohat, Armagh
By wife Rose, 4/23/1849 - 6/5/1924
Children:
Annie, 1872, 6 months
Catherine, 7 years
John, 1877, 2 years
Alexander C., 3/24/1877 - 4/21/1921
Mary J., 7/3/1934

Hughes
Mary E., 4/18/1891, 51
See Casey, James, 7/18/1852

Hull
Mary, 10/26/1883, 57, Waringstown, Down
By husband William, 9/17/1888, 58

Humbly
Julia, 10/25/1942
See Treacy, James, 5/10/1911, 51

Hunt
John, 1/19/1909, Roscommon
Children, Annie, Thomas M., William

Hunter
John, 9/16/1903
See Doherty, William

Hurley
Anna D., 4/23/1915, Kings
See Delaney, Joseph P., 1/28/1894

Hurley
Hanora, 10/10/1881, 58, Kerry
By son John F., 10/26/1922, 62
John Wright, 1939
James Wright, 1962
Aice, 1966

Hussey
George, 4/25/1895, 32, Roscommon
His sister Cecilia V., 3/21/1898, 40, Roscommon

Hussey
James, 2/5/1866, 27, Westmeath
His wife Mary, 8/7/1894, 63, Westmeath
By brother Thomas Hussey, 9/7/1897, 64

Hussey
Maria, 3/9/1929, Roscommon
Thomas P. Sr., 4/13/1931
Thomas Jr. killed in action in France, 9/29/1918
James, 1/14/1929
Patrick Kelly, 8/4/1894
Michael Kelly, 9/2/1937

Hyland
Francis J., 1/21/1913, 39, Ballycrana, Tipperary
By wife Elizabeth
Richard J. Larkin, 1876 - 1947
Joseph Larkin, 1884 - 1955
Anne F. Larkin, 1883 - 1964
Margaret T. Larkin, 1895 - 1966
Elizabeth Kenny, 1872 - 1967

Hylin
William, 1948
Catherine, 1969
See Keaney, John, 7/6/1911, 47

Hynes
Thomas, 11/16/1867, 35, Galway
Johanna Kennedy, 1871, Limerick

Indrizzo
Dorothy Belle, 11/4/1988, 86
See Harden, Edward, 5/25/1889, 76

Ivers
Mary, 12/3/1918, 48, Kiltamagh, Mayo
By husband John, 3/4/1867 - 10/3/1928, Kiltamagh, Mayo
Their daughter Mary, 8/14/1905 5 months

Jacob
Edward F., 3/18/1939, 65
Elizabeth, 4/1876 - 8/1957
M. Patricia, 2/16/1973
See McCawley, Eugene, 9/27/1886, 35-3-20

Jacob
George Martin, 9/17/1914, 71-6-0
Annie Cox, 11/9/1915
See Cox, Ann, 10/12/1880, 80

Jeffers
Edward, 11/19/1865, 55, Carrowbeg, Moville, Donegal
By sons Daniel, Richard, Thomas

Jeffers
Maria, 7/16/1886, Tyrone
By John

Johnson
Celeste M., 1916 - 1972
Celeste M., 1950 - 1973
See Edmunds, Thomas, 4/17/1881

Johnson
Edward J., 9/4/1905 - 4/5/1978
Anna C., 12/28/1906 -
See Kennelly, Dominick, 1802 - 9/28/1884

Johnson
Joseph, 4/17/1909, 38, Louth
By wife Bridget, 1/18/1939
Their children Alexander and May
Peter J., 10/5/1959

Jones
Christopher, 12/20/1906, 57, Longford
By dau. Delia Jones

Jones
Katie, 4/30/1891, 23, Tipperary
Margaret, 5/21/1897, 72
Nicholas Wolf, 2/21/1903, 38

Jones
Nora, 5/1/1925, 58, Fedamore, Limerick
By husband Patrick

Jordan
Michael, 9/24/1885, 54, Mayo
By wife Celia
Celia Jordan McTigue, 5/16/1902, 74

Jordan
Michael, 8/17/1893, Longford
Bridget Hanley Jordan, 5/27/1902, Longford
Mary Hanley, 4/1/1936
Thomas, 6/9/1941
By nieces and nephews of Manadarragh, Longford

Joyce
John, 3/22/1905, 45, Mayo
By wife Catherine, 1/21/1930, 64
Their children:
John, 3/9/1894, 2-7-0
Matthew, 9/9/1896, 1-4-0

Joyce
Patrick, 11/6/1904, 65, Mayo
By wife Elizabeth, 3/10/1918
Ellen, 7/27/1885, 1-7-0
Helen F. Ward, 7/30/1961
James J., 10/3/1964

Judge
Francis J., 3/14/1919, 32, Longford
By wife Bridget G.
Ellen Grifferty Sheridan, 3/28/1940
Bridget J. Ormsby, 3/15/1958

Judge
Jane, 11/6/1897, 60, Kings
By husband Patrick, 8/14/1912, 78, Kings
John, 5/24/1889, 60
Mamie Turner, 1873 - 1953
Mary Skelley, 1863 - 1933
Rose Volgarino, 1899 - 1963
Arthur Volgarino, 1888 - 1979
Senerino Giovannoli, 1885 - 1967

Judge
Mary, 12/14/1894, 46, Riverstown, Sligo
Husband John J., 8/1/1915, 67
Their son James J., 12/3/1910, 4
Husband of Ellen

Kalaher
William, 3/10/1878, 75, Kerry
By wife Mary
Son Thomas, 1/10/1890, 37, Kerry

Kallmeyer
Margaret, 6/23/1949
Andrew, --
Charles, 8/5/1938
Mary, 1/16/1942
See Coleman, Margaret, 5/21/1888

Kane
Bessie, 12/24/1900, Kilkenny

Kane
Francis, 12/24/1879, 26, Drumcliff Clare
By wife Lizzie F. Kane King, 3/19/1909
Son George Kane, 4/27/1913

Kane
James E., 12/3/1910
By wife Abbie, 1/5/1916, 69, Donegal

Kane
Margaret Harnett, 11/26/1913
See Harnett, Lawrence, 8/10/1910, 49

Kane
Mary, 8/29/1881 - 9/29/1882
Martin, 5/28/1883 - 12/7/1890
By father Martin of Castlerea, Roscommon

Kane
Patrick, 1/7/1851 - 1/23/1900, Newtown, Kilteevan, Roscommon
Bridget, 8/15/1879 - 10/25/1913, Newtown, Kilteevan, Roscommon
Bridget Hore 6/21/1840 - 10/2/1940, St. Johns Roscommon

Kane
Peter, 1911, 53, Derry
By wife Catherine, 11/23/1917, 55, Kilkenny

Kane
Thomas 4/11/1894, Leitrim
By wife Catherine
Thomas A. Clancey 11/21/1926, 33
Catherine Clancey 2/10/1936, 63

Kane
Thomas, 1/4/1900, 60
His wife Alice, 2/10/1878
His mother Ann, 11/7/1876, 75, Shinrone, Kings
Children of Thomas and Alice:
Thomas, 2/20/1871, 5-5-0
Mary, 2/28/1873, 5-11-0
Annie, 2/28/1873, 3-0-25
Thomas, 3/13/1873, 1-3-0
James, 12/25/1879, 6-5-0

Kavanagh
Edward J., 11/14/1907, 30, Welsh Island, Kings
By father James

Keaney
John, 7/6/1911, 47, Galway
By wife Mary, 1/3/1923
James, 11/10/1925
Margaret, 1937
John, 1941
Annie, 1943
William Hylin, 1948
Mary Keaney, 1951
Patrick J., 1951
Patrick Sr., 1959
Catherine Hylin, 1969

Kearney
Charles, 12/3/1858, 43, Doon, Limerick
By brother Michael
Their cousins Charles and Margaret

Kearney
Denis, 10/27/1878, 58, Carndonough, Donegal

Kearney
Edward, 67, Donegal
Susan
By Patrick

Kearney
Mary A., 8/10/1930
See McQuade, Michael, 6/3/1881, 60

Kearney
Mary, 11/20/1887, 70, Monaghan
By husband Patrick

Kearns
Mark, 3/10/1894, 31, Sligo
By father Mark
Patrick, 11/15/1895, 25

Keegan
James, 3/25/1884, 40, Cavan
By wife Catherine
Children:
Katie, 7/5/1881, 3-6-0
Lizzie, 9/5/1883, 10 months

Keegan
Mary McCauley, 12/1869, Longford

Keegan
Michael, 4/9/1887, 49, Tubberclare, Westmeath
By James, 6/12/1891, 47

Keegan
Michael, 9/28/1882, 50, Sligo Town, Sligo
By wife Margaret, 4/21/1901
Dennis, 12/21/1874, 11
William, 11/6/1881, 13

Keegan
Patrick, 8/30/1898, 67, Forgney, Longford
By wife Catherine, 12/25/1899
Dau. Mamie, 9/10/1878

Keenan
Catherine, 2/20/1912, Meath
By sister Annie Casey, 3/28/1919

Keenan
Edward 9/1866, 67, Ballymore, Westmeath
Mary 9/8/1866, 66, Ballymore, Westmeath
Their son Edward 10/6/1903, 63

Keenan
James, 6/22/1910, 62, Lagan, Longford

Keenan
Mary, 9/8/1866, Ballymore, Westmeath
By husband Edward, 10/6/1903, 63

Keenan
Thomas C., 11/14/1964, 74
See Delehanty, Patrick, 3/28/1889, 37

Keeren
Thomas, 9/26/1888 51, Killinvoy, Roscommon
Sarah Dolan, 8/31/1896 34
Svea L. Dolan, 1905 - 1985
Francis J. Dolan, 1901 - 1987

Keevan
By Mary for her mother, 3/30/1860 60, Tipperary
Father James died in Ireland
Mary Keevan, 4/27/1899

Kehoe
Daniel, 9/9/1865, 34, Kildare
By wife Rosanna, 6/19/1912, 85
Children: Daniel, Thomas, Mary died young

Kehoe
Genevieve, 72
Michael J., 86
See McNeely, Anthony Roe, 10/24/1891

Keleher
Mary, 4/11/1933, 68 dau. of the late
James and Ellen of Leitrim
By her sister Annie, 8/27/1949
Nellie, 7/10/1940

Kelleher
Dennis, 11/4/1887, Inch, Cork
Mary, 4/3/1916, Inch, Cork
William, brother of Dennis, 6/25/1925

Kelleher
Michael, 3/13/1929, 69
See Meehan, Catherine, 8/30/1893, 69

Kellesey
James, 4/1/1873, 23, Longford
See Cassidy, Patrick, 10/13/1901, 46

Kelley
Thomas, 12/11/1878, 56, Roscommon
By wife Bridget, 7/25/1900, 70

Kells
Edward, 9/16/1982
Gertrude
See Harvey, Samuel, 3/10/ no year

Kelly
Bridget, 8/3/1885, 85, Town of Kildare
By son James
His sister Maryann, 6/22/1885, 55, Town of Kildare

Kelly
Bridget, 7/2/1899, 86, Roscommon
John, 2/9/1915, 75, Roscommon
Martin, 5/17/1911, 66, Roscommon

Kelly
Bridget McEnroe, 8/27/1903, Killeevan, Monaghan
By sister Mary McEnroe, 1/28/1927, Killeevan, Monaghan
Niece Susan Donoghue, 8/5/1933

Kelly
Bridget McCarthy, 1855 - 1954, Donegal
See Phillips, Charles J., 12/20/1925 23

Kelly
Catherine Kane, 5/11/1886, Castlerea, Roscommon
By husband Thomas, 11/24/1919
John, 11/8/1885, Drumkeerin, Leitrim
John, 5/14/1909

Kelly
Edward, 2/9/1861, Aughmullen, Monaghan
Margarethe, 5/8/1884, Aughmullen, Monaghan

Kelly
Elizabeth, Culdaff, Donegal
By husband Peter

Kelly
Fergus, 11/27/1859, Mayo
By Patrick
Catherine Derrin, ?/20/1877, Ballinasloe?, Galway

Kelly
Hanora, 12/28/1876, 30, Bandon, Cork
Mary, wife of William Moffatt, 5/16/1879 30-2-0 Bandon, Cork
By sister Ellen Kelly
Also children of Daniel and Hanora Kelly

Kelly
James, 3/22/1898, 22, Ballinasloe, Galway

Kelly
John, 12/4/1906, 67, Donegal
By wife Margaret, 12/10/1913
Their children:
James, 3
Ellen, 7
Son-in-law Thomas F. Perry, 3/17/1915

Kelly
Maria, 11/17/1903, 52
See Wynne, Bernard D., 4/29/1901, 57

Kelly
Patrick, 8/4/1894
Michael, 9/2/1937
See Hussey, Maria, 3/9/1929

Kelly
Peter, 9/9/1913, 25, Abbeyknockmoy, Galway
Brother John, 5/6/1916, 22
By their sister
Children of John and Delia McHugh
Mary J. McHugh, 7/8/1916, 2
Catherine McHugh, 10/9/1916, 11 months
John McHugh, 10/15/1925

Kemple
Margaret, 3/25/1886, 45, Killasnet, Leitrim
By husband Thomas

Kennafin
Margaret, 5/30/1904, 78, Mitchellstown, Cork
By sons Thomas and James

Kennedy
Catherine, 8/19/1894, 36, Clonmel, Tipperary
By husband Michael P., 6/24/1918, 69

Kennedy
Johanna, 1871, Limerick
See Hynes, Thomas, 11/16/1867, 35

Kennedy
John J., 1914 - 1971
See McGoldrick, John, 8/15/1896, 38

Kennedy
John J., 5/6/1914, 70, Kerry
By wife Nora M. Ahearn, 3/3/1920, 74, Glin, Limerick
John F., 4/21/1920, 41
Edward J. Fitzgerald, 1901 - 1969

Kennedy
Lizzie
Julia
Eddie, died young
By parents Edward and Bridget of Ardcrony, Tipperary

Kennelly
Dominick, 1802 - 9/28/1884, Cork
Margaret Slattery Kennelly, 1810 - 10/4/1873, Cork
Edward Valentine Kennelly, 1852 - 1857
Albert Finbar Kennelly of the 17th N.Y.V. 1841 - killed in battle of Jonesboro, Georgia 9/1/1864
Margaret, 1839 - 1871
Mary Ellen, 1834 - 1878
Sarah F., 1850 - 1881
Kate L. Gallagher wife of J.F. Kennelly 1852 - 1891
Joseph F. Kennelly, 12/16/1837 - 11/13/1923
Joseph Jr., 1877 - 1939
James son of Joseph F., 1871 - 1874
Edward, 1888-1888
Maurice, 1889, infant
Dominick, 1891, infant
Frank I., 1846 - 1886
Dominick, 1836 - 1905
Walter DeGroat, 1873 - 1955
John J. Larkin, 1898 - 1969
Sarah U. Kennelly Tartaglini, 1879 - 1975
John O'Connor, 1885-1962
Rebecca K. O'Connor, 1875 - 1962
Mary O'Connor Guerra, 1914 - 1956
Edward J. Johnson, 9/4/1905 - 4/5/1978
Anna C. Johnson, 12/28/1906 -

Kennelly
Margaret, 1/4/1862, Cork
By husband David

Kenney
Thomas, 6/30/1896, 66, Robinstown, Longford
By wife Mary

Kenny
Elizabeth, 1872 - 1967
See Hyland, Francis J., 1/21/1913, 39

Kenny
James, 4/22/1886, 59, Longford
By wife Bridget, 73
Children:
Kate, 21
Willie, 15
Mary, 30

Kenny
Michael, 5/18/1886, 66, Ardagh, Longford
By wife Bridget, 8/13/1891

Kenny
Thomas, 5/12/1917, 40, Longford
By wife Catherine, 5/10/1877 - 10/1/1972
Thomas F., 9/14/1908 - 5/26/1981
James Murtagh, 5/29/1879 - 11/4/1961

Kenny
William, 2/16/1881, 52, Longford
By wife Mary, 60
James B., 20
Patrick Stanton, 26

Keough
Jeremiah, 3/4/1854 - 8/20/1914, Limerick
By wife Margaret, 7/24/1926, Bilboa, Limerick

Kerns
Dennis, 5/10/1917, 70, Killorglin, Kerry
By wife Margaret, 11/20/1922
William J., 11/20/1962
Mary A., 12/18/1973

Kerrigan
Anna, 2/18/1972
John J., 4/30/1988
See Barrington, Patrick, 7/3/1901, 73

Kerwin
Edward J., 4/13/1931, Kilkenny
By wife Nan
His mother Bridget, 1/23/1923, Kilkenny
Anna Walton Kerwin, 12/19/1956

Kiely
Margaret, 7/8/1892, 23, Glen of Arlough, Tipperary
By aunt and uncle
John Hickey, 1/31/1896, 67

Kiely
Mary, 8/15/1860 - 3/18/1902, Dungarvan, Waterford

Kiernan
Marcella, 1817 - 9/15/1881, Longford
Husband Joseph, 7/6/1896, 84, Longford
Kittie, their niece and adopted daughter 4/6/1878, 25
Joseph's niece Maryann Fagan, 2/27/1897, 50

Kiernan
Mary, 10/30/1884
See Clark, Susan, 4/19/1883

Kiers
Agnes L., 6/12/1967
See Connors, John, 8/27/1897, 36

Kilcoyne
James, 2/16/1896, Mayo
Wife Ellen, 8/7/1921

Kilfoyle
Mary, 1/31/1910, 67, Tyrone
By husband Michael
George Reinhardt, 12/18/1947

Kilpatrick
Ellen E., 4/17/1902 dau. of the late James and Ellen Kilpatrick of Dromore West, Sligo
Rev. Edward F. McGoldrick born 9/8/1870 ordained 6/24/1897, died 9/30/1930
Margaret Kilpatrick, 4/16/1941, 86
Maria J. Kilpatrick, 5/15/1945, 88
Both daus. of the late James and Ellen Kilpatrick

Kilpatrick
James, 4/2/1885 80, Dromore West, Sligo
Wife Ellen, 12/26/1894, 63
Dau. Kate, 4/2/1900, 47
Kate's husband James Simmons, 8/29/1900, 52

King
Bridget, 10/16/1897, 70, Galway
By dau. Mary A. Smith

King
Mary, 6/9/1862, 35, Gibstown, Kallare, Westmeath
Michael, 10/30/18?, 50
Dau. Ann, 4/10/1852, 23
By son and brother Patrick

King
Norah, 4/5/1886, 25, Roundstone, Galway

Kinnally
John, 1/3/1876, 65, Tipperary
John J., 12/17/1922, 73
Martha, 4/5/1924, 69

Kinsella
William, 12/8/1897, 56, Queens
By wife Ceceila
See McGiven, Philip, 5/5/1882, 78

Kirby
James, 12/7/1880, 52, Tipperary
By wife Hanora
Mary A. Casey, 3/30/1912, 45
John F. Casey, 3/4/1989, 64

Kirk
Charles V., 7/26/1935
See Henry, Thomas D., 1852 - 7/12/1914

Kirwin
Julia, 9/9/1887, 38, Cavan
By husband William
Margaret, 1905 - 1937
William, 1892 - 1949

Knee
William, 12/14/1895, 42, Leck, Donegal
By sister Rose

Ladley
James F., 11/9/1841 - 4/6/1911, Clonmel, Tipperary
By wife Ellen, 5/22/1851 - 9/15/1922, Clonmel, Tipperary
Anastasia Ladley Pitcher, 1/29/1928
Richard Ladley, 1871 - 1941
Martha, 7 months
Emma, 9 months

Lafferty
Robert, 9/8/1872, Errigal, Londonderry
By wife Sarah

Lahey
Mary, 6/7/1882, 40, Newport, Tipperary
By husband John
Their children died young, Ann, Martin, John, Michael, Wm. Margaret
John's mother Ann Lahey, 4/10/1887, 77

Lahey
Maryann, 6/8/1898, 40, Drogheda, Louth
By husband James, 10/24/1904, 66, Cavan
Robert P., 5/9/1877 - 10/22/1915

Lahey
Michael, 5/24/1892, 48, Bourney, Tipperary
Mary, 8/26/1930

Lally
Bridget, 11/19/1874, 52-8-0, Roscommon
Dau. Anna J., 4/30/1876, 28-8-0
By husband and father Patrick, 2/21/1898, 82

Lamb
Catherine 1865, St. John's?, Roscommon
By husband Thomas 12/1887, 68
Dau. Ellen 1855
Richard Dixon 1847-3/1923
His wife Matilda 6/3/1856 - 10/29/1919
Their children: Richard, Hilda, Cyril
Sarah Connaughton
Kate A. wife of Richard Dixon and dau. of the late Thomas Lamb
11/2/1888, 38
Children of Richard and Kate Dixon:
Richard 4/5/1886 - 9/12/1886
Thomas Coran 7/1887 - 11/11/1887 born Youghal

Landers
James, 1/8/1893, 46, Tipperary
By wife Mary, 3/29/1894, Meedian, Westmeath

Lane
Catherine, wife of Dennis, 11/11/1873, 28, Cork
See Murphy, Jeremiah, 1/18/1876, 77

Lane
John, 3/29/1895, 55, Cork
By wife Catherine, 4/22/1911, 74
Son Francis died young
Charles H., 10/21/1899, 33
John Jr., 4/24/1914, 52
William F., 5/29/1915, 49

Lane
Michael, 1873, Limerick
Catherine
Ellen
Julia

Lane
Patrick, Cavan
Bridget

Lantry
Rose, 1893 - 1962
See Byrne, Rose, 8/11/1885

Larkin
John J., 1898 - 1969
See Kennelly, Dominick, 1802 - 9/28/1884

Larkin
Julia, 58, Tipperary
Martin, 7/6/1890, 55
Pierce, 7/26/1909, 70
Mary, 10/2/?

Larkin
Maggie, No dates
See Sheridan, Bridget, 1/14/1892, 72

Larkin
Richard J., 1876 - 1947
Joseph, 1884 - 1955
Anne F., 1883 - 1964
Margaret T., 1895 - 1966
See Hyland, Francis J., 1/21/1913, 39

Larkin
Thomas, 8/1/1887, 37, Magheracloone, Monaghan
By brother Peter, 7/21/1921
Peter's wife Bridget, 11/24/1925
Their son James F., 11/16/1912, 23
Mary B. Myles, 8/17/1930
William T. Myles, 3/5/1945

Lavey
Edward, 7/5/1866
Eliza, 52
See McCann, Eliza, 9/5/1856

Lavin
Patrick J., 8/2/1913, Strokestown, Roscommon
By wife Catherine, 1/6/1932
Their son James P. 4/21/1886 - 9/26/1887
Her brother James White, 6/13/1881

Lawler
William, 8/27/1906, 44, City of Dublin
By wife Annie
Thomas Smyth, 4/28/1935, 40

Lawless
Ann, 2/1/1903, 50, Killinkere, Cavan
By husband James, 3/15/1924, 85
Catherine McKenna, 11/30/1910, 53
Edward A. Lawless, 1/12/1915, 30
Lawrence M. Lawless, 7/12/1919, 32
James J. Lawless, 11/20/1922, 33

Lawless
Mary J., 3/29/1841 - 7/5/1896, Dublin
By husband Charles J., 6/18/1838 - 6/18/1915, Dublin

Leahon
Margaret, 6/1/1886, 53, Tallow, Waterford
By daughters
Their sister Julia, 3/7/1887 26, Tallow, Waterford
Daniel F. Donoher, 11/17/1937
His wife Agnes J. Leahon, 12/5/1938

Leahy
Edward, 1/25/1885, 29, Clogheen, Tipperary
By sister Mary T., 12/30/1906, 50

Leavey
Elizabeth, 9/10/1919, Meath
See Greighton, Rev. Patrick

Leddy
Bridget T., 7/19/1908, Newmarket, Clare
Brother Patrick, 10/16/1916, 70, Newmarket, Clare
Sgt. William J. World War Vet. 7th Field Art. 1st Div., 1/23/1929
John F. Maher, 1/19/1947 husband of
Ann Maher, 2/4/1972
Francis R. wife of John Jr. 11/8/1958
1st Lt. Gerard S., 8/2/1977
John F. Jr., 11/20/1985

Leddy
James, 7/9/1918, Newmarket-on-Fergus, Clare
Catherine T., 10/30/1921, Newmarket-on-Fergus, Clare
John S., 11/9/1943
Thomas G., 9/7/1948
Timothy J., 4/7/1950
Mary C., 1/7/1961
Michael, 7/7/1961

Leddy
Mary F., 4/4/1924
See Dunne, Dennis, 10/4/1887, 64

Leddy
Michael, 10/28/1913, 47, Cavan
By wife Mary M., 1/2/1929
Her brother Matthew McCahill, 12/23/1912, 60, Cavan

Lee
James T.
Edna J.
See Ragan, Owen, 8/3/1869, 42

Lee
Marcella, 1/26/1899, 42, Longford

Lemmerman
Karen Ann 7/17/1965 - 11/13/1965
Julius, 1951
Elizabeth, 1958
Irene, 1959
See McKie, Thomas, 7/8/1899, 52

Lenehan
James, 10/21/1871, 45, Waterford
By wife Ann

Lennon
John, 10/6/1875, 54, Ballymahon, Longford
Catherine, 9/28/1852, 32
Margaret, 5/21/1862, 3
James, 1/22/1862, 11 months
Mary, 11/18/1883, 25
Kate Lennon, wife of George C. Tinker 10/17/1887
Mary Lennon, 6/19/1887

Leonard
Frank, 6/24/1906, 39, Longford
His brother Peter, 9/5/1889, 21, Longford
By Frank's wife Mary
Winifred Fayne, 12/24/1916, 29
John J. Fitzgerald, 3/22/1926, 64
Mary Leonard, 1905 - 1967

Leonard
Johanna, 12/2/1853, 26
See Cummings, Mary, 7/16/1861, 65

Leonard
John, 5/12/1888, Ballintubber, Roscommon
His son James, 12/25/1902, Ballintubber, Roscommon
By dau. and sister Rose Garvey
Catherine E. Behrend, 1886 - 1962
Emil, 1887 - 1971

Leslie
Eliza
Joseph, 4/10/1893
John S., 11/22/1927
John S. Jr., 7/9/1937, 47
Eliza B., 12/8/1939
See Bermingham, Maria, 7/27/1903, 63

Levey
Bridget, 10/28/1885, 93, Westmeath
See Murphy, Margaret, 7/5/1898

Lewis
Rose
See Fitzpatrick, Richard, 7/26/1877

Lillis
Margaret, 11/23/1893, 39, Tarbert, Kerry
By husband P.J.
Their children: Ellen, Mary, Catherine, Margaret, Hannah
and James, died young

Lindeman
William H., 9/4/1964
Anna M., 12/6/1967
See Berren, Mary, 7/5/1919, 73

Lindley
Mary E., 3/18/1920
See Clark, Thomas Jr., 2/22/1873

Line
James
William
See Sullivan, Timothy 10/1/1866, 55, Ardea, Kerry

Lineen
Cornelius J., 2/1/1930, Milltown, Clare
By wife Margaret, 2/11/1983

Little
Francis W., 7/11/1904, 4 months
Agnes J., 4/5/1912, 9
See Connors, Thomas, 7/4/1895, 33

Lloyd
John M., 1886 - 1945
See Farrell, Catherine, 3/3/1887, 53

Loftus
Rev. Martin, 2/2/1856 - 6/2/1901, Mayo
Founder Our Lady of Angels R.C. Church Bay Ridge

Logan
Mary, 11/30/1888, 65, Kildare
By children James and Kate

Logan
Mary, 5/1/1907, 39, Roscommon
By husband Luke
Her former husband Thomas Coughlin Sr., Roscommon
Her son Thomas Coughlin Jr., Roscommon
Her brother Robert Rogerson, Roscommon
Michael J. Rogerson, 12/10/1911
Robert J. Egan, 11/11/1907
Delia A. Egan, 3/20/1930, 79
Ellen T. Egan, 11/20/1932, 59
James J. Egan, 1/9/1953

Logue
Bridget, 12/28/1886, Maghera, Derry
Her sister Rose McKenna, 1/21/1904, 64
James McKenna husband of Rose, 3/20/1920, 71

Londrigan
Mary 1/24?/1873, 22
Catherine 2/25?/1873, 2 months
John 3/17?/1899, 45
See Hennessey, Richard 1?/1881?, Tipperary

Lonergan
Alice, 9/20/1894, 52, Cahir, Tipperary
By husband William, 5/27/1911, 70
John J., 11/5/1869 - 4/1/1913
Dennis A., 1/20/1873 - 8/11/1914
William A., 4/20/1940
Also children who died young

Loughman
Anne P.
See Riley, Mary, 12/28/1911, 96

Loughrey
S.Sgt. William J. USAF Killed in Action, 4/6/1945
See Dunn, Bridget, 4/4/1899, 70

Lowe
John, 5/12/1861, 26, Roscommon

Lowery
John, Monaghan
Bridget
John Joseph
John 8/9/1877
Rose A. Hayes 10/16/1908

Lunny
Mary A., 6/22/1932
See Rogers, Daniel, 3/11/1898

Lyden
John, 12/10/1910, Galway
Norah, 7/5/1893, Galway
James, 4/27/1934
John A., 12/24/1949

Lydon
Catherine, 8/6/1896, Galway
By sister Mary Lydon

Lynch
Catherine, 2/27/1916
See Tuite, Matthew, 3/26/1909, 22

Lynch
Daniel T., 5/7/1854 - 7/30/1875, Kilbonane, Cork
John H., 10/5/1860 - 4/8/1876, Kilbonane, Cork
By parents
Ellen, 12/25/1888, 64, Kilbonane Cork
John, 4/1/1912, 92, Kilbonane Cork

Lynch
John, 2/22/1916, 26
See Harvey, Bridget, 1/27/1910, 48

Lynch
John E., 1/21/1868, 4
Julia A., 10/28/1879, 22
See Coughlin, Daniel, 10/13/1963, 77

Lynch
Margaret Ryan, 11/10/1843 - 6/15/1918
See Ryan, Michael, 10/27/1920, 75

Lynch
Michael, 5/12/1838 - 5/28/1916, Carnaross, Meath
By wife Catherine
Bridget Hartz, 12/15/1929

Lynch
Thomas, 9/15/1858, 56, Forghney, Longford
Mary, Forghney, Longford
Michael, 3/1887, Forghney, Longford
Catherine, 8/26/1902, Forghney, Longford

Lynch
Thomas, 9/14/1877, 69, Cavan
Rose, 3/23/1893, Cavan

Lynch
William, 11/1/1850 - 3/28/1918
John J., 9/14/1883 - 3/8/1919
Elizabeth, 6/28/1860 - 6/12/1927 mother of John J.
Josephine T., 8/30/1942
See Bray, John, 7/29/1895, 66

Lyon
Sgt. George A., 9/28/1944
Robert C., 11/19/1955
Catherine M., 4/1/1973
See Meehan, James J., 12/24/1917, 59

Lyons
Mary, 12/23/1911, Ballyvourney, Cork
By husband Cornelius, 11/30/1923, Ballyvourney, Cork
Their son Michael, 11/12/1905, Ballyvourney, Cork
Hannah Lyons Winblade, 3/12/1928, 47, Ballyvourney, Cork

Lyons
Michael, 9/7/1918, 53, Roscommon
By Annie L., 1/23/1941, 77
John J. Roche, 6/23/1948, 56
John J. Lyons, 5/1/1975
Anne L. Roche, 5/24/1987, 97

Lyons
Patrick, 5/3/1898, 69, Westmeath
By daughter Catherine Halloran

Main entrance to the Cemetery of the Holy Cross, Flatbush, Brooklyn.
The first burial was in July 1849. The building on the inside right is the office.

The chapel at Holy Cross was dedicated by John Loughlin (1817-1891), first bishop of the Diocese of Brooklyn (1853-1891)

Most of the sections in Holy Cross are named in honor of saints. In some sections statues have been erected in honor of those saints. There are two statues of St. Patrick. One in the section named for him. The other seen here is outside the main office. St. Patrick is pictured here flanked on the right by St. Joseph and on the left by St. Cecelia.

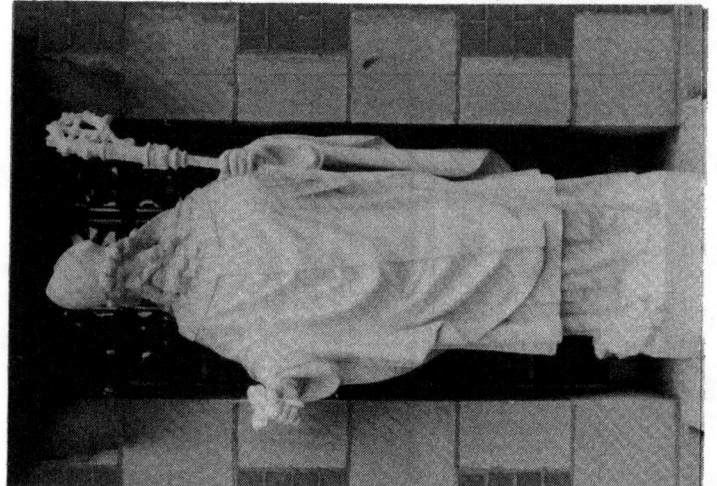

Here are two examples of the half dozen photographs placed on the tombstones of Irish-born. The tradition of placing photographs on tombstones was much more common among Italian-born and Italian-Americans at the time.

Patrick Sullivan 11 years old

Young Patrick Sullivan is seen here wearing what most likely is his "First Communion Suit". He was the son of John and Mary Quirk Sullivan. Patrick was born in Ireland and had been in the U.S. for seven years. He was admitted to Long Island College Hospital in Brooklyn, August 1, 1915 and died the same day. His death certificate lists his occupation as "School Boy". Once again because of the time in which they lived, another set of parents outlived their child.

Peter Kelly immigrated from Ireland only two years prior to his death in 1913. He was a native of Abbeyknockmoy, Galway. The photograph on his stone shows him wearing his motorman's uniform with number 2547 on the front of the cap. Mr. Kelly died in Holy Family Hospital, Brooklyn, September 9, 1913 aged 25.

Harry M. Supple was born in St. John's, Newfoundland. As a boy he moved with his family to the City of Brooklyn. During the construction of the Brooklyn Bridge he worked as a rigger foreman. On June 14, 1878 he was struck by a strand and fell from the anchorage on the Manhattan side. He suffered a compound fracture of the skull and fractures of both arms. He was taken to the Chambers St. Hospital where he died several hours later.

Shortly before his eighteenth birthday James Donlon was standing on the corner of Atlantic and Grand Avenues talking with two friends. The three young men and some other people noticed "an old lady" walking in the path of an oncoming steam car. Donlon and others shouted to her to watch out. She appeared not to hear. Mr. Donlon ran and tried to pull her away from the oncoming car. The woman who was identified several days later as Emma V. Barnes was killed instantly. Patrick and Ann Donlon, natives of Ireland, lost their son James several hours later due to a fracture of the skull. James was working as a journeyman plumber at the time of his death. What makes his death more tragic is that according to reports in the Brooklyn Daily Eagle, Miss Barnes may have attempted suicide. A funeral Mass was held for James Donlon at St. Joseph's Church, Pacific Street on December 13, 1877. His remains were laid to rest in the St. Edward's section of Holy Cross.

James B. "Diamond Jim" Brady was born on Cedar Street in New York City in 1856. As a young boy his family moved to the City of Brooklyn. His was a "rags to riches" story. He earned a fortune in the railroad industry. He loved good food and jewelry hence the name "Diamond Jim". He died in Atlantic City April 13, 1917. He was buried in the family plot in Holy Cross.

W. R. (William Russell) Grace was born in Riverstown, Cork in 1832. As a young man he travelled to South America and worked in several commercial houses. As he advanced he began the company which still bears his name today. After amassing a fortune he went to New York City in 1868. In 1880, running as a Democrat he was elected the first Roman Catholic mayor of New York. He did not run for re-election in 1882 but was elected again in 1884. After his retirement from politics he was involved in philanthropic causes. He died in Manhattan in 1904.

For centuries the Irish have been known for their poetry. In subjects from life to death they have left their mark. Pictured here are a few stones with definite 19th century flavors.

Ellen Cullum, the wife of David, was born in Ireland and immigrated to the U.S. in 1837. Forty of her fifty years in America were spent in Brooklyn. She died at her home, 877 Pacific Street. She was buried in Holy Cross after a Mass at St. Joseph's Church just a few block from her late residence.

Corkman William Greany has his first name inscribed as part of the poem on his stone:

THINK NOT MY DEAR WILLIAM, THOUGH FAR FAR AWAY
FROM THINE OWN NATIVE ISLE THOU ART SLEEPING
THAT NO HEART FOR THY LOSS DO MOURN TODAY
THAT NO EYE FOR THEY MEMORY IS WEEPING

Not only is there a poem on this stone but it also tells of another bit of history. James McAnally was one of the many thousands of Irish who died while crossing the Atlantic for America. Mr. McAnally died February 14th, 1850 aged 56 years. Mr. McAnally is not buried in this grave. This plot was bought in 1868 when his wife Ellen died on June 18th, aged 76 years. Their son James died January 30, 1869, 37 years old. The poem relating to James' death at sea is:

TOSSED ON A SEA OF DISTRESS
HARD TRYING TO MAKE THE BLESSED SHORE
WHERE ALL IS ASSURANCE AND PEACE
AND SORROW AND SIN NO MORE

The last two lines of the poem on this stone is enough to keep anyone from visiting the cemetery. I am sure that Mrs. Conklin knew that she was going to die, but to be reminded of it probably did not make it a pleasant day at the cemetery.

Mary Walsh was one of the thousands of Irish women who came to America and became domestic servants. She immigrated to America about 1860 and was in the service of the Patterson family of 140 McDonough Street, Brooklyn. In her will dated May 13, 1893, Miss Walsh made plans for the payment of her funeral. She also included payment for her grave, headstone and Masses. She left her watch, clothing and $25.00 to a Kate Kearny. The remainder of her estate went to her sister Mrs. Norah Ormand. Mary Walsh died May 27, 1893 at the home where she worked and lived for so many years. After a funeral Mass at Our Lady of Victory Church, Mary Walsh was buried in Holy Cross Cemetery May 29, 1893.

This stone does not mark the final resting place of May Rooney. Her final resting place is probably somewhere off the Irish coast. On May 1, 1915 Mary Rooney accompanied by her cousin Mary Agnes Ruppert went to the dock at the foot of West 14 Street. Miss Rooney boarded the SS Lusitania for Liverpool. It was the last time they would see each other. Miss Rooney was on her way home to be with her ailing mother who lived in Manor Hamilton, County Leitrim, Ireland. Years earlier Miss Rooney left Ireland and worked as a domestic servant in Brooklyn Heights. When she learned of her mother's illness she bought a ticket on the British owned Cunard Line steamship Lusitania. Despite warnings placed in newspapers by the German Embassy 1300 passengers and a crew of 700 sailed in the ship. It was almost one year since the start of the First World War. We do not know why she did it but Mary Rooney signed her Last Will and Testament the day before she sailed April 30, 1915. On May 7, 1915 the Germans torpedoed the Lusitania. Among the tremendous loss of life was Mary Rooney. She left an estate of over $5,000.00 plus property in Brooklyn. Not bad for an immigrant domestic servant. It is ironic that Miss Rooney had enough money to visit her mother only to be killed. Most immigrants were never able to return home. The following pages show more of the story of how one person was caught up in an historic event.

THE BROOKLYN DAILY EAGLE

NEW YORK CITY, FRIDAY, MAY 7, 1915.

LUSITANIA TORPEDOED AND SUNK BY GERMANS OFF IRISH COAST--PASSENGERS PROBABLY SAVED

Four Brooklyn and Queens Men Among Survivors; Others Missing

Out of nine Brooklyn and Queens residents known to have been aboard the Lusitania, four were definitely reported this afternoon to have been saved. The four are:

CLINTON BERNARD, 34 Herriman avenue, Jamaica, L. I.
ROBERT EWART, 1351 Broadway.
JAMES J. LEARY, 404 Eighth avenue.
WALLACE B. PHILLIPS, 29 Lefferts place.

The following other Brooklynites are yet to be accounted for:

Henry H. Meyers, or Herman A. Myers, Central avenue. (W. G. E. Meyers saved).

Miss Mary Rooney, maid at 255 Henry street (a Miss Loney saved).

Thomas Flaherty, 251 Court street.

May Locksters, 50 Nevins street (Harriet Judson, Y. W. C. A.).

Hannah Cunnis, 252 Gates avenue (maid of Dr. J. Richard Kevin).

No Word Yet From Mary Rooney and Thomas Flaherty.

The two Brooklyn passengers concerning whom word has not yet been received are Miss Mary Rooney, a maid servant, who was twelve years in the employ of Mrs. J. S. Hollinshead of 255 Henry street, and Thomas Flaherty of 251 Court street. Miss Rooney was booked in the second cabin, and was obliged to go to her mother, who, she had learned, was ill at Manor Hamilton, County Leitrim, Ireland. Mrs. Hollinshead is greatly concerned about the fate of the girl. There is a name of Miss Loney among those saved, but it is doubtful whether Miss Rooney and Miss Loney are the same person.

Thomas Flaherty of 251 Court street was one of the third cabin passengers on the ship. This was his third trip across the Atlantic to his home in Clifton, County Garvin, Ireland. His wife is there, and had been writing to him to come back to her ever since he came here last March.

WILL No. 114.　　　　　　　　John M. Bulwinkle, Stationer and Printer, 413 Fulton Street, Brooklyn, N. Y.

In the Name of God, Amen, I, MARY ROONEY, of #255 Henry Street, Brooklyn, New York, being of sound and disposing mind and memory, and considering the uncertainty of this life, do make, publish and declare, this to be my last Will and Testament as follows: First, after my lawful debts are paid, I give, devise and bequeath to my beloved brother, James Rooney, of Manor Hamilton, County Leitrim, Ireland, the real estate now owned by me on East 17th Street, near Avenue "U", Brooklyn, New York.

Second, I give and bequeath to my beloved Mother, Rose Rooney, of Manor Hamilton, Ireland, the sum of Five Hundred Dollars.

The first two paragraphs of Mary Rooney's Last Will and Testament.

In Witness Whereof, I have hereunto subscribed my name, and affixed my seal, the thirtieth day of April in the year of our Lord, one thousand nine hundred fifteen.

WITNESSES:

Josephine L. Malone
Louise B. Schattenkircher　　　　Mary Rooney

Subscribed by Mary Rooney the Testatrix named in the foregoing Will, in the presence of each of us, and at the time of making such subscription the above Instrument was declared by the said Testatrix to be her last Will and Testament, and each of us, at the request of said Testatrix and in her presence and in the presence of each other, sign our names as witnesses thereto, at the end of the Will.

The signatures of Mary Rooney and her two witnesses, Josephine L. Malone and Louise B. Schattenkircher. Eight days later Mary Rooney would die on the Lusitania.

This monument was erected by officers and members of the Brooklyn Fire Department. At the top stands a fireman holding a hose. There are three names and a poem inscribed on the stone.

Hugh McGowan who fell through the roof of a burning building December 4, 1891, 33 years old.

John F. Spaulding died during a fire at Harbeck's store November 12, 1892, Age 29.

Christopher D. Boyne died during a fire March 21, 1901 Age 33.

>"Died at his post like a hero brave
>Sweet in his sleep in a hero's grave
>Nobel unselfish and truly great
>He thought but of others, and met his fate"

Front reads:

In memory of
Francis S. Belton
Colonel of the 4th
Regt. of the U.S.
Artillery.
Born in Baltimore Md.
Aug. 9th, 1791
Died at Brooklyn
Sept. 10th, 1861

Back of Monument.

Back reads:

A soldier who illustrated the History of His Country by THE CONTINUOUS DEVOTION OF A HALF CENTURY MERITORIOUS SERVICES AND GALLANT CONDUCT IN THE WARS WITH GREAT BRITAIN AND IN FLORIDA AND IN MEXICO. HIS BRAVERY ON THE FIELD EQUALLED BY HIS SAGACITY IN COUNCIL. HE WAS OFTEN HONORED WITH POSITIONS OF HIGH TRUST AND DIGNITY AS GOVERNOR OF PUEBLA DE LOS ANGELES AND LIEUT. GOVERNOR OF MEXICO. HE DISCHARGED THE DUTIES OF A CIVIL MAGISTRATE WITH RARE ABILITY AND INTEGRITY. THE ARDOR OF THE PATRIOT THE PRIDE OF THE WARRIOR THE LEARNING OF THE SCHOLAR THE ACCOMPLISHMENT OF THE GENTLEMAN THE STEADFASTNESS OF THE FRIEND THE LOVING TENDERNESS OF THE HUSBAND AND THE FATHER WERE ALL MERGED IN THE SWEET HUMILITY OF THE FAITHFUL CHRISTIAN AND AS SUCH HE DIED.

Colonel Francis S. Belton was born in Baltimore and educated at St. Mary's College. At the age of 19 he was appointed to Gen. Scott's staff. He distinguished himself in the War of 1812 during the defense of Fort Erie (1813). He also played a role in the capture of Mexico City (War with Mexico). For his bravery he was breveted Colonel at Chorobusco. According to the Brooklyn Daily Eagle (9/13/1861) Col. Belton wanted to be buried "in the folds of the flag of that country which he fought for, with the cross of his faith upon his breast". After a solemn High Mass at St. Charles Borromeo Church, Col. Belton's remains were taken to Holy Cross Cemetery.

Albert Finbar Kennelly was the son of Cork natives. When President Lincoln called for volunteers during the Civil War, Mr. Kennelly joined the N.Y. 17th. He was killed at the Battle of Jonesboro 20 miles south of Atlanta, September 1, 1864.

Sgt. William S. Goodwin's stone is one of the few which shows the name of a veteran of the Spanish-American War. Mr. Goodwin's parents Francis and Mary were born in Ireland. Seen here, William Goodwin joined the 49th Company Volunteer Signal Corps. At the time of his death he was working as a store keeper. He died at the age of 63 in March 1928.

Andrew and James McVeigh both served in France during the First World War. During separate actions on the same day September 27th, 1918 both brothers were killed. Their bodies were returned home in 1921. Andrew was buried in Holy Cross on April 10th and James on September 4th. There were memorial services at their parish, Holy Rosary, Chauncey St. and Reid Ave. Both were buried with military honors.

S./Sgt. William J. Loughrey was 27 years old when he was killed in the European Theatre of operation during World War II. His death came just a month before the German surrender. His remains were brought back to Brooklyn and he was laid to rest in Holy Cross on June 4th, 1949.

Despite the fact that there are thousands of Irish-born buried in Holy Cross Cemetery there were few stones in the Irish language. Many people do not realize that the mother tongue of many of the famine and pre-famine Irish immigrants was not English but Irish. Yet there were no more than three tombstones of the Irish-born with Irish inscriptions. Below is the tombstone of William E. Clifford and his wife Mary. All the information pertaining to Mr. Clifford is inscribed in the Irish language. It reads: "William E. Clifford born Feb. 11, 1877 died August 15, 1930 Born at Ballina—, Co. Mayo Ireland". William E. Clifford was the son of Alfred and Mary Clark Clifford. He immigrated to the U.S. at the turn of the century. Mr. Clifford was employed as a letter carrier. He died at Long Island College Hospital. There is a poem in Irish at the bottom of the stone.

From the foot of the cross I look up
O Jesus Lord bend down
I profess the true faith
With heartfelt love and everlasting hope

On the following pages will be found stones in other languages.

Italian

Giuseppe Leto was the son of Stefano and Nunzia Leto, Italian immigrants. Their son was born in New York in 1904. He was employed as a salesman when he died accidentally at their Coney Island home at the age of 19 years. The parents names are the last two names above the Italian "Riposa in Pace" "Rest in Peace".

Polish

Here lies in sainted memory
Emilian Dobroskielski
born day 9 March 1852 year
died day 14 March 1914 year

May the earth be light upon him

Mr. Dobroskielski was a carpenter living in New York only three years prior to his death. He was born in what his death certificate described as Russian/Poland.

French

Here rests the body of
Joseph Demontreux
Died at Brooklyn
9 August 1914
At 71 years

Pray for him.

Mr. Demontreux was retired at the time of his death. He was born in France and had immigrated from there six years prior to his death.

German

Here rests in God
Nickolaus Hartung
of Bischofsheim on the Mountains
Bavaria Born Dec. 20, 1824
Died Feb. 12, 1891

Maria Anna Hartung
Born Beiner
of Herxheim Bavaria
born August 1, 1830
died June 21, 1905

Both Nickolaus and Maria Anna Beiner Hartung came to the U.S. about 1850. Mr. Hartung was retired when he died at their home on 18 St. in Brooklyn. Mrs. Hartung died fourteen years later.

Ukrainian

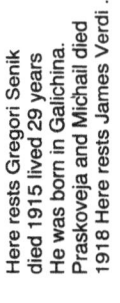

Here rests Gregori Senik
died 1915 lived 29 years
He was born in Galichina.
Praskoveja and Michail died
1918 Here rests James Verdi ...

Although the tombstone is inscribed in Ukrainian, Mr. Senik was born in Poland. He died in Holy Family Hospital in Brooklyn, November 1, 1915.

Lyons
Michael, 11/24/1901, 65, Tulsk, Roscommon
Wife Catherine Murray Lyons, 3/4/1899, 60, Tulsk, Roscommon
Dau. Margaret J., 11/19/1892 18, Tulsk, Roscommon
Michael J., 8/23/1923
Wife Margaret, 11/17/1948
Owen Murray, 4/2/1936 94, Roscommon
Sarah Lyons, 10/11/1947, Roscommon
Patrick J., 3/26/1952, Roscommon
Helen McGuire, 5/30/1956
John P., 1/25/1892
Maureen A. Collins, 1/26/1966
Timothy J., 11/22/1967
Loretta, 7/9/1975
Mary Murray, wife of Owen 3/23/1901 60, Williamstown, Galway
Dau. Catherine A. Fernie, 9/6/1901 33-7-0
Son Patrick J. Murray, 2/4/1928 56

McAleese
Rev. Msgr. James, 7/8/1847 - 11/3/1930, Antrim
Ordained 11/8/1874 Pastor St. Rose of Lima
Mary J., 2/16/1947, 91

McAlpine
Annie F., 6/13/1932
See Can. Code, Patrick, H., 1776 - 2/2/1851

McAnerne
Elizabeth, 9/20/1881 70, Keeloges, Inver, Donegal

McAuliffe
Bessie, 1/15/1926, 48, Lough Allen, Roscommon
By husband John, 9/14/1933, 60, Kerry

McAuliffe
Margaret, 11/18/1880, 10, Drumcollogher, Limerick
By father Timothy

McAvoy
John, 10/20/1912, 59, Kildare
Wife Catherine, 4/14/1913, 56, Dublin City
Children: Alfred, Mary, Francis
John J., 8/16/1937
Rose Helen, 10/24/1967

McAvoy
Peter J., 6/29/1822 - 9/2/1909, Cabbra Rathfriland, Down

McBride
Laurence, 7/1863, Sligo
By wife Rose
Dau. Mary E., 5/11/1859, 1-3-0

McCabe
Bridget, 10/3/1891, 87, Lurgan, Cavan

McCabe
Patrick, 1839 - 1909, Monaghan
Wife Ellen, 1853 - 1911, Monaghan

McCabe
Peter, Cootehill, Cavan
Wife Florence
Son Philip
His mother
Fredrick A. Wall, 12/6/1910 - 11/14/1988, Belfast

McCabe
Thomas, 3/11/1901, 55
Wife Mary, 3/14/1901, 50, Cavan

McCadden
Anthony, 6/2/1887, 62, Donegal
Grace, 38, Donegal
By dau. Annie McCadden

McCaffrey
Patrick, 12/4/1891, 34, Enniskillen, Fermanagh
By wife Susan, 5/28/1907
Dau. Bella, 12/10/1891, 5

McCaffrey
Peter, 4/19/1914, 30, Greencastle, Tyrone
Rose Boyle McCaffrey, 12/24/1971, Gweedore, Donegal
Thomas, 9/10/1976, Greencastle, Tyrone

McCaffrey
Sarah, 6/22/1904, 60, Fermanagh
By brother Edward, 3/17/1905, 58

McCahill
Matthew, 12/23/1912, 60, Cavan
See Leddy, Michael, 10/28/1913, 47

McCallig
Edward, 12/6/1895, 62, Inver, Donegal
By wife Mary, 2/23/1910
Sadie, 4/26/1928
Mary L. Gallagher, 7/19/1955

McCamley
John J., 5/14/1956
See Madigan, John, 3/2/1896, 54

McCann
Eliza, 9/5/1856 28, Aghallon, Antrim
By brother Edward Lavey, 7/5/1866
Eliza, 52

McCann
John, 6/19/1896, 35, Moville, Donegal
By wife Rose
Joseph McLaughlin, 3/3/1959
Neil Bonner, 11/4/1958
Daniel McNeill, 5/3/1963

McCann
John, 6/8/1906, 46, Bruff, Limerick
By wife Catherine, 3/28/1850 - 5/21/1915
Thomas F. Finn, 10/25/1888 - 10/7/1942
Arthur Philie, 8/7/1911 - 6/27/1959
Mary Finn, 1885 - 1906

McCann
Margaret, 3/12/1898, 47, Rathvilly, Carlow
By husband Thomas, 9/9/1903, 52, Meath
Arthur D., 3/19/1906, 22

McCann
Thomas, 2/10/1899, 60, Sligo
By wife Rebecca

McCarroll
Johanna, 9/23/1945
Walter J., 10/7/1950
See Murphy, Francis, 8/24/1892, 57

McCart
William, 4/1/1879, 68, Antrim
Mary, 3/17/1877, 65, Antrim
Mary, 9/19/1914, 64, Tyrone
By Alexander McCart son and husband

McCarthy
Charles, 6/8/1873 - 4/12/1916
By parents Daniel, 12/8/1832 - 11/14/1919, Clare
Mary, 10/12/1836 - 11/8/1926, Clare
Dau. Annie McCauley, 11/1/1863 - 9/21/1919
Catherine L. Durgo, 10/31/1871 - 6/7/1941
Daniel McCarthy, 10/31/1876 - 2/28/1956
Margaret A. McCarthy, 2/27/1888 - 1/22/1966
Mary V. Cillen, 11/2/1879 - 10/31/1965
Thomas F. McCarthy, 8/31/1918 - 5/24/1976

McCarthy
George H., 5/16/1954
Ann M., 9/29/1963
See Finn, Michael P., 4/18/1916, 45

McCarthy
Helen V., 6/10/1930
See Dunleavy, Thomas L., 5/7/1907, 38

McCarthy
John, 8/15/1893, 76, Cooneen, Waterford
By wife Mary, 5/25/1900, 59
Son Joseph
Joseph P. Mooney, 11/28/1887 - 7/28/1959
Jennie Mooney, 1966

McCarthy
James, 6/24/1896, Castlebar, Mayo
Anne, 5/30/1918, Castlebar, Mayo
See O'Donnell, James J., 5/11/1894

McCarthy
Nellie, 1/8/1903, Cork
By sister Mary McCarthy

McCarthy
Nora Ryan, 1867 - 1964
See O'Brien, Patrick, 1/12/1904, 51

McCarthy
Patrick, 8/16/1871, Clare
By wife Margaret nee White, 5/28/1927
Son Patrick Jr., 7/18/1903
Grandchildren died young

McCarthy
Patrick, 7/28/1885, 50, Kilkimmon, Kerry
By wife Mary, 4/23/1894, 60
Mary Bittel, 3/25/1884 - 5/28/1928
Frank Bittel, 5/19/1884 - 1/23/1953
Marie C. Bussinger, 1/1/1918 - 4/1/1990

McCartney
Mary, 7/22/1852, 45
Thomas McGlaughlin, 9/11/1860, Leitrim

McCarty
Bridget, 8/17/1881, 38, Longford
By husband John, 4/29/1919

McCarty
Mary, 6/20/1864, 32, Tralee, Kerry
By husband John
Dau. Mary

McCaul
Ellen Leweise, 2/26/1883, 31, Tyrone
Catherine, 12/16/1891, Poughkeepsie, N.Y.
By their husband Nicholas J., 3/31/1913, 60

McCauley
Annie, 11/1/1863 - 9/21/1919
See McCarthy, Charles, 6/8/1873 - 4/12/1916

McCawley
Eugene, 9/27/1886, 35-3-20, Tuam, Galway
By wife Bridget, 3/29/1930, 81
Her mother Margaret Horan, 12/17/1886, 75, Cappabane, Clare
Bridget's children:
Eugene, 9/23/1888
Margaret, 2/26/1884, 4 moths
John T., 5/14/1888, 2-1-2
Katie, 7/9/1890, 5-8-20
Edward F. Jacobs, 3/18/1939, 65
Elizabeth Jacobs, 4/1876 - 8/1957
M. Patricia Jacobs, 2/16/1973

McCloskey
Hugh, 8/28/1882, 45, Derry
By wife Bridget

McCole
Mary, 11/24/1859, 37, Moylagh, Meath
By Hugh her husband, 7/11/1891, 69, Moville, Donegal
His father Bryan, 10/14/1849, 60, Moville, Donegal
His sister Frances, 12/6/1881, Moville, Donegal

McCole
Timothy, 1896 - 1960
See McGoldrick, John, 8/15/1896, 38

McConnald
John, 5/30/?, 53, Culdaff, Donegal

McConnell
Sarah A., 7/9/1888, 59, Coal Island, Tyrone
Husband James, 5/2/1894, 75, Armagh
John J., 7/12/1910, 60

McCool
Bridget, 5/2/1911, 46, Moville, Donegal
By husband James

McCoppin
Edward, 11/1/1887, 45, Longford
By wife Mary T., 7/5/1919

McCormack
Catherine, 3/1865, 21, Galway
By husband Nicholas

McCormack
Hanora, 3/12/1935
Martin, 1965
See Spelman, John, 9/4/1887

McCormack
Margaret, 2/5/1909, 68, Kilkenny
By children: P.J. McCormack and M.F. Buggy
Michael McCormack, 3/12/1948, 69
Mary McCormack, 4/6/1889 - 8/18/1970

McCormack
Mary, 6/18/1918, 33
Her infant dau. Veronica
See Fogarty, John J., 2/4/1919, 70

McCormick
Ann, 11/19/1896, 60, Carrickedmond, Longford
Thomas Mullen, 10/19/1919, 53, Longford
Mary Mullen, 11/22/1931, 55
May Mullen, 10/15/1895, 3-5-0
Ensign Thomas A. Mullen USN 11/2/1918, 28
died for his country

McCormick
Bridget, 2/10/1892, 58, Greencastle, Donegal
Sister Grace Wisely, 10/23/1882

McCormick
Dennis, Legan, Longford
Ellen, Legan, Longford
Son James, 8/28/1867, 35, Legan, Longford

McCormick
James, 4/27/1887, Westmeath
By wife Ann

McCormick
John, 8/1871, 39, Killoe, Longford
By wife Ellen
Son Bernard, 1-3-0

McCormick
Patrick, 10/6/1876, 62, Westmeath
By sisters Marcella and Rose McCormick

McCormick
Patrick, 9/9/1877, 30, Ennis, Clare
By wife Margaret

McCoy
Kate, 1/15/1894, 32
See Shields, Ellen, 6/23/1874, 50

McCracken
Robert, 1815 - 1878, Tyrone
Mary, 1903

McCrory
William, 5/5/1876, 42, Antrim
John, 11/5/1876, 68, Antrim
See Mulholland, James, 2/23/1868, 19

McCue
John J., 1875 - 1945
See Bergon, Bridget, 2/4/1894

McCue
Maggie, 6/28/1896, 45, Killeshandra, Cavan
By brother and sister, Thomas and Katie

McCuirk
George, 11/25/1899, 67, Dublin

McCullough
Ann, 1884, Tyrone
By husband James, 3/2/1903, 70
Dau. Margaret, 9/17/1883
James, 11/22/1890, 29
Daniel F., 5/8/1891, 35
Mary, 10/25/1921, 66

McCullough
Mary, 8/10/1889, 55, Glenwoody, Tyrone
By husband James
James F., 2/1/1887 - 9/22/1953

McDaniel
Margaret, 9/12/1857, Toomevara, Tipperary
By brother Michael, 2/5/1895, 75
His wife Anne, 3/4/1895, 69
James, 1/18/1866 - 1/28/1896

McDavitt
Anne, 1/11/1885, 35, Convoy, Donegal
By sister Katie McDavitt
Joseph Sloane, 1910 - 1949
Sarah Boyle, 1879 - 1955
Joseph Boyle, 1924 - 1966
John Boyle, 1881 - 1966
Anna Boyle, 1921 - 1986

McDermott
Helen, 1910 - 1945
See McNamara, Catherine, 1883 - 1924

McDermott
John, 2/3/1871, 72, Headford, Galway
By son Patrick, 4/24/1873, 33, Headford, Galway
Catherine, 11/1/1890, 82

McDermott
John, 8/21/1872, 43, Dublin
By wife Ellen

McDermott
Mary, 5/13/1880, 33, Tyrone

McDermott
Patrick, 11/12/1886, 48, Sligo
By wife Mary

McDermott
William E., 1908 - 1965
See Hanley, Thomas, 2/10/1889, 50

McDevitt
Ellen Clarke, 11/18/1887, 24, Moville, Donegal
By husband Andrew McDevitt
Dau. Catherine

McDevitt
Mary, 8/15/1854, 72, Donegal
By Bridget

McDevitt
Mary, 5/8/1928, Drumaweer, Greencastle, Moville, Donegal
By husband Daniel

McDevitt
Patrick, 9/3/1898, 72, Donegal
Bridget, 3/30/1906, 70, Cavan
Son Patrick, 7/6/1899, 26
and other children who died young

McDonald
Christopher, 11/30/1854, 40, Dublin
Mary, 11/10/1881, 67, Wexford
See Dempsey, Patrick, 7/22/1848, 65

McDonald
James, 1848 - 1930, Clyde Court, Louth
Thomas A., 1886 - 1908
Rose A., 1873 - 1944
John J., 1883 - 1945
Viola wife of John, 1973
Elizabeth M., 1904 - 1980
Eileen R.V., 1906 -
Kathleen M. Murphy, 1922

McDonald
James, 1912 - 1976
Nora, 1914 - 1980
See Price, John, 7/19/1914, 40

McDonald
Mary Crowley, 12/20/1908, Youghal, Cork
By husband David McDonald
Dennis Crowley, 10/13/1907

McDonald
Maryanne, 11/29/1869
Patrick, 5/1798 - 2/21/1868, 70, Wexford
Their son Rev. John McDonald
Elizabeth, 8/14/1910

McDonald
Myra
Thomas
Margaret
See Bermingham, Maria, 7/27/1903, 63

McDonald
Peter, 11/1/1895, 70, Ardpatrick, Limerick
Mary, 3/3/1899, 58, Clare
By dau. Nellie McDonald

McDonnell
A., 1980; See Blake, James, 3/10/1885

McDonnell
Alice, 4/26/1893, 80, Kilkenny
By dau. Alice Jr., 10/18/1897, 40
Her nephew John J., 12/4/1873, 5
Richard J., 12/31/1907, 44

McDonough
(Rev.) James 10/3/1855, 61, Currin?, Monaghan
By the Congregation of St. James

McDonough
Julia, 1889 - 1953
See Foley, Thomas, 4/9/1909

McDonough
Margaret, 9/1866, 30, Leitrim
Katherine A. wife of Patrick J., 10/22/1901 51
Patrick J., 1/16/1911 84
Helen P., 2/22/1939
Mary Schultz, 12/31/1885 - 11/2/1964 79
William H. Gallagher Sr. 12/7/1882 - 7/16/1967, 84
Agnes E. Gallagher, 2/15/1882 - 1/18/1969, 86
Irene A. Goldenberg, 10/25/1910 - 7/7/1980

McElhenny
Patrick, 9/23/1901, 44, Moville, Donegal
By wife, 9/10/1937, 83
Their children:
Mary, 7/23/1895, 8 months
Patrick, 9/7/1906, 15
Delia, 2/28/1910, 21

McEntee
Bernard M.D., 1/22/1892
Catherine, 4/27/1899
See Murtaugh, John, 4/21/1899

McEvoy
John, 12/29/1906, 47, Knockseera, Leix

McFadden
Ellen, 10/18/1899, Kilcar, Donegal
Margaret, 11/24/1916, Kilcar, Donegal
By sister Mary McFadden
James, 6/1/1933

McFadden
John, Londonderry

McFadden
John J., 10/27/1928, 76
Mary McGinty mother of Mary E. McFadden 10/9/1905, Longford
Johnnie McFadden, 7/5/1884, 2 months - 15 days
Raymond, 8/11/1891, 5 months
Philip Pannone, 1896 - 1969

McGee
Patrick, 1/1/1906, 39, Tyrone
By wife Isabella

McGee
William, 12/13/1887, 52, Fermanagh
By wife Mary

McGeehan
William 70?, Donegal
By wife Mary

McGinness
Joseph, 1/21/1910, 27, Fermanagh
By sister Rose McGinness

McGinty
Mary, 10/19/1905, Longford
See McFadden, John J., 10/27/1928, 76

McGinty
Sarah, 11/27/1887, 46, Fanad, Donegal
By sons William and Bernard
Margaret M. Kyne wife of Bernard J. 4/1/1905 35

McGivern
Philip, 5/5/1882, 78, Down
His wife Anne and children
By niece Cecelia Kinsella

McGlaughlin
Thomas, 9/11/1860
See McCartney, Mary, 7/22/1852

McGlone
Mary A., 68-10-9, Glenturrett, Monaghan
By husband Robert, 6/7/1878 69-7-0, Monaghan

McGlynn
Edward, 12/2/1863, 76-9-0, Urlingford, Kilkenny
By Timothy

McGoey
Thomas 11/1/1835 - 9/5/1915, Longford
Wife Priscilla M. 12/3/1848 - 2/22/1925

McGoldrick
Rev. Edward F. born 9/8/1870 ordained 6/24/1897 died 9/30/1930
See Kilpatrick, Ellen E., 4/17/1902

McGoldrick
John, 8/15/1896, 38, Killymard, Donegal
William McGonnigle, 6/4/1917, 61, Killymard, Donegal
Timothy McCole, 1896 - 1960
John J. Kennedy, 1914 - 1971

McGoldrick
John J., 9/13/1913, Fernamenagh, Tyrone
By wife Catherine, 9/23/1923

McGoldrick
Maria, 11/1911, 51, Longford
By husband Thomas, 6/24/1923, 61
Children: Mamie, Thomas, John Stephen, Sabina, Lizzie

McGonnigle
William, 6/4/1917, 61, Killymard, Donegal
See McGoldrick, John, 8/15/1896, 38

McGovern
Ann, 10/23/1905, 65, Leitrim
By husband Patrick, 11/3/1907, 68, Cavan

McGovern
John, 3/5/1914, 47, Leitrim
By wife Ellen McDermott McGovern, 1/23/1938
Eunice, 5/23/1949, 48

McGovern
Rose, 2/15/1912, 73, Clonsilla, Dublin
Brother Patrick, 7/8/1912, 68

McGovern
Thomas J., 7/17/1923, Roscommon
Michael, 11/13/1907
Mary Mills, 9/13/1960

McGowan
Arthur, 8/15/1854, 71, Urney, Tyrone

McGowan
James F., 9/25/1897, 25, Son of Catherine and the late
    William, natives of Killargue, Leitrim
Rogder, 9/3/1898, 31
Mother Catherine, 10/17/1913, 62
Patrick, 1875 - 1918
Agnes M. Carroll McGowan, 1910 - 1936
Patrick Donohue, 3/16/1884, 78, Moydow, Longford
James, 1867, 30
Bridget, 9/18/1872, 75
John Donohue, husband of Louise C. Donohue, 4/1/1903;
73

McGowan
John, 10/20/1885, 52, Annaduff, Leitrim
By wife Elizabeth, 5/8/1844 - 6/30/1906

McGowan
Mary A., 2/26/1948
Anthony F., 11/15/1951
See Walsh, Mary E. McGowan, 3/8/1868 - 9/25/1910

McGrady
Daniel 12/27/1887, 62, Lissaine, Tyrone
By wife Ann
Catherine 7/19/1886, 34

McGrane
Annie, 4/23/1879/77, 28
Mary, 11/20/1881, 32
Their mother Mary, 6/7/1888, 80, Templemichael, Longford

McGrath
Annie, Killymard, Donegal
Her 2 children
Mother and father Catherine and Henry Gallinagh

McGrath
Bridget, 1880, Leitrim
By husband Anthony, 10/11/1893
James, 50

McGrath
Henry J., 1904 - 1958
See Walsh, John, 6/25/1865, 40

McGrath
John, 8/7/1890, 70, Knock Roe, Limerick
By brother and sisters
Michael, 12/18/1895, 66
Bridget, 3/23/1898, 70

McGrath
Mary, Colry, Westmeath
James Farrell, 10/19/1947, 76
By Lawrence McGrath

McGrath
Mary, 1/29/1908, 60
See Finnegan, Annie, 5/11/1893, 34

McGrath
Michael, 4/11/1900, 50, Leitrim
By wife Anne, 9/17/1906, 51, Longford
Their sons:
Charles J., 7/8/1915, 38
Francis X., 3/13/1965, 77

McGrath
Patrick, 2/9/1885?, 48, Leitrim
Mary, 4/18/1936

McGreal
Michael, 12/15/1908, 47, Drumkeerin, Leitrim
By sister Elizabeth, 3/4/1925
Ann E. Brown, 4/13/1968

McGuigan
Henry T., 2/19/1908, Rathcline, Longford
By wife Catherine, 1/6/1909

McGuiness
Mary, 7/2/1901, 58, Lurganboy, Castlerahan, Cavan
Frank, 12/23/1939
Delia, 12/4/1947
Frank Jr., 1/26/1950

McGuire
Helen, 5/30/1956
John P., 1/25/1982
See Lyons, Michael, 11/24/1901, 65

McGuire
James, 2/18/1910, 61, Ballybay, Monaghan
By wife Delia

McGuire
James, 7/25/1918, 57
See Hoye, Thomas, 8/3/1871

McGuire
Susan, Longford
By husband Edward
Philip
Edward Francis
Mary T., 7/1/1945

McGuire
Thomas, 12/31/1896, Tullamore, Kings
By wife Kate, 5/9/1931, Fermanagh

McHenry
Patrick, 5/22/1890, Drumuck, Derry
By dau. Eliza J.
Her dau. Mary Maria McHenry, 3/26/1901, 2-3-26

McHugh
Denis J., 1939 - 1969
See Monaghan, Patrick J., 2/13/1916, 34

McHugh
Hugh V., 1918 - 1974
See Harrigan, Maurice, 4/4/1884, 50

McHugh
Mary J., 7/8/1916, 2
Catherine, 10/9/1916, 11 months
John, 10/15/1925
See Kelly, Peter, 9/9/1913, 25

McInerney
John, 8/22/1884, 72, Tubber, Clare
By wife Ann

McInerney
Kathleen Mannix, 3/7/1901 - 4/28/1952
Thomas F., 4/12/1899 - 7/7/1978
See Minihan, John, 4/2/1911, 35

McInerney
Thomas, 12/23/1889, 50, Limerick
Catherine, 11/21/1890, 75
Michael, 11/12/1901, 53
Ellen, 2/10/1963, 53

McKay
Rose, 9/7/1887, 53, Down
Son James, 8/20/1894, 32
Rosanna, 2/14/1928, 60

McKellop
Mary, 10/18/1908, 84, Westmeath

McKenerney
Elizabeth, 7/16/1891, 56, Bourney, Tipperary
By husband Thomas
Their children: Michael J., Nicholas, Thomas and Elizabeth died young

McKenna
Ann, 5/17/1889, 50, Arthurstown, Louth
By husband John J.

McKenna
Catherine, 11/30/1910, 53; See Lawless, Ann, 2/1/1903

McKenna
Patrick J., 5/22/1901, Knockballyroney, Monaghan
By wife Mary
Son James, 8/9/1892, 10 months
Marguerite M., 8/3/1966, 71
Joseph P., 3/24/1976, 83

McKenna
Rose, 1/21/1904, 64
James, 3/20/1920, 71; See Logue, Bridget, 12/28/1886

McKeon
Michael, 66, Streete, Westmeath

McKeon
Patrick, 11/27/1904, Ballymahon, Longford
Grandson Joseph Charles McKeon, 2 months
Joseph P., 5/28/1912, 28

McKeown
Annie, 3/12/1927, 59, Leitrim
See McNamara, Margaret, 6/24/1855 - 12/4/1915, 60

McKie
Thomas, 7/8/18991, 52, Westmeath
By wife Ellen, 7/18/1905, 54;
Twin sons John, 39
George L., 5/31/1943
Edward J., 3/19/1912, 30
Thomas E. Rhatigan, 8/11/1943
Karen Ann Lemmerman, 7/17/1965 - 11/13/1965
Ellen E. Seitz, 5/9/1937
Martin F. Rhatigan, 2/21/1950
Julius Lemmerman, 1951
Elizabeth, 1958
Irene, 1959

McKinley
Jane, 7/2/1892, 71
Michael, 9/29/1898, Tyrone
William, 1855 - 1927
His wife Barbara, 1863 - 1928
Their son William, 1903 - 1944
His wife Margaret, 1907 -

McLaren
Peter, born 9/25/1805, Blairdrummond, Scotland
Margaret born 6/25/1818
See Corrigan, Mary, 8/19/1895, 79

McLaughlin
Ellen, 1859, Donegal
Patrick, Donegal
Annie, Donegal
Mary, Donegal

McLaughlin
Hugh, 2/9/1835, 50, Cloncar, Donegal
Grace, 3/12/1868, 88, Cloncar, Donegal
Hugh, 1827 - 12/7/1904, Brooklyn, N.Y.
Sarah Ellen Kays, wife of Hugh born at Lafayette, Sussex, New Jersey died Brooklyn, N.Y. 4/2/1915, 85
Hugh Harvey only son of Hugh and Ellen 6/6/1878, 14-1-0
Mary Grace dau. of Hugh and Ellen, 3/5/1868, 1-11-0
Ann McLaughlin, wife of Maurice Fitzgerald, 10/10/1880, 59
Luke McLaughlin, 6/19/1849, 32
Patrick, 3/17/1867, 54
Sarah, 10/10/1850, 42

McLaughlin
James, 7/23/1866, 37, Westmeath
By wife Rosanna
Son Michael
James' mother Mary, 1871

McLaughlin
John, 12/16/1867, Moville, Donegal
By wife Catherine

McLaughlin
Joseph, 3/3/1959
See McCann, John, 6/19/1896, 35

McLaughlin
Margaret, 3/18/1857, Longford
By brother Thomas, 1875

McLaughlin
Mary, 7/17/1895, 74, Drung, Cavan
By husband Michael
Mary dau. of Patrick Clark

McLaughlin
Neil, 10/25/1918, Donegal
By wife Bridget, 10/9/1924, Donegal
Her sister Annie Gallagher, 2/14/1921
Hannah Bonner, 1892 - 1967

McLaughlin
Patrick, 1/30/1869, 71
Rosanna, 5/9/1866/68, 74, Moville, Donegal
Their dau. Catherine Daly, 4/1875
By their son William McLaughlin

McLaughlin
Thomas B., 2/27/1882, 62, Bellmullet, Mayo
By wife Catherine, 1/1/1911
Their son John J., 4/16/1894, 37
William T., 3/25/1919
Catherine F., 11/19/1924
Julie M.V., 1/11/1955
Edward C., 8/22/1957

McLaughlin
Thomas, 5/1/1858 - 7/9/1924, Carrowmenagh, Donegal
By children:
Roger, 6/24/1890 - 3/15/1936
Mary M., 5/31/1887 - 11/21/1962

McLean
Hannah Shanahan, 10/11/1881, 29, Kilvemonon, Mullinahone, Tipperary, Wife of Henry

McLoughlin
Peter, 7/5/1892, 90, Longford
Bridget, 6/1/1861, 30, Longford

McMahon
John, 8/29/1887, 48, Clare
By wife Mary

McMahon
Kate, 9/16/1901, 24, Tulla, Clare
By husband John, 6/21/1865 - 5/28/1932
Ann, 2/6/1908, 75
Della, 8/13/1900 - 6/25/1949

McMahon
Mary, 1890 - 1981
See Shannon, Michael G., 7/27/1859 - 1/16/1912

McMahon
Patrick, 10/3/1894, 62, Clonduff, Down
By wife Bridget, 3/4/1926, 88
James, 9/28/1903, 35
Cornelius, 3/31/1911, 47
Children: John, Rose, Alice died young
Maryann, 1855 - 1932
Margaret, 9/30/1940

McMahon
Patrick Henry, 1929
Annie A. Dau. of Denis Farren, 1846 - 1922
See Farren, Denis, 7/17/1857, 52

McMahon
Thomas, 2/4/1877, 42, Clare
By wife Ellen

McMahon
Thomas, 7/6/1889, 57, Glenduff, Down
Mary, 12/5/1887, 54, Glenduff, Down
Their children: John, Stephen, Thomas, Bernard, John
Patrick H., 2/5/1945

McMahon
Tim, 1953
Margaret, 1963
Sgt. John, 1983
See Barrett, Mary, 9/2/1926

McMahon
William, 10/12/1920, 55
See Raleigh, Thomas F., 8/4/1903, 30

McManus
Annie, 5/2/1898, 52, Lisnaskea, Fermanagh
Gormley Family

McManus
Patrick, 8/17/1877, 67, Remelton, Donegal
Roseanne

McManus
Thomas, 10/22/1868, 37, Longford
By wife Mary, 8/15/1833 - 5/14/1905, Galway

McMenoney
John, 2/24/1877, Donegal
Wife Mary, 10/26/1894, Donegal

McMorrow
Bernard, 10/29/1916, Leitrim
By wife Annie, 12/29/1924, 64

McMullen
Ellon, 9/18/1881, 70, Armoy, Antrim
By sisters Rose and Margaret

McNally
Edward, Monaghan
By Catherine

McNally
Margaret, 5/21/1900, 61, Longford

McNally
Matilda, 10/14/1903, 48
See Sexton, John, 2/19/1902, 72

McNally
Patrick, 5/23/1871, Leitrim
By wife Alice

McNally
Thomas, Westmeath

McNamara
Bridget, 3/22/1882, 70, Newmarket, Clare
By son Michael
John J. Bukouski, 12/18/1892 - 11/8/1920

McNamara
Catherine, 1883 - 1924, Lixnaw, Kerry
Anna, 1912 - 1916
James, 1883 - 1953
Helen McDermott, 1910 - 1945

McNamara
John Jr., 4/29/1883, 28-0-27, Kings
By parents
Ann, 4/21/1885, 58
John, 6/15/1899, 75
Dennis, 9/10/1900, 42

McNamara
Kate, 1/2/1916, 32, Doon, Limerick
John O'Donnell, 6/24/1920
Mary, 4/29/1938

McNamara
Margaret, 6/24/1855 - 12/4/1915, 60, Leitrim
Dau. of Thomas and Mary McNamara
Annie McKeown, 3/12/1927, 59, Leitrim
Ellen McKeown Mele, 1896 - 1964

McNamara
Mary 2/1871, 50?, Killuran?, Clare
By husband James 5/30/1879, 73

McNamara
Mary, 80?, Clare; By husband James, 5/10/1870

McNamara
Michael B., 1/4/1915, 24, Ballina, Mayo

McNamara
Patrick J., 1/24/1889, 55, Clare
By wife Mary, 12/24/1890, 46, Cappabane, Clare
John J., 11/7/1908, 43
Her children: John J., Mary, George W., Charles B., died young
Mary Ward, 6/16/1943

McNamara
Sylvester J., our father, 6/14/1849, 38, buried in Finloe, Clare
Matthew, our brother, 12/29/1852, 14
Anne, our sister, wife of James O'Donnell, 12/9/1875 41
Bridget, our mother, 8/11/1881 79
John McNamara, 5/4/1911, 78
Sarah A. wife, 4/6/1918
Maria T., 1/20/1935
Mildred A., 7/8/1965
Eleanor D. dau of Sarah and John, 8/18/1970
Ellen, wife of Patrick, 7/22/1908 73
Mary H., their dau., 5/25/1866 - 5/21/1905
Patrick, 12/28/1828 - 4/4/1919
Sylvester J., 5/14/1869 - 1/31/1943
Mildred M., 9/30/1885 - 6/30/1978
Michael A., 2/14/1929
Elizabeth A., 3/9/1926
Angelo N. Rommo, 1963
Sylvester A. McNamara, his wife Jennie
Their children: Mary, Margaret, Katherine A., Catherine A., a loving wife and mother, 1/31/1874 - 1/10/1943
Matthew T., 11/20/1875 - 10/23/1950
Sylvester J., 8/11/1882 - 1/21/1954
Adele, 9/4/1884 - 6/27/1964
Helen A., 8/28/1976

McNamee
Daniel, 8/21/1899, 53, Armagh
By wife Mary, 3/24/1904, Monaghan

McNamee
Marguerite 2/23/1923, 14
John J., 6/15/1941, 58, Cranky More, Edgeworthstown, Longford

McNeely
Anthony Roe, 10/24/1891, 53, Mount Charles, Donegal
By wife Mary, 7/10/1894, 59
Thomas F., 1/4/1897, 25
Gustave Carlson, 4/19/1926, 39
Irene V. Carlson, 4/16/1976, 84
Geneieve Kehoe, 72
Michael J. Kehoe, 86

McNeely
Mary, 7/13/1883, 55, Donegal
By husband Michael, 2/8/1899
Their sons:
John, 3-6-0
Michael, 1-9-0

McNeil
Maryann Spillane, 4/1/1891, 54, Cork
By husband Capt. Roderick

McNeill
Hugh, 10/15/1889, 55, Louth
By wife Kate
Their son Daniel, 8/24/1868, 1
Hugh, 8/4/1918
Rose A., 11/17/1933

McNeill
Daniel, 5/3/1963
See McCann, John, 6/19/1896, 35

McNerney
John, 12/26/1912, 51, Clanmore, Longford
By wife Bridget
John, 2/28/1950
John, 1/6/1988

McNichols
Michael 3/24/1910, Bohola, Mayo
By wife Ann 2/7/1951

McNoble
Mary, 5/25/1882, 37-9-0, Kilrush, Clare
By husband Thomas, 1/7/1892, 57, Leitrim
Their children: Alice, Elizabeth, Catherine, Thomas
Charles H. died young
Laura E., 1/18/1897, 20-8-0

McNulty
Anna, 9/16/1914, Fawnaboy, Donegal

McNulty
Bridget, 6/6/1897, 47, Naas, Kildare
By husband Martin

McNulty
Celia, 4/7/1871, 30, Dundoran, Dundooan, Donegal

McNulty
John, 12/9/1914, 52, Naas, Kildare
By sister Mary (Nona) Thompson, 5/20/1940, 92

McPadden
Daniel, 5/21/1898, 22
John, 6/5/1900, 1
Peter, 7/11/1907, 7
James J., 4/25/1915, 13
Peter, 4/30/1918, 51, Leitrim
Patrick, 4/30/1936, 78
Bridget, 11/13/1939, 68

McPadden
John, 6/23/1877, Leitrim
Bridget, 5/11/1916, Leitrim
By dau. Margaret, 1873 - 1946
Emily M. Foy, 1/3/1946

McPadden
Michael, 4/11/1899, 33, Leitrim
By sister Mary, Leitrim

McPartland
Annie A., 5/19/1914, 50, Leitrim
By sister Mary McNiff

McPartland
John, 8/19/1901, Leitrim
By wife Catherine, 8/24/1951
Son John Jr., 2/23/1907

McPartland
Mary, 9/29/1891, Roundwood, Wicklow
Her children Eddie and Mamie
See Brown, John, 3/21/1905, 77

McPartland
Peter, 10/22/1898, Leitrim
Ann, 7/30/1917

McQuade
Michael, 6/3/1881, 60, Tyrone
Wife Mary, 12/8/1900, 82, Tipperary
Children: Isabel, Cornelius, Michael died young
Sarah F., 11/27/1926
Mary A. Kearney, 8/10/1930

McSherry
Rev. Eugene 4/21/1879, 39, Clogher, Tyrone
Pastor of Our Lady of Loretto Hempstead, L.I.

McTernan
Catherine, 7/12/1901, 54, Killargue, Leitrim
Kathleen M., 8/22/1907, 3-0-1
Mary, 1/10/1910, 38
Kathleen, 1/31/1926
Patrick H., 9/6/1928

McTernan
Mary, 11/16/1932, Killargue, Leitrim

McTighe
Patrick, 10/19/1896, 42, Sligo
By wife Ann

McTigue
Celia Jorden, 5/16/1902, 74
See Jordan, Michael, 9/24/1885, 54

McVeigh
Mary E. dau. of Patrick and Bridget Hoben,
  8/25/1861 - 10/4/1913, Lisgormin, Mayo
By husband Patrick
Patrick, 1/10/1902, 3 months
Pvt. Andrew, Co. A 313 I.N.F. A.E.F., 27
Pvt. James, Co. E 106 I.N.F. A.E.F., 21
Both killed in action, 9/27/1918

Mackey
Julia Dollard, 1/18/1931, Ennis, Clare
Michael, 12/7/1933, Kilnamona, Clare
By son Joseph M. Mackey, 5/7/1979
John T., 4/18/1961
Mary M., 9/26/1970

MacKinnon
John A., 5/21/1964
Anne Byrne, 9/6/1986
See Byrne, Edward, 9/1/1887, 55

Mackin
Delia, 5/13/1890, 56, Ballymoran, Edenderry, Kings

Macklin
Bridget, 4/25/1910, 46
See Garvin, John, 8/2/1893, 31

Macklin
Elizabeth, 6/12/1836 - 2/6/1905, Westmeath
By husband Thomas, 5/17/1916, 85, Westmeath

Madden
Ann, 11/17/1879, 45, Dublin
By husband Hurbert

Madden
Delia C., 6/26/1914, Killala, Mayo

Madigan
Bridget, 2/13/1909, 34, Limerick
By husband John
Henry Drew, 12/15/1958

Madigan
John, 3/2/1896, 54, Clare
By wife Catherine, 1/27/1909
Son John F. died young
Mary Norton F.E., 11/1/1932
James L. Madigan, 5/7/1933
Catherine Maloney, 11/27/1954
John J. McCamley, 5/14/1956
Francis M. Hanihan, 1921 - 1982

Magee
Twins Roseanna and Mary, by their parents Patrick and Ann
Patrick's sister Mary Hammill, 2/11/1883, Ballinderry, Antrim
Patrick, 9/12/1897, 75
Ann, 7/26/1906, 80

Maguire
Anna M., 1/7/1973, 73
See Grant, Michael, 3/5/1884, 60

Maguire
Bridget, 6/7/1925, 81
See Carlin, Alice, 5/13/1920

Maguire
Edward, 5/15/1863, 67, Longford
By wife Catherine

Maguire
Elizabeth; See Quinn, James, 6/8/1866

Maguire
John, 5/20/1894, 31, Leitrim
By sisters Rose and Annie

Maguire
Rose, 12/16/1891, 60, Cavan
By husband John, Longford
Mary Maguire Stickevers, 6/30/1941, 77
Bill Stickevers, 11/22/1941, 2

Mahady
Mary, 3/3/1902, 33
See Collins, Mary, 6/28/1897

Mahaney
Ellen, 5/12/1916, 40, Leitrim
By husband John D.

Maher
John F., 1/19/1947
Wife Anne, 2/14/1972
Frances R., 11/8/1958
1st Lt. Gerard S., 8/2/1977
John F. Jr., 11/20/1985
See Leddy, Bridget T., 7/19/1908

Maher
Julia, 5/11/1872, 80, Johnstown, Westmeath
By son James, 7/30/1887 ?, 48

Maher
Patrick, 8/5/1888, Ballinakill, Queens
By wife Alice, 12/8/1912, Queens

Maher
Rita A., 12/27/1988, 54
See Delehanty, Patrick, 3/28/1889, 37

Maher
Thomas Joseph, 12/24/1895, 49, Enniscorthy, Wexford
By wife Margaret, 1/18/1907, 65, Enniscorthy, Wexford

Mahon
Mary, 9/5/1909, 91, Roscommon

Mahon
Michael, 2/8/1893, 65, Kiltoghert, Leitrim
By sister Mary Mahon
Frank J. Ryan, 9/14/1914, 11
Thomas R. Ryan, 1/3/1945
Catherine M. Ryan, 7/5/1957

Mahon
Patrick, 8/20/1860, 70, Moveagh ?, Meath
By wife Ellen
Alice, 6/22/1864, 41, Toomevara, Tipperary
Ellen Mahon Bates, 7/6/1880
Her dau. Ellen

Mahon
Patrick Joseph, 7/22/1901, 22-2-0
By father Patrick J., 5/4/1903
Margaret Walsh, 4/4/1846 - 12/1/1909, Dunboyne, Meath
Marion P., 8/31/1880 - 8/3/1945
James E., 1906 - 1970

Mahoney
Thomas, 9/26/1889, 66, Donaghmore, Cork
By wife Margaret

Mahony
Mary, 11/15/1825 - 5/30/1893, Waterford
Cornelius, 5/10/1824 - 6/13/1900, Waterford
Henrietta, 8/5/1860 - 2/1/1897
Francis J., 12/6/1860 - 1/15/1928
Mary, Bridget, Kate, Henry, Mary, James died young

Malley
John, 6/18/1891, 62, Roscommon
By wife Catherine, 6/21/1898, 60
John, 2/24/1909, 32
Thomas, 7/4/1911, 49
Patrick, 6/22/1914, 46
James J., 11/3/1904 - 2/23/1970
L. Marie wife of James, 11/16/1915 - 8/6/1975

Mallon
John, 1834 - 6/4/1890, Tyrone
By wife Catherine, 11/23/1915, 82
Their children:
Joseph E., 3/24/1903, 34
Thomas F., 3/16/1912, 45
Also children: Francis, Peter, Edward and Mary died young
Catherine's sister Mary Feely, 4/18/1902, 70, Longford

Mallon
Patrick, 1/6/1909, 70
By wife Ann, 3/14/1922, 85
His parents:
James, 1859, 75, Tyrone
Mary, 2/4/1889, 85, Tyrone

Mallory
Arthur Thomas, 5/9/1886, 4
John Lawrence, 5/25/1886, 3
By their mother Mary A.
Her mother Bridget, 9/27/1886, 75, Longford

Malone
Bridget Dinnigan, Killashee, Longford
By son Patrick Malone
Marian Malone O'Rourke, Killashee, Longford
Catherine Malone Keating, Killashee, Longford

Malone
Ellen Shea, 7/24/1907, 50, Fethard, Tipperary
By husband Thomas, 3/9/1921, Kilkenny
Their children:
James V., 12/15/1918, 34
William H., 7/5/1905, 22
Nellie, 2/9/1892, 21
John, 1902 - 1973

Malone
Mary Jane, 6/3/1888, 56, Dundalk, Louth
Husband John, 7/13/1910

Maloney
Bessie, 3/16/1930, Easky, Sligo
Brother James, 3/23/1930, Easky, Sligo
Ellen, 9/21/1967
Belinda Connolly, 4/23/1987
Matthew Maloney, 7/27/1990

Maloney
Catherine, 11/27/1954
See Madigan, John, 3/2/1896, 54

Mangan
Annie, 2/17/1912, 45, Longford
By children: Mary, Bernard, Anna
Their brother John, 8/2/1899, 3
Patrick, 3/9/1936
John A. Cleary, 10/1/1968

Mannix
Matthew, 9/30/1917, Tulla, Clare
By wife Annie

Mannix
Patrick, 1/25/1917, 48, Tulla, Clare
Wife Delia, 9/19/1951, 70
Son Emmett D., 9/12/1931, 25
Delia, 10/10/1942, 78
Michael Dennis Mannix, 5/8/1953, 11
Virginia Rita Mannix, 9/25/1957, 25
William P. Mannix, 2/22/1989, 80

Mannon
Thomas, 7/29/1866, 38, Ardagh, Longford
By wife Eliza
Their son Thomas, 11/11/1866, 5-8-10

Mansell
Ellen, 1/25/1893, Tipperary
By sister Mary, 3/9/1931

Mansell
Tobias, 4/26/1892, 55, Tipperary
By wife Ellen, 3/31/1905, 63

Mantz
Julia Donovan, 6/29/1922, 48, City of Cork

Mara
Maria, 6/3/1902, 35, Nenagh, Tipperary
By sister Norah Boland, Nenagh, Tipperary
Their mother Winifred Mara, 55, Nenagh, Tipperary
Their sister Maggie Reilly, 27, Nenagh, Tipperary

Markey
Francis, 3/18/1892, 73, Tullacorbet, Monaghan
Margaret, 10/19/1892, 73, Tullacorbet, Monaghan

Markham
Annie, Tulla, Clare
Elizabeth, Tulla, Clare

Marrin
Margaret P., 12/11/1938, 58
See Monahan, John, 5/28/1899, 60

Martin
Alice, 9/13/1885, 60, Westmeath
By husband John, 7/24/1894, 65
Their dau. Mary A., 3/25/1908, 56
Margaret A. wife of Silias A. Ott, 1/1/1918, 63

Martin
James, 9/1/1891, 67, Johnstown, Kilkenny
By wife Bridget
Son Michael, 10/4/1884, 25

Martin
Mary, 7/4/1898, 55
See Mullaney, John, 1/27/1888, 45

Martin
Mary, 11/9/1948, 84
See Ward, William, 9/30/1904, 65

Martin
Michael, 2/8/1820 - 12/4/1896, Kildare
Anastasia, 3/31/1830 - 6/9/1883, Waterford
Their children:
James F., 12/25/1868 - 3/17/1911, Stellarton, Nova Scotia
Andrew M.F., 4/16/1871 - 8/10/1909, Stellarton, Nova Scotia

Matthews
Mary 7/1866, Westmeath
By brother John

Maxwell
Thomas, James and John
See Canwan, Mary, 10/21/1870

May
Mary, 1/6/1892, 54, Tyrone
By husband Dennis, 6/21/1892, 65

Meagher
John M. Sr., 8/12/1953
See Ryan, Phoebe, 3/1860 - 9/1897

Mee
John J., 3/28/1904, Longford
Wife Margaret Pettit, 11/14/1916
Michael P. Cunningham, 1/14/1949
John P. Mee, 3/24/1951
Mary Mee Cunningham, 5/11/1965
Cecelia Mee, 8/11/1973

Meehan
Catherine, 8/30/1893, 69, Knockscur, Carlow
Michael Kelleher, 3/13/1929, 69

Meehan
James, 4/22/1901, 58, Lakyle, Clare
Michael, 6/25/1905, 71
By their sister Annie, 6/17/1924, 75

Meehan
James J., 12/24/1917, 59, Westmeath
By wife Anna M., 8/17/192
Sgt. George A. Lyon, 9/28/1944
Major Donald F. Osterburg, 4/22/1947
Robert C. Lyon, 11/19/1955
Catherine M. Lyon, 4/1/1973

Meehan
John, 9/12/1896, 38, Leitrim
By wife Bridget, 5/12/1941, 76

Meighan
Cornelius, 1864, Donegal
Elizabeth

Mele
Ellen McKeown, 1896 - 1964
See McNamara, Margaret, 6/24/1855 - 12/4/1915, 60

Mella
Mary A., 4/12/1908, 34, Roscommon
By husband Peter

Merrick
Mary C., 1/29/1899, 63, Geevagh, Sligo
By husband William, 2/18/1912, 75
Their dau. Annie, 4/29/1870, 14 months
Their son John J., 12/13/1901, 36
Their dau. Mary A. Barrett, 7/13/1934
Their son William J. Merrick, 8/17/1872 - 11/11/1950
John T. Byrne 3rd, 1926 - 1971

Messerschmidt
Mary O'Connell, 1878 - 1972
See O'Connell, John, 1/1/1909, 28

Meyers
Mary McGrath, Waterford
By husband August Meyers
Dau. Lillian, 7/21/1906
John J., 3/26/1899 - 3/30/1925

Millea
Denis, 2/27/1844 - 10/3/1906, Castlecomer, Kilkeeny
By wife Ellen, 3/2/1933

Millea
Elizabeth, 8/26/1905, Danville, Kilkenny
By mother Mary, 4/20/1920, Danville, Kilkenny
Maria, 9/1/1927, Danville, Kilkenny

Miller
Felix J., 8/26/1888, 32-7-0
See Scanlon, Timothy, 9/7/1879, 50

Mills
Mary, 9/13/1960
See McGovern, Thomas J., 7/17/1923

Mills
Patrick J., 1968
Rita A., 1973
See Murphy, Matthew, 6/6/1890, 65

Miner
James, 1/23/1892, Tyrone

Minihan
John, 4/2/1911, 35, Tulla, Clare
Michael, 10/24/1917
Mary, 2/25/1935
Annie, 7/22/1943
Kathleen Mannix McInerney 3/7/1901 - 4/28/1952
Thomas F., 4/12/1899 - 7/7/1978

Mitchell
Annie Dillon, 12/8/1924
See Woodlock, Elizabeth Keating, 12/11/1914

Mitchell
Catherine, 2/25/1864, 35, Galway
By husband Patrick
His parents: Thomas, 1/15/1867
Mary, 9/21/1868

Mitchell
Timothy, 3/4/1860 - 8/13/1922, Kildare
By wife Mary, 1/29/1959
Infant son John
Timothy M., 4/22/1976
Catherine, 3/17/1991

Mockler
Ann, 9/5/1853, 25
By husband John, 8/8/1897, 63, Bennetts, Fethard, Tipperary

Mockler
Patrick, 4/11/1891, 58, Turles, Tipperary
His wife Catherine
Children: Mary, Edward, Mary and Catherine
Their son John, 1/18/1919
Anna, 1/12/1957

Moclair
Michael J., 10/2/1916, 33, Cashel, Tipperary
By brother William, 1881 - 1964
Wife of Wm., Sarah, 10/17/1951
Nancy, 1949 - 1955
William M., 1912 - 1985
Grace D., 1988
Michael J., 1942 -

Moffatt
Mary, 5/16/189, 30-2-0
Wife of William
See Kelly, Hanora, 12/28/1876

Moldenhauer
Christian, 10/16/1953
Mary J., 10/3/1971
See Coleman, Margaret, 5/21/1888, 63

Moley
Robert J., 9/22/1927, 19
William J., 11/23/1934, 60
Mary C., 12/1/1965, 86
William S., 7/1/1986, 80
See Tuohey, Bridget, 2/5/1889, 47

Molloy
Margaret, 1/16/1861, 34, Westmeath
Son Bernard, 6/8/1885, 34
Mary, 2/26/1931
Matthew, 12/6/1938

Molloy
Michael, 9/28/1909, 40, Kilmain, Mayo
By wife Katie
Norah, Michael, Mary died young

Molloy
Thomas Francis, 7/19/1872, 46, Abbey, Longford
By wife Catherine
Their children:
Francis Joseph, 7/2/1871, 20-1-7
George, 10/3/1868, 2-6-18

Moloney
Daniel J., 4/6/1926
Mary J., 5/29/1927
See Devaney, John J., 7/3/1890

Moloney
Daniel 11/1864, 60, Limerick
Wife Mary 10/2/1860, Limerick
Children: Thomas, Maryann, Daniel H.

Monaghan
Bridget, 9/12/1874, 63, Killann, Cavan
By son Michael, 2/6/1891, 48
His son William, 11 months
John and Hugh died young

Monaghan
James, 9/4/1885, 77, Longford
By son James, 2/3/1888, 38
Mary, 12/21/1913, 76

Monaghan
Mary, 12/4/1883, 52, Longford
By children Mary, Joseph, John

Monaghan
Patrick J., 2/12/1916, 34, Blackbog, Fermanagh
By brother James J.
Denis J. McHugh, 1939 - 1969

Monahan
John, 5/28/1899, 60, Longford
Wife Alice, 11/9/1904, 61
Their children Patrick and Ellen died young
Margaret P. Marrin, 12/11/1938, 58

Monahan
Mary, 9/24/1880, 56, Galway
By husband John

Monnia
Margaret, 1881 - 1974
See Phillips, Charles J., 12/10/1925, 23

Moody
Thomas Abraham
By wife Bridget, 11/7/1897, 62
Children: Mary A., Richard, Thomas
Bridget's mother Rose Duffy, Monaghan
James, 4/4/1880

Mooney
John, 4/5/1890, 54, Dublin
Wife Mary A., 11/23/1896, 68
Children:
Beatrice, 5/25/1882, 26
Mary Agnes, 4/30/1885, 19
Constantine, 12/22/1885, 32
Charles T., 8/1/1886, 24

Mooney
Joseph P., 11/28/1887 - 7/28/1889
Jennie
See McCarthy, John, Coonean, Waterford

Moore
Christopher, 5/2/1904, 51, Kildare
By wife Margaret
His mother Ann, 2/9/1898, 65
William A., 4/7/1915, 33

Moore
Thomas, Westmeath
Mary, Westmeath
By dau. Margaret Bourdy

Moran
James, 6/22/1888, 26, Ballinabrackey, Meath
By his sisters
Christopher, 7/1/1892, 32
His wife Kate, 11/9/1905, 45

Moran
James, 3/26/1893, 51, Westmeath
By wife Ann, 10/2/1898, 50
Son John, 5/18/1905, 23
Dau. Mary, 6/12/1909, 37

Moran
John, Tubber?, Westmeath
By wife Margaret

Moran
Mary
Michael, 5/18/1915
John T.
See Rourke, Thomas, 8/28/1891, 78

Moran
Patrick, 11/23/1873, 38, Roscommon
See O'Reilly, Patrick, 6/23/1870, 42

Moran
Roger, 7/7/1854, 26, Edgeworthstown, Longford
Catherine, 7/31/1887, 96
By sister and dau. Margaret Gallagher, 1/23/1899, 67

Moriarty
Thomas F., 1/17/1880 - 3/19/1900
By parents:
Margaret V., 8/29/1855 - 2/28/1928, Kerry
Patrick J., 3/30/1933
Joseph, Irene, Robert Emmitt, William

Moroney
Bridget, 7/6/1868, 1-9-28
By father Dennis, Herbertstown, Limerick

Morris
Kate, 5/3/1908, 55
By husband Thomas, 7/13/1919, Meath

Morris
Joseph, 7/7/1889, 64
By wife Bridget, 3/30/1904, 70, Kings
Son William J., 7/17/1905, 50
Joseph F., 6/14/1913, 45
Bridget's children: Rose, 10/1856
Roseanna, 10/3/1862
John, 12/5/1866
Bridget, 3/6/1870
All died young
James Kennedy, husband of Annie Morris, 12/8/1913
Annie Morris Kennedy, 2/22/1931
Frank M. Heaney, husband of Mary Kennedy, 11/5/1939
Theresa Morris, wife of William J., 2/22/1895, 35
William J., Jr., 2/18/1895
Rose Kennedy, 1/1/1895
William, son of Joseph F., 7/15/1913, 20 months
Rose O'Dea, wife of Thomas P.O.'Dea, 1874 - 1964
Thomas P. O'Dea, 1895 - 1974

Morris
William, 7/24/1881, 73, Cavan
Dau., 4/20/1884, 36

Morrisey
Bridget, 4/10/1904, 47, Modelligo, Waterford
By husband Richard, 1/12/1921, 74
Children: Richard, Helen, Joseph died young

Morrissey
Margaret, 9/23/1885, 45, Limerick
By husband James, 8/7/1888, 50
Their two children Maggie and Hugh

Morrissey
Patrick C., 12/9/1905, 60, Galway
By wife Bridget

Mortlby
Hanora
See Hennessey, Richard 1?/1881?, Tipperary

Mowen
John, 3/21/1891, 49, Fermanagh
By wife Margaret, 6/13/1910, 75, Fermanagh
Grandson Willie Bennett died young
Johnnie Bennett, 12/30/1892, 6-8-11

Moylan
Ellen, 11/15/1887, 42, Kings
Brother Michael, 7/11/1888, 48
By sister Ann
Bridget, 2/2/1891, 38
Francis E. Price, 8/3/1948

Mulaney
Michael, 5/27/1881, 46, Galway
By wife Bridget, 3/18/1883

Mulcahy
Catherine, 7/16/1890, 54, Cork
Husband John, 7/7/1904, 69, Cork
Alton F. Currey, 12/31/1911 - 2/1/1913

Mulholan
Margaret McKew, 5/1882, 60, Leitrim
Owen, 3/24/1891, 76, Armagh

Mulholland
James, 2/23/1868, 19, Antrim
Lizzie, 5/15/1868, Antrim
John, 7/18/1873, Antrim
By parents Ambrose and Isabella, Antrim
William McCrory, 5/1/1876, 42, Antrim
John McCrory, 11/5/1876, 68, Antrim

Mulick
John, 7/4/1899, 36, Leitrim
By Minnie
Cornelius J., 4/26/1920

Mulkalr
Thomas, 12/1/1829 - 2/4/1867, City of Dublin
By wife Margaret, 6/13/1833 - 3/9/1907
Daughter Theresa, 1861

Mullaney
John, 1/27/1888, 45, Galway
By wife Johanna, 11/10/1923, 83
Her sister Mary Martin, 7/4/1898, 55
Mary Mullaney, 4/24/1926, 49

Mulledy
Patrick, 12/27/1891, 73, Longford
Wife Maria, 3/9/1924, 88
Margaret, 5/26/1930
P.F. Mulledy, 3/25/1897, 42
His wife Maud C. Duncan, 4/15/1899, 26

Mullen
Bridget, Castlerock, Derry
By Sarah O'Doherty, 3/26/1948, Castlerock, Derry

Mullen
John, Roscommon

Mullen
Michael, 7/1/1868, 60
His dau. Bridget, 5/15/1861, 20, Longford
James, 1881 - 1965
Augusta, 1893 - 1972

Mullen
Thomas, 10/19/1919, 53, Longford
Mary, 11/22/1931, 55
May, 10/15/1895, 3-5-0
Ensign Thomas A. U.S.N., 11/2/1918, 28
Died for his country
See McCormick, Ann, 11/19/1896, 60

Mullery
Edward, 5/26/1897, 43, Galway
Delia Mullery Fox, 5/12/1914
Edward J. Mullery, 1876 - 1947
Bertram E. Mullery, 1879 - 1951
George Mullery, 1/6/1898
James C. Fox, 5/5/1901
Eleanor Philips, 10/9/1932
Margaret Dooley, 2/11/1936

Mulligan
John, 12/17/1899, Bree, Wexford
His sister Anne, 2/19/1908
His niece Kate Whalen, 6/3/1907
His newphew Martin Whalen, 6/26/1909
John T. Mulligan, 5/7/1925
Marion Mulligan, 4/20/1937

Mulligan
Julia, 3/9/1877, 29, Cavan
By husband John J.

Mullin
Kate, 9/4/1883, 40, Clonmel, Tipperary
By husband Michael

Mullins
Patrick, 8/10/1912, Tipperary
Ann V., 1861 - 1953
See Daly, Thomas, 5/13/1893, 48

Mullins
William F., 8/31/1917
Mary A., 8/17/1939
James J., 10/13/1955
See Doyle, James, 8/23/1877, 44

Mulrennen
Bridget, 1/22/1911, Roscommon
Sister Mary, 9/22/1921
Margaret, 1/27/1925

Mulroy
James, 9/1893, 24, Mayo
By parents John and Ellen

Mulvanney
Patrick, 1/15/1876, 72, Westmeath

Mulvany
Martin, 1/6/1888, 73, Westmeath
Wife Ann, 1/20/1884, 63, Westmeath

Mulvey
Catherine Murray, 2/19/1873, Ballymacormack, Longford
By husband Patrick Mulvey

Mulvey
Mary Todd 2/1868?, 63, Westmeath
By husband John
Dau. Eliza 1839?, 25
John 4/22/1869?, Leitrim

Murphy
Beatric, 10/31/1918
By husband Patrick, 7/22/1926, Kilnacarrow,
Carrickedmond, Longford
Dau. Marion M., 10/31/1899, 2-4-0

Murphy
Catherine A., 3/8/1892, 30
John T., 1/12/1912, 63
See Curtin, John, 6/17/1870, 60

Murphy
Daniel, 1/14/1930, 49, Ballyhoulahan, Boherbee, Cork
By wife Bridget, 3/16/1931

Murphy
Francis, 9/11/1866, 55, Lady's Island, Wexford
By sisters Ellen Murphy and Margaret Stafford
Also his nephew Patrick W. Devereux, 6/26/1886

Murphy
Francis X., 8/24/1892, 57, Wexford
Wife Johanna, 8/1/1905
Johanna McCarroll, 9/23/1945
Elizabeth A. O'Brien, 6/13/1948
Walter J. McCarroll, 10/7/1950

Murphy
Hannah, 3/16/1910, 49, Dublin City
Patrick, 12/21/1902, 57, Dublin City
John, 4/17/1914, 49
Joseph M. Conlon, 1905 - 1958
Ethel G. Conlon, 1910 - 1969

Murphy
Hanora, 8/11/1899, 55, Clare
By the estate of her sister
Mary Egan, 6/20/1910, 70, Clare

Murphy
Hanorah, 1/24/1883, 62, Killahora, Glanmire, Cork
See Murray, Ann, 8/29/1880, 66

Murphy
James, 7/20/1864, 36, Westmeath
By wife Ellen
Son Willian
Ellen Ann

Murphy
James, 2/5/1915
By wife Mary, 5/12/1920
Her sister Margaret Prescott, 10/20/1907, Wexford
William P.J. Murphy, 5/14/1920 son of James and Mary Murphy
Caroline Murphy, 10/12/1918
Son William V. Murphy, 1/27/1937
James W. Murphy, 8/20/1956

Murphy
Jane
See O'Toole, Patrick, 1/7/1874

Murphy
Jeremiah, 1/18/1876, 77, Cork
By dau. Ann
His dau. Catherine Lane, wife of Dennis Lane, 11/11/1873, 28, Cork
Dennis J. Crowley, 7/11/1914
His wife Mary F., 8/29/1959
Richard A., 1/23/1981

Murphy
John
Ellen
Elizabeth
Joseph
All died young
By parents Thomas and Mary, Kells, Meath
Mary, 11/12/1892, 63

Murphy
John, 6/29/1895, 30, Forkhill, Armagh
His sister Rose, 8/10/1896, 29
John Devine, 8/23/1908
Wife Kate, 3/5/1911

Murphy
John, 12/4/1910, 36, Clifden, Galway
By wife Maria, 1/6/1965, 92

Murphy
Kathleen M., 1922
See McDonald, James, 1848 - 1930

Murphy
Margaret, 7/5/1898, Westmeath
By husband William
Her mother Bridget Levey, 10/28/1885, 93, Westmeath
Children of William and Margaret: Daniel P., Catherine
Hanora, William died young

Murphy
Margaret, 7/1898, 57, Waterford City
By husband John J.

Murphy
Mary, 6/30/1900, 65
See Crogan, Margaret, 3/26/1863, 33

Murphy
Mary, 1/16/1903, 61, Sligo
Husband Michael, 11/1/1906, 70
Their son Thomas H., 9/5/1916, 46

Murphy
Mary, 1/24/1908, Ballybunion, Kerry
Martin J., 6/16/1951

Murphy
Mary, 1/16/1937
See O'Brien, Margaret, 3/11/1905

Murphy
Mary H., 5/11/1879, 38
John, 12/26/1881, 42
By Timothy Hartigan for sister Mary H. Murphy
Timothy Hartigan, 2/17/1885, 50, Doneraile, Cork

Murphy
Matthew, 8/2/1884, Wexford
By wife Rebecca T., 1/30/1912, 83

Murphy
Matthew, 6/6/1890, 65
By wife Ann, 12/29/1891, Clare
Patrick J. Mills, 1968
Rita A. Mills, 1973

Murphy
Maurice, 8/16/1890, Glanahin?, Limerick
Wife Ellen, 3/9/1890, Glanahin?, Limerick
See Vaughn, Thomas, 8/1/1894

Murphy
Murtha, 6/21/1909, Wexford
By wife Catherine, 3/6/1927, Wexford

Murphy
Owen, 1/18/1878; See Harvey, Ellen

Murphy
Patrick, 1/5/1888, 72
See Donohue, Margaret, 12/13/1877, 38

Murphy
Patrick, 12/15/1890, 70, New Abbey, Kildare
By wife Ann
Julia A. Thompson, 8/8/1889, 26, New Abbey, Kildare
Delia, Mary, Patrick died young
Francis J., 1901 - 1977

Murphy
Patrick, 1/5/1903, 81, Glanmire, Cork
Ellen, 3/21/1899, 73, Glanmire, Cork
Children:
Matthias, P., 1/31/1855 - 10/8/1880
William S., 11/28/1856 - 11/14/1880
Ellen, 5/21/1861 - 10/2/1862
Mary, 6/21/1859 - 2/25/1871

Murphy
Patrick H., 2/3/1867, 43, Wexford

Murphy
Sarah, 1/7/1910, Ballybeg, Ferns, Wexford
Anne, 1/3/1913
Dennis J., 1863 - 1930
Mary Quirk Wilhoit, 1892 - 1944
Rosanna M. Quirk, 1860 - 1948
Sarah B. Quirk, 1897 - 1949
Patrick J. Murphy, 1865 - 1951
Kathryn P. Braithwaite, 1889 - 1954

Murphy
Thomas, 1/26/1855, 1
William, 9/15/1865, 1-3-0
By parents:
Mary, 2/20/1889, 64, Litter, Wexford
Miles, 7/6/1890, Litter, Wexford

Murphy
William, 6/16/1919, 79, Bansha, Tipperary
Wife Delia Raymond, 11/16/1923, 72
Henrietta Oliver, 1/11/1939, 53
See Sheridan, Daniel A., 7/13/1909 - 7/29/1911

Murray
Ann
See Hickey, Mary, 3/13/1872, 50

Murray
Ann, 8/29/1880, 66, Killahora, Glanmire, Cork
Elizabeth, 4/5/1885, 11 months 12 days
Ann, 4/10/1885, 5-8-10
Patrick J., 4/13/1885, 2-1-0
Mary, 4/20/1885, 4-0-25
Hanorah Murphy, 1/24/1883, 62, Killahora, Glanmire, Cork
George M., 10/11/1890, 3 months 7 days
Timothy J., 9/17/1891, 3
Patrick J. Murray, 9/4/1911, 60
Mary, 11/10/1926, 71
Mary Wright, 8/8/1880, 5 months 26 days
Hanorah Wright, 7/19/1882, 1-2-19
Michael John, 9/10/1890, 6 months 4 days
Charles H. Jr., 7/14/1899, 27
Mary A., 12/28/1899, 47
Annie F., 10/7/1895, 19
Charles H. Sr., 2/19/1903, 60

Murray
Ann, 12/27/1901, 59, Kilnoe, Clare
By husband Patrick, Kilnoe, Clare
Son Edward J., 11/23/1915, 39

Murray
Anna, 3/12/1917, 49, Ballyduffy, Roscommon
See Breslin, Bridget, 3/19/1912

Murray
Annie, 7/17/1911, 55, Cashel, Longford
By husband John
Their children John, Thomas, Bernard and James

Murray
Bridget, 9/8/1894, 75, Rathcline, Longford
Husband John J., 11/29/1902, Rathcline, Longford
John F., 7/25/1929, 62
Annie, 2/15/1939, 86

Murray
Bridget, 10/23/1906, 55, Roscommon
Patrick, 4/5/1903, 90

Murray
Francis, 10/10/1851, 42
Margaret, 12/23/1883, 84, Kiltoghert, Leitrim
By son Garrett, 12/5/1896, 65
His wife Eliza, 4/15/1877
Dau. Mary Ellen
Mary T., 10/18/1918, 62

Murray
Henry, 1/3/1885, Lissonuffy, Roscommon
By sister Ann
His son Tim died young
Patrick Coyle husband of Margaret, 2/18/1947
Margaret M., 9/17/1962

Murray
John, 3/4/1885, 47, Donegal
Wife Margaret, 8/4/1899, 62, Donegal
John, 8/8/1931
Catherine A., 11/30/1942
Ellen Flanagan, 12/5/1924

Murray
Mary, 2/19/1882, 80, Armagh
By son John J.
Her son Hugh, 4/1/1891, 37
John, 10/4/1897, 45

Murray
Mary, 3/16/1887, 50, Westmeath
By children
John

Murray
Owen, 4/2/1936, 94, Roscommon
Mary, 3/23/1901, 60, Williamstown, Galway
Patrick J., 2/4/1928, 56
See Lyons, Michael, 11/24/1901, 65

Murray
Richard J., 1899 - 1963
See Waldron, Mary, 7/22/1887

Murray
Rose, 1/16/1866, 18
By Patrick, 8/1869, 58, Cashel, Longford
Mary, 4/16/1878, 60, Cashel, Longford

Murry
John; See Donovan, Richard, 3/4/1861

Murtagh
John, 5/11/1868, 39, Rathcline, Longford

Murtaugh
John, 4/21/1899
By wife Catherine, 4/20/1926
Mary Ellen
Loretta Catherine
Bernard McEntee M.D., 1/22/1892
Catherine McEntee
Rev. Hugh Hand, 1845 - 7/27/1908, Monaghan
Founder and First Rector of our Lady of Presentation Church Brooklyn

Murtha
Catherine Navilla, 2/10/1908, Wexford
By husband Thomas Murtha, 2/23/1911, 76, Ballycolgan, Edenderry, Kings

Murtha
Mary, 8/17/1911, 30, Westmeath
By husband Thomas, 1883 - 1967
Hannah, 1896 - 1970

Murthagh
James, 5/29/1879 - 11/4/1961
See Kenny, Thomas, 5/12/1917, 40

Myles
Mary B., 8/17/1930
William T., 3/5/1945
See Larkin, Thomas, 8/1/1887

Mylet
James, 8/24/1896, 50, Galway
By wife Jane, 3/10/1901, 53, Ballyfarnan

Nee
Elizabeth, 11/1/1976
See Conway, John, 12/29/1897, 35

Neff
William, 5/6/1889, 65, Kilkenny
See Feeney, Catherine

Nelson
Rose, 12/25/1913, 52, Ballinamore, Leitrim
By dau. Mary E. Nelson
Catherine Gallagher, 5/13/1921, 63
James. G. Stroud, 10/26/1962, 69
Alice C. Stroud, 12/22/1966, 72

Nerney
Bridget Fitzsimons, 1/3/1866, 65, Edgeworthstown, Longford
Husband Bernard, 12/7/1901, Longford
Annie, 1/17/1860
Mary Jane, 10/4/1888
Michael J., 12/21/1910
His dau. Mollie, 7/20/1891
William B., 7/26/1924
Margaret, 2/12/1932
Anna Nerney Cornell, 4/16/1952

Nevins
Ellen, 8/22/1883, 48, Westmeath
By husband Patrick

Nevins
Mary, 11/9/1877, 30, Tyrone
By husband Patrick

Newell
Hannah, 1876 - 1964
See Ahearn, William, 12/27/1913, 41

Newman
Ellen, 1/19/1875, 65, Drinan, Longford
By brother Thomas

Newman
Mary, 7/21/1897, 38, Wonho ?, Monaghan
Dau. of Peter and Bridget Woods
By husband Thomas, 3/24/1906, 46

Nichols
Michael, 3/24/1910, Bohola, Mayo
By wife Ann, 2/7/1951

Niemann
Agnes, 12/19/1965
See Freeman, Bernard, 4/16/1888, 60

Nolan
Ann, 7/9/1868, 77, Carrickedmond, Longford

Nolan
John, 1/20/1883, 62, Templemichael, Longford
By son Thomas

Nolan
Mary, 11/27/1854, 36, Ballyporeen, Tipperary
William, 11/15/1877, 77, Ballyporeen, Tipperary
By children
Margaret, 1/4/1897

Nolan
Owen, 3/2/1900, 64, Carrickedmond, Longford
By wife Mary

Nolan
Michael J., 8/8/1910, 41
See Feegan, Michael, 10/16/1882, 52

Noonan
Ellen, 12/26/1887, 55, Ballisodare, Sligo
By dau. Mary, 6/9/1912
Andrew A., 3/12/1936

Noonan
John, 3/5/1895, 65, Jamestown, Leitrim
By wife Anna, 11/22/1919, 74
Children: Mary and Mary Louise
Grandchild Francis Noonan
Son William, 10/7/1920, 42
Zita, 1881 - 1957
James A., 1882 - 1957
J.J. Campbell, 1873 - 1938

Noonan
Mary, 3/21/1909, 63, Limerick
By children Thomas and Bridget
Timothy, 8/28/1931
Thomas, 2/11/1951

Noonan
Nellie, 1/31/1915, Dublin
See Byrne, Mary A., 4/18/1914

Noone
Catherine, 7/6/1926
See Feeney, Joseph P., 11/30/1910

Norton
Mary F.E., 11/1/1932
See Madigan, John, 3/2/1896, 54

Norton
Michael, 11/6/1883, 55, Galway
By wife Catherine, 12/30/1915, 77

Norton
Peter, 11/29/1864, 40, Galway
Dau. Ellen, 15 months
By wife Bridget, 6/21/1893, 63
James J., 12/21/1903

Nugent
Annie Moore, wife of William Nugent, 7/10/1890, 44, Kildare
Margaret Moore 7/15/1926, 75

Nugent
Annie Moran, 25, Lagan, Longford
John D., 64, Russagh, Westmeath
Their infant dau. Mary
By dau. Catherine, 1/27/1921

Nugent
Catherine Thompson, 9/15/1958
See Thompson, Ellen Judge, 5/3/1921, 58

O'Beirne
Nora, 9/25/1973
Joseph, 2/6/1976
See Conway, Elizabeth, 12/30/1896, 78

O'Beirne
Timothy, 1836 - 1914, Sligo
Wife Bridget Finan, 1839 - 1915, Sligo
Also their children

Obrey
J. Leonard, 5/4/1956
See Weldon, William, 7/15/1869, 32

O'Brien
Catherine, 5/21/1891
See Reid, James, 9/1/1867, 2

O'Brien
Eliza, 5/5/1891, Queens
By niece Sarah O'Brien, 9/30/1903
Sarah's brother William O'Brien, 4/4/1914

O'Brien
Elizabeth A., 6/13/1948
See Murphy, Francis X., 8/24/1892, 57

O'Brien
Hugh, 7/7/1863, 31
Thomas, 12/29/1863, 51, Drumlane, Cavan
Ann, 11/7/1886, 62

O'Brien
James, 5/6/1916, Carberry, Cork
Mary C., 8/19/1931, 8

O'Brien
James J., 12/22/1920, 57
Elizabeth, 7/5/1931, 61
Elizabeth C., 12/5/1954
Mary E., 4/13/1955
See Scully, Simon, 5/28/1898

O'Brien
Margaret, 3/11/1905, Limerick
Mary Murphy, 1/16/1937

O'Brien
Maria, 3/17/1918, Clare
By husband John, 3/28/1946, Clare
Mary Corroll O'Brien, wife of John, 3/2/1924, Tipperary
Granddau. Eileen F. O'Brien

O'Brien
Mary, 10/15/1889, 25
By parents:
Ellen, 12/30/1908, 65, Roscarberry, Cork
Patrick, 2/17/1910, 70, Roscarberry, Cork

O'Brien
Michael J., 5/25/1917, 35, Limerick
By wife Catherine, 8/17/1951
Their son James M., 6/24/1905 - 3/14/1924
Joseph M., 3/8/1910 - 8/1/1926
William P., 3/1/1957, 49
Husband of Genevieve M.

O'Brien
Patrick, 1/12/1907, 51, Clare
By wife Catherine, 9/16/1919, 58, Limerick
Nora Ryan McCarthy, 1867 - 1964, Limerick

O'Brien
Patrick, 7/26/1898, 60, Kilteely, Limerick
By wife Mary

O'Brien
Patrick, 1/30/1902, 70, Tipperary
Wife Johanna, 8/3/1900, 68, Limerick
Son John C., 1/1/1905, 37

O'Brien
William, 8/6/1890, 39, Feakle, Clare
By wife Mary

O'Connell
John, 1/1/1909, 28, Carrigeen, Croom, Limerick
Wife Mary O'Connell Messerschmidt, 1878 - 1972
William and Patrick died young

O'Conner
Patrick J., 3/15/1827 - 7/13/1892, Clonmel, Tipperary
By wife Margaret

O'Connor
Eliza, 6/26/1903, 74, Kilbeggan, Westmeath
Niece Eliza O'Connor, 11/3/1928

O'Connor
Francis J., 3/25/1907, 60, Roscommon
His wife Mary, 6/15/1895, 40, Roscommon
James, 2/10/1872, Roscommon
By their cousin Annie, 5/23/1929

O'Connor
James J., 1/9/1876 - 1/18/1902
Wife Helen, 1/25/1878 - 4/10/1912
Their son James J., 3/10/1902 - 8/1/1902
See Coyne, John, 11/13/1895, 56

O'Connor
John, 1885 - 1962
Rebecca K., 1875 - 1962
See Kennelly, Dominick, 1802 - 9/28/1884

O'Connor
John C., 10/14/1882, 56, Rooskey, Roscommon
Peter, 3/20/1883, 54, Rooskey, Roscommon
Hanora, 3/26/1894, 70, Rooskey, Roscommon
By brother Patrick, 4/25/1913
Anne, 2/22/1901, 72

O'Connor
Joseph P., 1875 - 1946
Josephine D., 1875 - 1947
See Dalton, Thomas and Rose
Thomas, 7/1/1914

O'Connor
Pierre M., 1876 - 1956
Mary E., 1880 - 1976
See Bergen, Bridget, 2/4/1894

O'Dea
Michael, 2/28/1868, 37, Mayo
By wife Ellen
Son Thomas H., 4/4/1868
Dau. Mary Jane, 12/24/1870, 12

O'Doherty
Sarah, 3/26/1948, Castlerock, Derry
See Mullen, Bridget

O'Donnell
Edmond, 4/16/1881, Cahir, Tipperary
By wife Alice

O'Donnell
James J., 5/11/1894, Limerick
James McCarthy, 6/24/1896, Castlebar, Mayo
Ann McCarthy, 5/30/1918, Castlebar, Mayo

O'Donnell
John, 2/1/1871, Limerick
By wife Margaret
Dau. Ellen, 6/28/1867

O'Donnell
John, 6/24/1920
Mary, 4/29/1938
See McNamara, Kate, 1/2/1916, 32

O'Donnell
Michael, 12/20/1868 - 5/16/1917 49, Tipperary
By wife Nora and John
John, 12/25/1929, 62
Patrick, 9/25/1953
Nora O'Donnell Beary, 3/7/1965

O'Dwyer
Maria, 8/5/1890, 62, Dublin
By husband Thomas N., 2/27/1900, 76, Dublin

O'Gara
James, 11/15/1878, 73, Claremorris, Mayo
By wife Ann
Grandson Joseph Scully, 5/26/1871, 10

O'Gorman
Mary Stevens, 4/30/1930, 76, Clare
See Eckman, Catherine M., 9/1/1904, 11 months

O'Hara
Wife of James, 4/1872, Sligo
His two sisters Mary and Ann Dennedy
Margaret O'Hara Carey, 9/1/1964
Harry W. Carey, 11/15/1954
Harriett Carey, 2/14/1972

O'Hare
Bridget, 2/18/1878, 80, Monaghan
By Michael, 1/9/1918
His wife Margaret, 4/25/1913
Patrick, 7/1/1877, 12
Patrick, 2/21/1922
Delia, Terance, Lizzie and Sarah died young

O'Hare
Elizabeth, 1/21/1900, 56, Wexford
By husband Patrick

O'Hare
Hugh, 7/2/1906, 65, Armagh
Mary, 2/19/1911, 69, Monaghan
Their children:
Edward T., 5/18/1902, 28
Margaret, Maggie J., Ellen died in infancy
Henry, 2/7/1872 - 10/14/1932

O'Hare
Margaret, 10/29/1903, 54, Dromara, Down

O'Keefe
James, 7/12/1907, 48, Kilkenny
By wife Mary
William B., 2/22/1964
Angela, 5/16/1968

O'Leary
John, 8/19/1910, Kerry
By sister Nora Daly

O'Leary
Michael, 1/25/1869, Wexford

O'Leary
Nora, 1/20/1885, 31, Cork
Maggie, 1/18/1887

O'Mahoney
John, 12/11/1815 - 6/5/1889, City of Cork
Founder and First President of the St. Patrick's Society
of the City of Brooklyn

O'Neil
Ann, 11/15/1914
See Cusack, Thomas, 11/26/1909

O'Neil
Bernard, 1/13/1886, 93, Cavan
By wife Ann
Daughter Margaret, 1/25/1865, 30
Hugh, 1/15/1930, 70

O'Neil
James, 6/9/1887, 54, Londonderry
James Jr., 7/20/1895, 44
By dau. and sister Mary Jane O'Neil

O'Neil
William, 4/30/1891, 56, Ferns, Wexford
By wife Ann

O'Neill
Alice, 8/28/1889, 56, Dungarvan, Waterford
By husband Patrick
Their children: Mary E. and Joseph
Thomas, 2/25/1899, 31
John W., 1/24/1900, 24

O'Neill
Ann, 3/1/1869, 29
See Hughes, James, 3/8/1868, 30

O'Neill
Anne, 3/25/1861, 35-9-21, Killashandra, Cavan
By husband Charles, 3/29/1812 - 2/16/1887

O'Neill
Margaret
Maria
See Byrne, Patrick J., 3/5/1901, 62

O'Neill
Mary see Delahanty, James, ?/29/1878?, Westmeath

O'Riley
Patrick, 3/10/1867, Limerick
Johanna, 11/12/1881, 70, Limerick
By dau. Catherine, 2/18/1905, 51
Margaret, 6/1/1904, 49

O'Reilly
Ellen, Castlecomer, Kilkenny

O'Reilly
Patrick, 6/23/1870, 42, Aughmullen, Monaghan
By wife Jane
Michael, 10/27/1867, 2 months
Margaret, 6/1861, 1 year
James Joseph
Patrick Moran, 11/23/1873, 38

Ormsby
Bridget J., 3/15/1958
See Judge, Francis J., 3/14/1919, 32

O'Rourke
Elizabeth, 12/17/1933, Roscommon
By husband Michael, 1/23/1970
Mary Farrell, 11/8/1859

O'Rourke
Mary, Moville, Donegal
Catherine
William
James
Mother Bridget

Orr
Bridget, 5/23/1893, 45, Ballyrogan, Derry
By husband Allen, 4/29/1901, 57, Cooley, Moville, Donegal
Son Allen J., 4/29/1883, 9 months 4 days

Orr
Daniel, 5/11/1896, 71, Culdaff, Donegal
By wife Margaret
Their children:
William, 10/30/1864, 1 month
Patrick, 11/10/1870, 11
Rosie, 5/16/1872, 1-7-0
Patrick J., 4/16/1956, 54
James D., 4/29/1969, 56

Osborne
Mary E. Reilly, 1906 - 1988
See Shields, Ellen, 6/23/1874, 50

O'Shaughnessy
Fannie, 11/24/1886, 66
See Curtin, John, 6/17/1870, 60

Osterburg
Major Donald F., 4/22/1947
See Meehan, James J., 12/24/1917, 59

O'Sullivan
Mary J.B., 8/28/1905
See Frewen, Mary, 6/17/1904

O'Toole
Patrick, 1/7/1874, Dublin
By wife Mary, 8/20/1898
Katie
Maria A.
Jane Murphy

Ott
Margaret A., wife of Silas A., 1/1/1918, 63
See Martin, Alice, 9/13/1885

Owen
James, 12/7/1901
By wife Margaret, 5/21/1918, City of Cork

Pannone
Philip, 1896 - 1969
See McFadden, John J., 10/27/1928, 76

Parke
Francis, 8/6/1893, 29, Glencar, Leitrim
By sister Annie Parke
His wife Delia, 1893

Parker
Rebecca P.
See Ragan, Owen, 8/3/1869, 42

Parks
Anne Marie, 1914 - 1984
See Hayes, Thomas, 1/9/1900, 60

Parks
Patrick, 4/5/1821 - 12/14/1887, Dundalk, Louth
In the patriotic struggles of his native land he took an active part and being forced into exile in 1848 he found on these shores the freedom for which he conceived a most ardent love.

Parters
Mary Shields, 3/15/1874 - 4/7/1957
See Clay, Charles, 11/27/1889, 92

Perry
Thomas F., 3/17/1915
See Kelly, John, 12/4/1906

Phair
Michael, 11/5/1877, 27, Rahan, Cork

Phelan
Jane, 8/15/1852, 54, Kilkenny
Her son John, 3/31/1870, 30, Kilkenny

Phelan
William, 3/3/1918
See Whalen, Mary, 1/7/1894, 62

Philie
Arthur, 3/7/1911 - 6/27/1959
See McCann, John, 6/8/1906, 46

Philips
Eleanor, 10/9/1932
See Mullery, Edward, 5/26/1897

Phillips
Charles J., 12/10/1925, 23
Charles Sr., 1875 - 1947
Wife Mary A., 1870 - 1959
Bridget McCarthy Kelly, 1855 - 1954, Donegal
Helen Phillips Giger, 1905 -
Son F.X. Giger, 1898 - 1970
Margaret Monnia, 1881 - 1974

Pierce
Bridget, 3/30/1892, 52, Castlejordan, Meath
By husband Patrick R., 9/4/1894, 52, Edenderry, Kings
Dau. Maggie, 7/13/1879, 7-4-0
Joseph P., 7/10/1901, 26

Pitcher
Anastasia Ladley, 1/29/1928
See Ladley, James F., 11/9/1841 - 4/6/1911

Plunkett
John, 9/24/1890, 35, Drumreilly, Leitrim
By wife Maria
Maria Goggin, 10/29/1938, Wife of James Goggin

Potter
Herbert, 6/2/1949
See Reilly, Rose, 3/8/1915

Powers
James, 3/19/1892, 9-4-0
By parents James F., 2/26/1920, 69
Elizabeth C., 11/21/1924, 60
Thomas Haughton, 8/15/1862, 26, Edenderry, Kings
Wife Anne, 9/24/1904, 66
George J. Powers, 1932, 40
Daniel G. Grady, 3/8/1886 - 9/27/1938
Catherine N. Grady, 1897 - 1970

Powers
John H., 6/4/1906, 50, City of Waterford
By wife Mary, City of Waterford

Powers
John J., 9/30/1894, 40, Waterford
By wife Margaret, 8/12/1911, Belfast
Arthur J., 12/16/1960

Powers
Nora, Tipperary
By sisters Alice and Margaret Leahy
John J. Powers, 1/2/1940
Margaret Powers, 10/1/1952

Powers
William, 4/2/1879, 45, Waterford
By wife Bridget

Prescott
Margaret, 10/20/1907, Wexford
See Murphy, James, 2/5/1915

Price
Francis E., 8/3/1948
See Moylan, Ellen, 11/15/1887, 42

Price
John, 7/19/1914, 40, Clifden, Galway
By wife Norah, 1874 - 1959
James McDonald, 1912 - 1976
Nora McDonald, 1914 - 1980

Price
Michael, 5/4/1866, 62, Shellumsrath, Kilkenny
See Downey, Bridget, 4/15/1876, 74

Priest
Simon, 9/30/1930, 55, Newtown, Ballivor, Meath
By wife Mary Stephen Priest 4/7/1944, Dailybridge, Roscommon

Purcel
Ellen, 10/17/1889, 62, Derry
Dau. of Michael and Sarah Cammel
By husband Michael, 12/9/1905, 64, Kings
Son of Thomas and Bridget Purcel

Purcell
John, 3/19/1876, 73/53, Kilkenny
Margaret, 5/4/1883, 65, Queens
John, 12/15/1886, 33
Nellie, 4/22/1895, 18
Lucy, 11/22/1900, 44
William, 2/17/1907, 25
Patrick, 8/25/1916
Ellen Hanigan, 12/5/1920

Purchell
Catherine, Queens
By husband Patrick

Pye
Sadie Agnes, 10/25/1912, 12
Julia, 8/9/1900 - 5/15/1959
William J., 5/7/1890 - 6/3/1961
See Walsh, John, 6/25/1865, 40

Quigley
Ann, Longford

Quin
John, 8/17/1856 ?, 88, Blessington, Wicklow
By wife Ann

Quinn
Anne, 5/1862, Roscommon

Quinn
Bridget, 1/23/1901, 68, Strolar, Tipperary
By sister Norah Quinn

Quinn
Catherine 36?, Longford
By husband John
Roseanne
Edward, 2

Quinn
Edward, 7/8/1906, 50, Clonmore, Kings
By wife Jane, 11/20/1913

Quinn
James, 1/2/1879, 52, Ballymachugh, Cavan
By wife Bridget
Margaret J. Woods, 12/24/1945
C. Doyle, 2/19/1952

Quinn
James, 6/8/1866, Noughaval, Westmeath
John, 8/8/1866, Noughaval, Westmeath
Elizabeth Maguire, 2/1869?, Noughaval, Westmeath
By sister Mary Rock
Margaret Regan 11/26/1901, wife of Partick and dau. of Mary Rock

Quinn
James, 2/8/1915, 48, Drumkeeran, Leitrim
Patrick J., 3/24/1927
Mary, 1874 - 1946

Quinn
Jane, 1873 - 1955
See Halpin, William, 8/1/1878, 68

Quinn
John, 3/15/1883, 64, Kilgefin, Roscommon
By sister Mary, 5/28/1909
John F. Burke, 5/15/1918

Quinn
Mary E. McGrath, 3/11/1913, 43, Clogheen, Tipperary
Robert Quinn, 2/3/1870 - 5/11/1961
Victor C., 4/8/1906 - 9/8/1974

Quirk
Andrew, 1/31/1892, 44, Limerick
Wife Mary, 6/5/1892, 42, Limerick
Edna M. Cronin, 1885 - 1943
John J., 1876 - 1945
Edna A., 1913 - 1984

Quirk
Rosanna M., 1860 - 1948
Sarah B., 1897 - 1949
See Murphy, Sarah, 1/7/1910

Ragan
Owen, 8/31/1869, 42, Sligo
By wife Alice, 6/4/1913, 87
Rebecca P. Parker
James T. Lee
Edna J. Lee
Herome J. Guerrin

Raleigh
Thomas F., 8/4/1903, 30, Limerick
Son of Thomas and Mary Raleigh
William McMahon, 10/12/1920, 55
Husband of Mary Raleigh McMahon

Randolph
Augusta Reilly, 5/10/1977
See Dennington, John, 9/12/1885, 52

Ratigan
Michael, 1/27/1895, 61, Kilcommuck, Longford
By dau. Annie Ratigan
Bridget, 3/29/1912, 74, Kilcommuck, Longford

Rawl
Thomas, 4/16/1882, 67, Templemichael, Longford
Son Thomas F., 6/16/1854 - 10//30/1888
Wife of Thomas Sr., Catherine, 2/11/1916, 84
Elizabeth Courtney, 11/7/1917
John Y. Fletcher, 7/12/1960

Rawl
William, 3/18/1878, Dromard, Longford
By wife Bridget
T.A.B. Society R.C. Church Our Lady of Victory

Rawle
Michael, 3/22/1882, 71, Templemichael, Longford
Bridget, 7/8/1891, 69, Kilcommuck, Longford
Mary E., 2/20/1900

Raymond
Catherine, 10/31/1939
James H., 3/9/1952
See Carney, Elizabeth, 3/14/1939

Reardon
Mary 11/20?/1889
See Dunn, Julia 18??, Roscrea, Tipperary

Recht
Amalie Louise, 4/15/1951
See Hansin, Peter, 7/5/1909, 61

Redican
Laurence, 1908 - 1975
Kevin T., 1938 - 1981
See Ederton, Frank, 7/16/1913, 48

Reed
William, 5/8/1870, 45, Tynan, Armagh
By wife Catherine, 12/30/1888, 68
Son William, 1910

Reehil
Francis E., 3/30/1957
Florence M., 1/7/1965
See Weldon, Hugh, 12/23/1887, 64

Regan
Margaret 11/26/1901
See Quinn, James 6/8/1866, Noughaval, Westmeath

Regan
John S., 10/23/1958
See Fennesey, Daniel, 12/4/1917, 72

Reid
James, 9/1/1867, 2
John T., 11/27/1871, 6
Lizzie A., 12/8/1871, 2-8-0
By parents Thomas F. and Eliza A. of Kiltoghert, Leitrim
Mrs. Catherine O'Brien, 5/21/1891, 20

Reid
Mary dau. of James and Mary, 9/27/1908 - 3/1/1919
Mary, 11/22/1927
James, 6/3/1939
Jennie, 8/30/1941
See Cavanagh, Hugh, 3/11/1877 - 2/17/1921

Reid
Samuel, 11/15/1889, 40, Dublin
Wife Catherine, 2/24/1918, 68, Dublin

Reilly
Annie, 11/9/1954
Patrick, 7/5/1955
See Gill, Michael, 3/20/1899, 42

Reilly
Bridget, 1/24/1914, 76
Husband John, 11/30/1917, 79
See Goggins, Patrick, 4/29/1887, 75

Reilly
Charles, 2/1857, Rathmore, Noughaval, Longford
Dau. Ellen, 4/25/1856

Reilly
James, 8/30/1880, 48, Granard, Longford
Joseph, 4/21/1883, 47

Reilly
Maggie, 27, Nonagh, Tipperary
See Mara, Maria, 6/3/1902, 35

Reilly
Mary, 4/7/1886, 62, Annagh, Cavan
Her dau. Rose A. Brady, 2/28/1870, 19, Annagh, Cavan

Reilly
May, 8/1/1888, 1-6-0
Augusta Dennington, 1/19/1918
Peter F., 5/2/1862 - 1/18/1936
Margaret D., 12/21/1947
Peter F. Jr., 9/15/1960
See Dennington, John, 9/12/1885, 52

Reilly
Michael, 4/20/1864, 25, Carrymore Cross Rd., Cavan
Patrick, 7/22/1879, 43, Carrymore Cross Rd., Cavan
By their sister Bridget R. Harden

Reilly
Patrick, 6/8/1913, Cavan
By wife Mary C., 3/9/1921

Reilly
Peter Francis, 12/19/1882, 56, Meath
By wife Mary Jane

Reilly
Rose, 3/8/1915
By husband Owen, 7/19/1917, 65, Killinkere, Cavan
Herbert Potter, 6/2/1949
Bertha Evans, 3/7/1965, 41

Reinhardt
George, 12/18/1947
See Kilfoyle, Mary, 1/31/1910, 67

Reirdon
John, 3/29/1861 ?, 49, City of Cork
By wife Elizabeth
Dau. Elizabeth, 7/15/1875, 21
Dau. Ellen

Reynolds
Marion E., 1901 - 1968
See Daly, Mary, 2/14/1895, 53

Reynolds
Mary Jane, died young
Patrick, died young
By parents Thomas and Catherine, both of, Westmeath
Catherine, 10/20/1887
John E., 6/18/1903, 30
Thomas, 2/6/1906, 75

Rhatigan
James, Longford
By Bridget Rhatigan

Rhatigan
Patrick, 3/15/1916, Longford
See Cusack, Thomas, 11/26/1909

Rhatigan
Thomas E., 8/11/1943
Martin E., 2/21/1950
See McKie, Thomas, 7/8/1899, 52

Rhawl
Ellen, 4/14/1894, 63
By son Thomas, 7/30/1922, 63, Derryharrow, Longford
James, 9/24/1921, 64

Rice
Owen, 11/22/1886, 69, Dublin
By children

Riley
Mary, 12/28/1911, 96, Bansha, Tipperary
By niece Anne P. Loughman

Ring
Patrick, 11/13/1890, 72, Kilkenny
Julia, 6/14/1907, 88, Kilkenny
Their children: Thomas, Terrance, Annie, Maria, John
Julia died young
Patrick, 4/28/1877, 26
James, 11/18/1880, 24
Mary, 12/24/1893, 28

Riordan
Michael, 6/15/1951
See Ryan, Phoebe, 3/1860 - 9/1897

Riordan
Timothy, 3/31/1909, 40
Eleanor, 4/8/1934
See Downing, Michael, 6/15/1908, 40

Ritter
Mary, grandchild of Mary Fogarty died in infancy 1927
See Fogarty, John Jr., 2/4/1919, 70

Roach
Patrick, 4/14/1894, 40, Limerick
By wife Margaret, 7/21/1911

Roche
John J., 6/23/1948, 56
Anna L., 5/24/1987, 97
See Lyons, Michael, 9/7/1918, 53

Roche
Patrick, 1/9/1894, 42, Castlekevin, Cork
By wife Catherine

Rock
Mary
See Quinn, James, 6/8/1866

Rodney
Claire, 5/11/1940, 63
See Harden, Edward, 5/25/1889, 76

Roe
Claire Indrizzo, 2/18/1976, 46
See Harden, Edward, 5/25/1889

Roe
Mary A., 8/10/1887, 65, Monaghan
Catherine, 8/4/1922, 55
Her husband Michael Roe, 12/23/1930, 70
Michael J., 11/3/1890 - 2/1/1955
Wife Florence, 11/30/1891 - 2/3/1957

Rogan
James, 2/10/1900, 74, Louth
By wife Mary, 6/2/1903

Rogers
Bridget, 4/15/1891, 65
Maria R.J. Anderson, 11/11/1891, 55
Husband Robert J. Anderson, 11/16/1899, 57, Cookstown, Tyrone

Rogers
Daniel, 3/11/1898, Tyrone
By wife Sarah, 3/29/1916
Children: Sarah, Daniel, Annie and Elizabeth
Mary A. Lunny, 6/22/1932

Rogers
Michael J., 7/4/1932, Lisbrack, Longford
By wife Catherine M.
His mother Bridget, 12/13/1903
His sister Mary, 12/5/1902
His brother James, 7/5/1916
His aunt Margaret Guy, 11/2/1927

Rogers
Patrick, 2/28/1881, 53, Tulla, Clare
By sister Sarah, Tulla, Clare

Rogers
Sarah, 8/12/1885, 52, Ballyregget, Kilkenny
By husband Samuel

Rogerson
Robert, Roscommon
Michael J., 12/10/1911
See Logan, Mary, 5/1/1907, 39

Ronnenberg
Catherine, 2/5/1943
See Dougherty, John, 1/9/1910, 50

Roper
Terrence, 8/19/1903, 62, Ballyshannon, Donegal
By wife Catherine, 12/2/1916
Children: Terrence, Mary, James, Catherine who died young

Rossiters
Joseph, 4/1/1915, 71, Wexford
By wife Mary
William Browers died at sea 1880, 42
Joseph F. Browers Co. K 14th N.Y. Vol. 1870 - 1939

Rourke
Thomas, 8/28/1891, 78, Longford
By niece Mary Moran
Her husband Michael, 5/18/1915
Their son John T.

Rouse
Jane, 4/24/1876, 62
See Finnegan, Annie, 5/11/1893, 34

Rouse
Patrick, 4/16/1888, 28, Carn, Sligo
Dau. Ellen, 11/10/1886, 1

Rowan
John J., 7/1/1916, 35, Queens
By brother Dennis, 7/8/1930
Husband of Isabella Rowan

Ruddy
Mary, 2/14/1893, 30, Armagh
By husband Patrick

Russell
Elizabeth, 10/7/1913, 60, Dublin
By husband William, 5/27/1936, 85
Sara, 9/11/1937
James J. Ryan, 3/12/1941
Anna E. Russell, 10/29/1960
Mary M. Ryan, 7/28/1967

Russell
John, 1/7/1907, Six Mile Bridge, Clare
By wife Annie

Ryan
Bridget, 6/26/1886, 43, Bree, Wexford
By Thomas

Ryan
Bridget, 12/24/1917, 82
Her dau. Bridget
Daniel, 9/11/1875, 46
His wife Mary, 8/11/1863, 30
See Walsh, Mary, 12/17/1873

Ryan
Dennis, 9/10/1871, 52, Bartholemew ?, Cork
By wife Mary, 8/5/1895, 65
Elizabeth G., 7/15/1933

Ryan
Edward, 8/2/1869, 48, Kilkenny
By Patrick Hoynes

Ryan
Ellen, 9/17/1871/74, Kilrush, Hospital, Limerick
By husband Michael
Son John, 7/19/1855

Ryan
Frank J., 9/14/1914, 11
Thomas R., 1/13/1945
Catherine M., 7/5/1957
See Mahon, Michael, 2/8/1893, 65

Ryan
Hanora Considine, 9/18/1919, 54, Fedamore, Limerick
By husband John J., 2/21/1933
Infant dau. Katie
Hilda L., 10/12/1900 - 8/8/1961
John A., 4/6/1899 - 9/23/1971

Ryan
Hannorah, 8/4/1858, 34
See Cummings, Mary, 7/16/1861, 65

Ryan
James, 11/1/1908, Pallas, Limerick
Matthew K., 3/3/1911, Pallas, Limerick
John, 3/1/1913, Pallas, Limerick
See Harnett, Lawrence, 8/10/1910, 49

Ryan
James J., 3/12/1941
Mary M., 7/28/1967
See Russell, Elizabeth, 10/7/1913, 60

Ryan
Johanna T., 1/24/1917, Kerry
Michael S., 8/10/1898
John T., 8/4/1919

Ryan
John, 5/3/1891, 87, Nenagh, Tipperary
Wife Johanna Holmes, 8/3/1895, 77, Newcastle, Westmeath

Ryan
John, 1863 - 1933
See White, Mary, 11/27/1897, 57

Ryan
John J., 12/24/1849 - 5/26/1908, Westmeath
By wife Mary E. Quinn
Their dau. Mollie died young
Frank H. Weiteckamp, 8/9/1964
His wife Margaret Ryan Weiteckamp, 9/15/1969

Ryan
Joseph, 10/2/1916, 28
See Hackett, James, 2/2/1917, 70

Ryan
Joseph H., 11/16/1935
Mary E., 5/27/1937
See Sweeney, Miles, 6/22/1884, 60

Ryan
Kathleen Finneran, 1971
See Finneran, Catherine, 6/6/1907, 74

Ryan
Margaret, 11/1/1892, 40, Kileroe, Nenagh, Tipperary
By husband Patrick, 9/11/1915, 72

Ryan
Margaret, 10/13/1902, 72, Dublin
By husband Francis, 9/2/1915, 86, Dublin

Ryan
Margaret, wife of Patrick J., 7/4/1913, 38, Limerick

Ryan
Margaret, 4/7/1918, 46, Tipperary
Dau. Winifred, 1/19/1920, 20

Ryan
Mary, 5/1/1885 78, Thurles, Tipperary
Timothy, 11/13/1890, 77, Thurles, Tipperary
Their nephew Patrick Cassidy, 11/16/1898, 37, Thurles, Tipperary
By dau. and son-in-law of Ryans
Ellen and William Conrahn

Ryan
Michael, 11/1/1918, 35, Cashel, Tipperary
His mother Ellen, 2/4/1930, 95
Thomas J. Butler
Margaret M. Butler
Donald A. Galvin
Francis J. Horn, 1915 - 1981

Ryan
Michael, 10/27/1920, 75
Elizabeth Hopkins Ryan, 9/1/1864, Borrisoleigh, Tipperary
Peter J., 4/24/1883 - 6/16/1905
James, 1/12/1840 - 5/6/1904
William J., 9/15/1872 - 5/5/1894
Thomas F., 12/5/1874 - 1/19/1908
Catherine, 7/30/1924
Elizabeth Ryan Beyrer, 8/25/1916
Margaret Ryan Lynch, 11/10/1843 - 6/15/1918

Ryan
Phoebe, wife of Nicholas 3/1860 - 9/1897, Dublin
Thomas, 7/1867 - 9/1898, Ballylongford, Kerry
Timothy, 9/6/1915, 54, Kilrush, Clare
Nicholas, 6/27/1917 60
Michael Riordan, 6/15/1951
John M. Meagher Sr., 8/12/1953

Ryan
Rose McDonnell, 11/19/1916, 54, Louth
By husband Patrick Ryan
His friend Michael Archibold, 12/15/1919, 64, Dublin

Ryan
Thomas, 1/1/1893, 52, City of Dublin
By wife Sarah, 4/26/1920

Ryder
Patrick, 12/25/1800 - 8/9/1871, Dublin
Patrick Horrigan
James Horrigan
Mary Horrigan

Sagendork
Mary, 10/25/1933, 40
See Cooley, Elizabeth, 6/6/1923

Sampson
Elizabeth Deegan, 4/25/1916
James, 5/30/1937
See Deegan, Michael, 9/21/1911

Samsony
Ellen, 12/9/1952
See Weldon, Hugh, 12/23/1887

Sanger
Emil Joseph, 3/19/1942, 69
See Cooney, William, 10/10/1917, 68

Sanguinetti
Veronica A., 12/3/1894 - 8/13/1960
See Graham, Ann, 11/3/1913

Savage
Catherine, 5/24/1941
Elizabeth M., 4/4/1948
See Heslan, Mary, 6/15/1908

Savage
William, 12/4/1895 58, Noel, Longford
By wife Catherine, 8/8/1913, 70, Longford
Safronia, wife of Patrick Savage, 11/8/1909, New Orleans, La.

Scanlan
Mary Teresa, 12/20/1908, Waterpark, Catleconnell, Limerick
Second dau. of the late Edward and Hanora Scalan
Her uncle James Haley, 4/18/1913, 85
Her aunt Sarah Haley, 11/27/1913, 84

Scanlon
Mary, 3/7/1882, 44, Kerry
By husband Timothy, 6/12/1882, 58
Timothy J., 11/2/1890, 20
Son Lawrence, 2 years-10 days

Scanlon
Timothy, 9/7/1879 50, Bagenalstown, Carlow
By daughter
Her husband Felix J. Miller, 8/26/1888 32-7-0
Her uncle, husband of Margaret Glander, 5/23/1884 50-3-0

Schultz
Mary, 12/31/1885 - 11/2/1964, 79
See McDonough, Margaret, 9/1866, 30

Scott
Bernard, 5/26/1893, 74, Longford
Ellen, 9/20/1875, 55, Longford
By their daus. Katie and Ellen

Scott
William, 1/19/1850, 35, Westmeath
By wife Ellen
Son James, 16
Son Thomas, 4/9/1871, 22

Scott
William, 3/10/1874, 67, Limerick
By son John

Scully
Ann, 11/27/1887, 63, Castlejordan, Meath

Scully
Dennis, 12/10/1882, 69, Edenderry, Kings
By wife Bridget, 1/9/1899, 62, Monaghan
Grandchild Thomas Dowd
Dennis Dowd, 6 months
Owen Boyle, 3/10/1904, 65
Ellen Dowd Coffin, 12/8/1934, 30

Scully
Joseph, 5/26/1871, 10
See O'Gara, James, 11/15/1878

Scully
Mary and Thomas died young
Patrick, 4/21/1917
By father and brother Timothy, 4/22/1935, Tipperary

Scully
Simon, 5/28/1898, 58, Adare, Limerick
By wife Eliza, 3/23/1901, 66
James J. O'Brien, 12/22/1920, 57
Elizabeth O'Brien, 7/5/1931
Elizabeth C. O'Brien, 12/5/1954
Mary E. O'Brien, 4/13/1955

Seery
John, 4/26/1889, 88, Navan, Meath

Seery
John, 4/25/1899, 73, Navan, Meath
His wife Bridget; His son Peter, 31

Seery
Julia, wife of William, 2/19/1897, 34
By her sister Bridget Caulfield
Julia's child Mamie, 4/17/1894, 11 months
Margaret, 12/24/1912, 60, Tobberclaire, Westmeath
William Seery, 2/5/1918, 56
Mary Seery, 1852 - 1937
Thomas, 9/4/1895, 21
Bridget Caulfied, 7/23/1925, 79
Marcella, 1856 - 1939

Seitz
Ellen E., 5/9/1937
See McKie, Thomas, 7/8/1899, 52

Sexton
John, 2/19/1902, 72, Kilrush, Clare
By sister Matilda McNally, 10/14/1903, 48
Wife of Michael McNally

Shanley
John, 5/29/1881, 73, Kiltoghert, Leitrim
By wife Ellen, 10/8/1889, 74

Shanley
Margaret, 3/27/1936
See Dunne, Dennis, 10/4/1887, 64

Shannon
Michael G., 7/27/1859 - 1/16/1912, Galway
By wife Margaret, 1861 - 1946
Mary McMahon, 1890 - 1981

Sharpe
Michael J., 11/17/1906, 30, Roscrea, Tipperary

Shaw
Elizabeth, 10/25/1865, 66, Rathconnell, Westmeath
By son Peter, 6/29/1827 - 11/14/1908 81
His children:
Francis Joseph, 12/25/1864, 3
Mary infant, 1/1869
John Paul, 1/15/1894, 21-11-20
Emily A., 2/14/1828 - 11/19/1908, 80, N.Y. State

Sheehan
Ellen, 6/10/1957
Michael J., 7/18/1961
See Cuff, Peter, 9/2/1883, 56

Sheehan
Geraldine, 1903 - 1974
See Devaney, John J., 7/3/1890, 44

Sheehan
James, 7/24/1872, 62, Bansha, Tipperary
By son Patrick J.

Sheehan
William, 5/22/1889, 59, Limerick
By Margaret
Four children

Sheehy
Rev. Daniel J., 6/23/1850 - 2/4/1895, Banora, Caher, Tipperary
Founder and Pastor St. Ambrose Church

Sheridan
Bridget, 1/14/1892, 72, Aughmullen, Monaghan
By dau. Bridget Sheridan
Sister Mary Sheridan
Anie Squires
Maggie Larking

Sheridan
Celia Haran, 2/5/1901, Crossmolina, Mayo
By sister Maria Maran
Celia's niece Mary Sheridan, 12/18/1902, Crossmolina, Mayo
Mary Sheridan Jr., 3 days

Sheridan
Daniel A., 7/13/1909 - 7/29/1911
William Murphy, 6/16/1919, 79, Bansha, Tipperary
His wife Delia Raymond Murphy 11/16/1923, 72
Henrietta Oliver Murphy, 1/11/1939, 53
Dennis J. Sheridan, 1876 - 1949
Margaret E., 1882 - 1962

Sheridan
Ellen Grifferty, 3/23/1940
See Judge, Francis J., 3/14/1919, 32

Sheridan
Kate, 1891 - 1913, Breaffy, Mayo
Thomas, 1895 - 1900

Sheridan
Mary M., 4/21/1907, 85, Roscommon

Sherlock
Thomas
See Feeney, Ann, 9/19/1862, 48-7-0

Sherlock
William, 9/15/1836 - 11/11/1886, Tipperary
By wife Johanna, 2/12/1912
Stephen, 2/2/1914
Edward H., 1/30/1929, 39
Thomas H., 4/30/1933, 73
Jane C.,, 8/16/1949, 26
Children of Johanna:
Katie, 2-4-0
Francis, 2-7-0
Loretta, 5-3-0
Edward, 8
George W., 5/28/1899, 34

Shields
Catherine, 8/22/1849, 24, Castleblaney, Monaghan
Peter, 8/20/1855, 34

Shields
Catherine, 12/1871, 76, Down
By sons Dennis and Charles
Charles J., 11/2/1898, 59

Shields
Ellen, 6/23/1874, 50
Martin, 9/8/1887, 65, Queens
Nellie, 1/10/1885, 27
Kate McCoy, 1/15/1894, 32
Mary E. Osborne nee O'Reilly, 1906 - 1988

Short
Catherine, 6/12/1894, 75, Grogan, Queens
By husband Edward

Shortell
Julia, wife of Richard, 1/1888, Galway
See Hamilton, James, 1/11/1886, 60

Simmons
James, 3/18/1889, Limerick
By wife Margaret

Simpson
Bridget, 12/22/1874, 56, Ardagh, Longford
By husband Patrick

Six
Walter J., 5/29/1947, 30
Walter A., 1894 - 1952
Margaret A., 1890 - 1981
See Egan, Mary, 1/1/1887, 44

Skelley
Mary, 1863 - 1933
See Judge, Jane, 11/6/1897, 60

Skelly
Catherine, 12/24/1872, 29, Longford
By husband Michael, 1/4/1886, 64
Mary Hardcastle, 4/16/1914, 43
James Hardcastle, 7/22/1953

Skelly
James, 9/25/1897, 51, Cashel, Longford
By wife Margaret
Agnes E., 7/15/1945

Skelly
John, 12/2/1898, 49, Longford
Ellen, 8/15/1924
Children:
William J., 2/14/1881, 2-0-4
Anna M., 2/21/1890, 1-7-21
Ellen E., 5/8/1894, 3-3-8
Noreen, 7/20/1913
James L., 12/18/1938
Noreen C., 4/19/1955
James Joseph, 11/16/1962
Francis L., 3/26/1964
Elizabeth Irene Moan, wife of J.W. Skelly, 12/19/1897, 21

Skelly
Kate, 1/19/1882, 38, Ireland
For their mother by J.J. and Mary M. Skelly
James B., 4/20/1920, 84, Longford

Slattery
Patrick, 6/9/1895, 35, Kilkenny
By wife Annie

Slattery
William A., 1/19/1897, 28
Brothers and sisters:
Ellen, 5
Mary, 5
Dennis, 7
Edward, 3
Agnes, Kate, James, Annie and Theresa died young
By parents James, 4/22/1903, 68, Clare
Mary, 6/17/1928, 83, Clare
Agnes Slattery Madigan, 12/20/1985, 84

Slevin
Jane, 1/3/1910, Kingscourt, Cavan
Resident of Mt. Vernon N.Y.

Sloane
Joseph, 1910 - 1949
See McDavitt, Anne, 1/11/1885, 35

Smith
Catherine, 11/11/1896, 47, Tuam, Galway
By husband James T.

Smith
Edward, 1/28/1874, 25, Cavan
By brother Christopher, 3/1/1897, 42, Cavan

Smith
James, 1873, Cavan; By nephew Bernard Smith

Smith
John, 11/28/1882, 58, Cavan
By wife Jane

Smith
Lucy Dwyer, 1/18/1917
See Dwyer, Mary, 7/22/1886

Smith
Martha J., 1/30/1941, 78
See Cunningham, Hugh, 7/25/1900, 62

Smith
Michael J., 1/3/1882, 48, Longford
Elizabeth, 12/9/1872, 39, Longford
Dau. Maggie

Smith
Peter, 1/17/1870, 45
James, 11/10/1871, Mughna, Monaghan
By sisters Catherine and Mary Smith

Smith
Sarah, 3/18/1888, 54, Cavan
Bernard, 3/21/1891, 80, Cavan
By sister of Sarah, Annie Cowell

Smith
Thomas, 11/20/1877, 73, Doon, Meath
By son Edward J.

Smyth
Thomas, 4/28/1935, 40
See Lawler, William, 8/27/1906, 44

Spellman
Mary, 4/12/1918, 79
Mary, 1/30/1929
See Coffield, Mary A., 4/21/1882, 15-7-0

Spelman
John, 9/4/1887, Cork
His wife Anastasia Ryan, 75, Nicker, Limerick
Hanora McCormack, 3/12/1935
Martin McCormack, 1965

Squires
Annie
See Sheridan, Bridget, 1/14/1892, 72

Stack
John, 11/23/1907, 49, Lisready, Limerick
By wife Norah, 2/13/1913, 43
His mother Mary, 11/27/1915, 85
Thomas Boyle, 12/7/1944, 70
Mary Boyle, 7/18/1946, 75

Stanley
William, 10/2/1871, 43
See Cullen, Patrick, 5/27/1881

Stanton
John, 5/23/1902, 63, Limerick
By wife Catherine, 2/18/1903, Limerick
Michael F. Gibbons, 9/23/1913, Limerick
His wife Josephine, 3/29/1919, 46

Stanton
Patrick, 5/6/1888, 57
Ann, 10/14/1890, 54
See Celsh, John, 5/13/1882

Stanton
Patrick, 2/25/1895, 36
Alice, 12/27/1890, 3
Mary E., 3/5/1918
See Connors, John, 8/27/1897, 36

Stanton
Patrick, 26
See Kenny, William, 2/16/1881, 52

Stern
Margaret
See Freeman, Bernard, 4/16/1888, 60

Stickevers
Mary Maguire, 6/30/1941, 77
Bill Stickevers, 11/22/1941, 2
See Maguire, Rose, 12/16/1891, 60

Stoddard
Thomas Francis, 5/18/1893 - 1/28/1908
By parents:
Richard H., 12/13/1943, Clare
Margaret E. Walsh, 4/4/1954
Grace, 8/22/1907 - 11/11/1908

Stokes
Michael, 9/8/1892, 78, Cappagh, Limerick
By wife Bridget, 5/7/1916, 76
Also children: Martin, Edward, Robert died young

Stroud
James G., 10/26/1962, 69
Alice G., 12/22/1966, 72
See Nelson, Rose, 12/25/1913, 52

Sullivan
Anastasia, 12/8/1885, 53
See Doyle, Michael, 5/6/1893, 58

Sullivan
Ellie Callaghan, 5/3/1902, 30, Inniscarra, Cork
By husband James

Sullivan
Hannah, 7/8/1907, 44, Kerry
Bridget Walsh, wife of Thomas, 1/22/1919

Sullivan
Hanora, 7/1/1905, 65
William, 5/24/1899, 48, City of Cork

Sullivan
James, 2/17/1866, Kenmare, Kerry
Wife Catherine, 3/30/1869, 56
Their dau. Maryanne, wife of J.H. Mullarky, 5/15/1874, 34
George Sullivan husband of Catherine A., 1/16/1886
Catherine A., 1/22/1901, 35
Kate Anastasia dau of Ellen M. and John Treanor 8/10/1861, 17

Sullivan
Maurice, 9/11/1900, 26, Ballyhea, Cork; By brother Michael

Sullivan
Patrick, 7/15/1883, 45, Kerry
Catherine, 7/28/1871, 54, Wexford
By son Patrick S., 3/29/1920, 72
His wife Mary, 5/6/1884, 30

Sullivan
Timothy, 10/1/1866, 55, Ardea, Kerry
By his grandsons William and James Line

Sunny
James H., 6/13/1889, 34-8-0
By parents:
Bernard, 11/28/1897, 80, Coloney, Sligo
Margaret, 2/17/1904, 67, Tullamore, Kings

Suter
Kate, 11/27/1896, 54, Limerick
By husband William, 12/10/1942, Louth

Sweeney
Ann, 8/27/1886, 64, Mallow, Cork
By husband James
Son James Jr., 8/1866, 4 months, Mallow, Cork
Ann's sister Catherine Flynn, 11/16/1861 53, Mallow, Cork
Her dau. Hanora Flynn

Sweeney
Ellen, 1/28/1905, 30
By mother Catherine, 1839 - 7/18/1906, New Ross, Wexford
Mary dau. of Catherine, 8/21/1924
Patrick Deasy, 5/23/1928
Anne Deasy, 2/2/1941

Sweeney
Hugh, 6/10/1869, 40, Kilmacrenan/Kilmagrannon, Donegal
His wife Maryann, 11/23/1868, 38
Their sons:
Hugh, 4/1871, 6
Joseph, 6/5/1885, 26
By James brother of Hugh

Sweeney
James, 3/13/1860, Westmeath
Margaret, 3/29/1908, Westmeath
By son John F.
His brothers and sister: John, Lawrence, Lizzie, Bernard, Thomas,
Joseph, Patrick, Terence
His wife Lizzie, 4/4/1885, 23
Two children:
Mary, 9 months ?
Joseph, 2 days

Sweeney
Michael, 1/5/1902, Kilmaine, Mayo
Edward, 6/24/1928, Kilmaine, Mayo
By their sister Mary, 6/1/1938

Sweeney
Miles, 6/22/1884, 60, Donegal
Wife Mary E., 11/17/1914, 75
Joseph H. Ryan, 11/16/1935
Mary E. Ryan, 5/27/1939

Sweeney
Miles, 9/6/1888, 31, Roscrea, Tipperary
By mother Mary

Sweeney
Patrick, 7/5/1908, 57, Watergrasshill, Cork
By wife Bridget

Sweeney
Rose, 8/21/1907, 90 ?
See Fitzpatrick, Richard

Taaffe
James, 5/2/1888 50, Enniskillen, Fermanagh
Sarah, 6/8/1892 65, Enniskillen, Fermanagh
By their cousin Ellen O'Donnell
Minnie E. Little, 6/8/1940
Husband Francis W. Little, 12/25/1940

Taaffe
John, 1/27/1909, 60, Drougheda, Louth
Wife Catherine A., 11/13/1922, 76

Taiff
James 1867?, Londonderry
Maryann

Tartaglini
Sarah U. Kennelly, 1879 - 1975
See Kennelly, Dominick, 1802 - 9/28/1884

Teevan
James, 8/26/1872, Cavan
By dau. Catherine
Mary, 10/12/1880, Cavan
John, 3/22/1886, Cavan

Thomas
Julia, 10/8/1856, City of Cork

Thompson
Ellen Judge, 5/3/1921, 58, Queens
By husband James, 10/10/1923, 60, Queens
Son Patrick, 11/22/1909, 17
James, 11/13/1903, 1
George, 8/19/1932
Catherine Thompson Nugent, 9/15/1958

Thompson
Mary (Nona), 5/20/1940, 92
See McNulty, John, 12/9/1914, 52

Thompson
Julia A., 8/8/1889, 26, New Abbey, Kildare
Delia, Mary, Patrick died young
Francis J., 1901 - 1977
See Murphy, Patrick, 12/15/1890, 70

Thompson
Thomas, 6/7/1841 - 8/30/1866
Patrick, 9/14/1869, 51, Longford
Michael, 11/12/1885 - 9/16/1856

Thorsen
Nelis C., 1/28/1927, Norway
By wife Elizabeth, Carrickedmond, Longford

Thorton
Mary, 6/30/1907, Kill, Kilmaine, Mayo
Bridget, 1/24/1917, Kill, Kilmaine, Mayo
Patrick F. Donlon, 6/19/1932
Delia, 9/12/1961
John J. M.D., 6/18/1965

Tierney
Anna Tracy, 12/17/1873, 40, Nenagh, Tipperary
Michael Joseph, 7/20/1886, 48, Ennistimon, Clare
By son George Tierney

Tierney
Bridget Kearns, 2/17/1922, Louth
Dau. Mary, 3/8/1942

Tierney
Margaret, 12/3/1893, 67, Kilkenny
By son John

Tierney
Patrick, 4/2/1884, 91, Tipperary
Elizabeth
Dau. Mary died young
By children Kate and John Tierney
John, 1/15/1904, 73

Timm
John, 12/31/1874, 56, Ballymore, Westmeath
By wife Julia

Timony
Patrick J., 8/29/1900, 28, Donegal

Tinker
Kate Lennon, wife of George C. Tinker, 10/17/1887
See Lennon, John, 10/6/1875, 54

Tobin
Joseph, 11/4/1853 - 12/11/1890, Cork
By his shipmates U.S. Navy

Tobin
Peter, 3/11/1905, 46, Ballyduff, Waterford
By wife Kate

Tobin
Philip, 8/6/1860, 46, Tipperary
Arthur, 2/8/1868, 20
John, 3/18/1869, 26
James, 5/10/1886, 42

Toomey
Patrick J., 1860 - 9/27/1914, Rathkeal, Limerick
Ellen, 1956 - 8/6/1898, Cork
Mary, 1874 - 1932, Mungret, Limerick

Tracy
Patrick, 10/14/1845, 37, Fintona, Tyrone
Catherine, 11/20/1878, 70, Fintona, Tyrone
Margaret, 1/18/1901
Thomas, 10/21/1910, 68

Trainor
Mary, 11/15/1896, 30, Moville, Donegal
By husband James, 2/17/1938, Monaghan

Travers
John, 12/20/1902
Margaret, 10/23/1911
See Gilroy, Eliza, 3/12/1876

Travers
Mary, 1/22/1883, 75, Inishmagrath, Leitrim
By son John, 4/15/1901
Katherine, wife of John 9/14/1900
John Jr., 11/14/1927
James L., 1892 - 9/17/1943 V.F.W.

Treacy
James, 5/10/1910, 51, Roscrea, Tipperary
By wife Mary, 5/31/1939, Roscrea, Tipperary
Julia Humbly, 10/25/1942

Trehy
Thomas 3/28/1922, 45, Finnoo, Ballynahill?, Limerick
Michael 1/12/1936
Anna 12/2/1946, 62
Katharine V. 4/15/1950
Ann 12/30/1962

Tucker
Margaret, 4/14/1886 (first wife), Down
John, 7/2/1891, 52, Columbkille, Longford
By Bridget, second wife of John, 2/19/1894

Tults
Matthew, 3/26/1909, 22, Newcastle, Meath
His aunt Catherine Lynch, 2/27/1916
Margaret Forrester, 1884 - 1967

Tunney
John M., 2/11/1897, 49, Bellmullet, Mayo
By wife Elizabeth

Tuohey
Bridget, 2/5/1889, 47, Kilkeedy, Clare
By husband Patrick, 11/26/1890, 52
Robert J.Moley, 9/22/1927, 19
William J., 11/23/1934, 60
Mary C., 12/1/1965, 86
William S., 7/1/1980

Tuohy
Delia, 3/3/1912, 32, Knock, Mayo
By sister Margaret Lally
Nephew John Gerard Tuohy, 15 months

Turnbell
Maryann, 12/23/1904, 68, Cork
By son William
Wife of William, Sarah Ann, 3/3/1930
His sister Margaret Cowley, 6/30/1940

Turner
Mamie, 1873 - 1953
See Judge, Jane, 11/6/1897, 60

Turner
Peter, 12/21/1862, 75, Wexford
Wife Mary Jane, 9/1869, Dublin

Turner
Peter E., 12/5/1908, 29
By wife Katie, 1/14/1919
Her sister Hanora Carmody, 4/20/1904, Kilkee, Clare

Tynan
Lucy M., 7/6/1911, Kells Grange, Kilkenny
Josephine, 8/3/1958
Catherine, 3/21/1971
James Clarke, 11/2/1942
Elizabeth, 7/3/1955
Thomas F., 9/2/1982

Urell
Edward
See Gaynor, Ellen, 1858

Vasaturo
Laura B., 1977 - 1979
See Burns, Andrew, 7/10/1905, 58

Vaughan
Nora O'Neil, 6/28/1913, 29, Mullingar, Westmeath
By husband William, 3/15/1950
Thomas J., 6/1/1908 - 3/4/1971

Vaughn
Thomas, 8/1/1894, Broadford, Limerick
Catherine, 12/13/1904, Broadford, Limerick
Her brother Maurice Murphy, 8/16/1890, Glanahin ?, Limerick
His wife Ellen, 3/9/1890, Glanahin ?, Limerick
Katherine R. Vaughn, 4/14/1945
Richard Vaughn, 2/16/1955

Vesey
Catherine, 5/12/1881, 50, Rathcline, Longford
By sister Ann Vesey

Vesey
Vesey family; See Elliott, Patrick, 11/27/1878, 40

Victory
Catherine Dunne, 4/29/1892
See Dunne, Michael, 12/14/1869, 64

Volgarino
Rose, 1899 - 1963
Arthur, 1888 - 1979
See Judge, Jane, 11/6/1897, 60

Wade
Catherine, dau. of James and Ellen Wade, 3/21/1871; 15-4-0
See Hennessey, Mary, 9/5/1884 58

Wade
Patrick, 5/1/1895, Tipperary
By wife Margaret, 2/21/1912, 67
His children: Charles and John died young
Michael J., 1874 - 1952
Elizabeth M., 1880 - 1967

Waldron
Mary, 7/22/1887, 49, Mayo
Dau. of Michael and Mary
Catherine Curley, 9/21/1896, 61
Richard J. Murray, 1899 - 1963

Walker
Michael, 10/2/1861, Skehana, Castlecomer, Kilkenny
James, 10/5/1880, Skehana, Castlecomer, Kilkenny
Henry, 12/8/1898

Wall
David J., 8/15/1906, Kilmallock, Limerick
By wife Mary
Their son James, 4/27/1906, 1-8-0

Wall
Fredrick A., 12/6/1910 - 11/14/1988
See McCabe, Peter

Wallace
Margaret, 3/20/1895, 30, Leck, Donegal
By husband John

Walsh
Ann, 3/10/1869, 97, Clonbroney, Longford
Son Francis, 1/24/1881, 58
His wife Catherine, 12/15/1882, 54

Walsh
Annie F. Cowen, 1/24/1873, 24
Dau. of Richard and Mary Cowen
and wife of Andrew, 7/9/1890, 50, City of Cork

Walsh
Bridget, 1/22/1919
See Sullivan, Hannah, 7/8/1907, 44

Walsh
Francis, 10/21/1853, 55, Rathcline, Longford
Maria, 8/2/1877, 70, Rathcline, Longford
By son James

Walsh
Genevieve, 2/10/1895 - 11/9/1940
James J., 11/11/1889 - 1/23/1954
See Gillen, Michael J., 7/31/1908 3

Walsh
John, 6/25/1865, 40, Wexford
Wife Mary Agnes Sutton, 12/19/1901, 70, Wexford
Sadie Agnes Pye, 10/25/1912, 12
Julia Pye, 8/9/1900 - 5/15/1959
William J. Pye, 5/7/1890 - 6/3/1961
Henry J. McGrath, 1904 - 1958

Walsh
Margaret, 4/4/1846 - 12/1/1909, Dunboyne, Meath
Marion P., 8/31/1880 - 8/3/1945
James E., 1906 - 1970
See Mahon, Patrick Joseph, 7/22/1901, 22-2-0

Walsh
Mary, 12/17/1873, Drumsally, Limerick
By dau. Bridget Ryan, 12/24/1917, 82
Also her dau. Bridget Ryan, No date
Daniel, 9/11/1875, 46
His wife Mary, 8/11/1863, 30

Walsh
Mary, 8/13/1906
Dau. Margaret, 7/20/1907
James, 7/31/1920, Wexford

Walsh
Mary E. McGowan, 3/8/1868 - 9/25/1910, Mayo
Mary A. McGowan, 2/26/1948
Anthony F. McGowan, 11/15/1951

Walsh
Michael, Gohilly/Gubilyn, Kilkenny
By wife Catherine

Walsh
Michael, 4/7/1877, Golmoy, Kilkenny
By his wife Catherine

Ward
Ann, 5/27/1897, 82, Longford
By brother John Martin

Ward
Ann, 4/29/1905, 55, Cork
By husband John, 7/26/1921, Cork
Son Richard, 4/10/1887, 19

Ward
Bernard, 12/15/1872, 73, Ballymore, Westmeath
Dau. Annie, 2/6/1868, 25

Ward
Helen F., 7/30/1961
James J., 10/31/1964
See Joyce, Patrick, 11/6/1904, 65

Ward
Mary, 10/21/1879, Longford
Children: John, Ann, James, Katie, Thomas Jr.

Ward
Mary, 4/20/1901
See Feeney, Joseph P., 11/30/1910

Ward
Michael, 70, Longford
Patrick
Ellen Wiliam, 8/1878

Ward
Mary, 6/16/1943
See McNamara, Patrick J., 1/24/1889, 55

Ward
Patrick, Clonduff, Down

Ward
Patrick, Derry

Ward
Patrick, 8/1855, 60, Forgney, Longford
Mary, 2/1870, 70, Forgney, Longford
By daus. Mary and Margaret

Ward
Peter, 1/17/1886, 78, Longford
Marcella, 8/14/1873, 51, Longford
Peter Jr., 7/29/1866, Longford
By dau. Catherine E. Ward Campbell
Her sister Teresa A. Ward, 3/3/1875, born Brooklyn
Thomas Francis Campbell, husband of Catherine E.,
4/11/1918, 74, son of the late Robert and Margaret
Campbell, Fermamagh

Ward
Thomas, 4/6/1889, 62, Carrickmacross, Monaghan
Mary, 8/24/1885, 65, Carrickmacross, Monaghan

Ward
Thomas, 8/2/1874 - 3/21/1914, Westmeath
Patrick, 3/22/1942
Catherine, 11/24/1956
Frank S. Houston, 10/28/1973

Ward
William, 9/30/1904, 65, Longford
By wife Mary, 5/25/1917, 65, Kilkenny
Son Willie
Dau. Mary Martin, 11/9/1948, 84

Watson
John Joseph, 1/31/1909, Dublin
Elizabeth, 6/17/1908, Dublin
Christ'na E. 12/25/1894 - 12/3/1909

Watson
Ma.y, 9/12/1929, 42
Husband Foster B.
See Costello, Bernard P., 12/14/1908, 51

Watt
Robert, 1885 - 1935
See Coffey, Patrick, 3/4/1909

Watters
Peter, 3/18/1888, 35, Castleblaney, Monaghan
Wife Mary, 4/2/1891, 29, Kanturk, Cork
See Burke, Deborah, 7/29/1885, 56

Weadock
Margaret, 10/29/1858, 68, Wexford

Weaver
Fred, 1888 - 1969
Eulalie, 1899 - 1976
See Dwyer, Mary, 7/22/1886

Weltekamp
Frank H., 8/9/1964
His wife Margaret Ryan, 9/15/1969
See Ryan, John J., 5/16/1908

Weldon
Hugh, 12/23/1887, 64, Antrim
Wife Abagail, 12/13/1896, 70
Abbie C., 3/7/1925, 66
Ellen Samsony, 12/9/1952
John J. Cunnion, 1/9/1879, 34
Anna Cunnion, 5/13/1925
Francis E. Reehil, 3/30/1957
Florence M. Reehil, 1/7/1965

Weldon
William, 7/15/1869, 32, Clones, Monaghan
By wife Bridget, 12/17/1899
J. Leonard Obrey, 5/4/1956

Whalen
Ellen, Clogheen, Tipperary

Whalen
Kate, 6/3/1907
Martin, 6/26/1909
See Mulligan, John, 12/17/1899

Whalen
Mary, wife of Patrick, 3/6/1889, 48, Killan, Wexford
By her sister Catherine Cavanagh

Whalen
Mary, 1/7/1894, 62, Ballyragget, Kilkenny
By sister Margaret, 11/30/1912, 88
William Phelan, 3/3/1918

Wheeler
Thomas, 1822 - 1874, 52, Meath
By wife Ann, 1/27/1893, 67, Edenderry, Kings

White
Alice Barry, 5/6/1914, Wexford
By husband John C., 3/23/1918, 47, Wexford

White
James, 6/13/1881
See Lavin, Patrick J., 8/2/1913

White
Mary, 11/27/1897, 57, Drummore, Waterford
By husband William, 3/18/1918, Youghal, Cork
John Ryan, 1863 - 1933

White
Mary E., 1863 - 1920, Longford

White
Patrick, 12/25/1857, 28, Portarlington, Queens
By wife Sarah
Their son Edward Patrick White, 2/28/1867, 13

Whitehead
Walter E. V.F.W., 5/30/1895 - 3/10/1936
Susan, 8/23/1969
See Flynn, Catherine, 2/28/1907, 47

Wilholt
Mary Quirk, 1892 - 1944
See Murphy, Sarah, 1/7/1910

Williams
Catherine Curran, 11/24/1927, 28
See Gill, Bridget, 11/19/1895, 65

Williams
Ellen, 8/1878
See Ward, Michael, 70

Williams
Maria, 9/9/1887, 35, Leitrim
By husband Thomas
His father Daniel Williams, 1/17/1890, 75, Westmeath

Winblade
Hannah Lyons, 3/12/1928, 47
See Lyons, Mary, 12/23/1911

Winters
Catherine, 12/11/1884, 45, Monaghan
John, 2/8/1894, 35, Monaghan
By sister Ellen, Monaghan

Wisely
Grace, 10/23/1882
See McCormick, Bridget, 2/10/1892, 58

Wolf
Nicholas, 2/21/1903, 38
See Jones, Katie, 4/30/1891, 23

Wolfe
Anthony, 22, Glounagh, Galway
John, 26, Glounagh, Galway
By sister Nora Wolfe

Woodlock
Elizabeth Keating, 12/11/1914, Cahir, Tipperary
Anne Dillon Mitchell, 12/8/1924

Woods
Margaret J., 12/24/1945
See Quinn, James, 1/2/1879, 52

Wright
John, 1939
James, 1962
Alice, 1966
See Hurley, Hanora, 10/10/1881, 58

Wright
Mary, 8/8/1880, 5-0-26
Hanorah, 7/19/1882, 1-2-19
Michael John, 9/10/1890, 0-6-4
Charles H., Jr., 7/14/1899, 27
Mary A., 12/28/1899, 47
Charles H. Sr., 2/19/1903, 60
Annie F., 10/7/1895, 19
See Murray, Ann, 8/29/1880, 66

Wrinn
Jeremiah, 2/14/1900, 24, Kerry
By members of L.I. State Hospital

Wylie
Mary F., 6/8/1870 - 10/28/1958
See Howley, Richard, 3/7/1885, 75

Wynne
Bernard D., 4/29/1901, 57, Roscommon
By wife Ellen, 7/18/1905, 55
Son John H., 4/9/1899, 23
Her sister Maria Kelly, 11/7/1903, 52
Helen M. Wynne, 9/14/1930
Joseph L. Wynne, 3/28/1932

York
Ann, 11/2/1894, 68, Carrickedmond, Longford
John J., 11/11/1899

Zwick
Marie C., 1923 - 1980
See Carroll, Annie, 2/7/1916

COUNTIES OF IRELAND

Number of Appearances on Tombstones

The Counties of Ireland and the number of times they appeared on tombstones at Holy Cross.

COUNTY	Number	Percentage
Longford	256	12.2
Donegal	147	7.0
Tipperary	141	6.73
Westmeath	139	6.64
Cork	122	5.8
Roscommon	112	5.3
Limerick	98	4.6
Clare	88	4.2
Cavan	79	3.7
Mayo	73	3.4
Galway	70	3.3
Leitrim	70	3.3
Monaghan	63	3.0
Wexford	59	2.82
Kilkenny	58	2.77
Dublin	56	2.67
Kings/Offaly	51	2.4
Meath	49	2.3
Waterford	42	2.0
Kerry	39	1.8
Tyrone	39	1.8
Sligo	36	1.72
Queens/Leix	30	1.4
Kildare	27	1.29
Derry	25	1.19
Louth	22	1.05
Antrim	21	1.0
Fermanagh	21	1.0
Down	20	.95
Armagh	19	.90
Wicklow	10	.4
Carlow	8	.3
Total	2,091	

Please note that the total of 2,091 is greater than the number of counties associated with surnames in this book. Because some stones were illegible many surnames were not copied. However in some cases the place of origin in Ireland was legible. In those instances the counties were added for statistical purposes.

Also note that either all or part of 1,492 tombstone inscriptions were copied which included 5,363 names.

Cemetery of the Holy Cross.

One Grave.

This is to Certify, That _Edward Gallagher_ is the Proprietor of the right of Burial in that certain Lot, known as No. _198_, Range, _A, Diamond_ Square, Part 3rd, on a certain Map entitled

"CEMETERY OF THE HOLY CROSS."

Surveyed September 15th, 1888, by SAMUEL H. McELROY, City Surveyor, subject to the rules and regulations to be made by the Right Reverend Bishop of Brooklyn, relating to said Cemetery:

PROVIDED that nothing herein contained shall be construed to grant any other right or privilege whatever than the right of burial therein; and provided further, that the said right shall not extend to the burial of any deceased person who shall have departed this life not in communion with the Catholic Church

Dated Brooklyn, _27_ day of _July_ 188_9_

John Loughlin

Cemetery of the Holy Cross

✝

Full Aug 6 - 1913

One Grave

This is to Certify, That _____
is the Proprietor of the right of Burial in that certain Lot, known as **No.** _____
Section _St Albans Sq_ on a certain Map, entitled

"CEMETERY OF THE HOLY CROSS"

Surveyed August 10th, 1869, by GEORGE ANSTICE, City Surveyor, subject to the rules and regulations to be made by the Right Reverend Bishop of Brooklyn, relating to said Cemetery.

Provided that nothing herein contained shall be construed to grant any other right or privilege whatever than the right of burial therein; and provided further, that the said right shall not extend to the burial of any deceased person who shall have departed this life not in communion with the Catholic Church.

Dated, **Brooklyn,** ___ day of _March_ 1905.

C. E. McDonnell

Jno. J. Barrett

HOLY CROSS CEMETERY

Holy Cross Cemetery is located in Flatbush, Brooklyn. The Cemetery embraces 100 acres and the remains of more than 500,000 are interred there. Holy Cross is under the jurisdiction of the Roman Catholic Diocese of Brooklyn. I became interested in Holy Cross more than ten years ago, when I began tracing my Family tree, I discovered a number of ancestors there,

In June 1991, I conducted a tour of Holy Cross as a member of The New York Irish History Roundtable. My research, while preparing for the tour, uncovered for me a wealth of history I had not known. The history I write of is not just of the 100 acres of land. It is the history of every one of the more than one-half million people interred there. Each of those 500,000 plus has a history of their own. They may have been rich or poor. They may have once stood at the top of the social ladder or they may have been at the lowest rung of that ladder. Their span of life may have been several hours or nearly a century. No matter what their previous conditions, they now rest side by side in Holy Cross. Diamond Jim Brady may be buried just a few feet from an immigrant laborer who never had a stone marking his grave. At Holy Cross, it seems, that the peacefulness of the consecrated grounds embraces all, their previous status being totally irrelevant. Brooklyn and its people have never been humble. However, as you walk up and down row after row of graves you will not see the ostentatiousness you will see in other local cemeteries. As you walk towards the center of the cemetery, you get the feeling that you are not in the City any longer. It is the feeling of the quiet of a small town at the beginning of the day. The fact is that when Holy Cross opened its gates in 1849 it was in a small town. The town of Flatbush, Kings County, New York.

By the middle of the 19th Century, the population of the City of Brooklyn was growing rapidly. This growth was due in large part to heavy immigration. In the mid 1840's hundreds of thousands of Irish-Catholics were fleeing Ireland. This was caused by mass starvation during the potato famine. For many, America was their last hope.

Brooklyn was not part of New York City until the consolidation of 1898. Before that, Brooklyn was a City within Kings County. Besides the City of Brooklyn, the towns of New Utrecht, New Lots, Flatbush, Flatlands and Gravesend made up the remainder of the County of Kings. In the mid 1850's the City of Williamsburg and the town of Bushwick became part of the City of Brooklyn.

The 1840 census showed the City of Brooklyn with about 36,000 people. By 1850 the number had grown to over 96,000. The population of Brooklyn in 1860 was 266,000. Of that number, 104,000 were foreign born, of the foreign born over 56,000 were natives of Ireland. That is slightly less than fifty percent. It is fair to assume that the vast amount of the Irish born were Roman Catholics.

Poor, uneducated and with little or no training in any trade or profession. the Irish crowded into neighborhoods along the waterfront and the Navy Yard. They turned certain wards into Irish enclaves. By 1860, the leader of the Kings County Regular Democratic General Committee was Hugh McLaughlin, the son of immigrants from Donegal. By 1870, one-third of the aldermen of the City of Brooklyn were Irish-Catholics, e.g. William Dwyer (2nd Ward), John Clancy (5th Ward), James Dunne (6th Ward), James Boland (8th Ward), John McGroarty (9th Ward), Michael Coffey (12th Ward) and Francis Nolan (14th Ward).

With the large numbers of people crowding into the above mentioned areas, many problems arose in connection with employment, education, housing and health care. These problems concerned this life. But what about the next life? What happens when someone wants to be buried according to the traditions of his or her faith? The civil authorities were not concerned. The church took action. The original burial ground for Roman Catholics in Brooklyn was the yard at St. James Church on Jay Street. The parish was founded in 1822. Today it is know as St. James Cathedral-Basilica. By the 1840's space was running out at the St. James' grave yard. The Diocese of Brooklyn was not created until 1853. Until that time, Brooklyn and all the areas east to the tip of Montauk Point were part of the Archdiocese of New York. Father James McDonough, Pastor of St. James was asked by the Archdiocese to find a suitable final resting place for Roman Catholics in Brooklyn.

The land which composes Holy Cross has a history of its own. The 100 acres which make up the cemetery were not bought all at once, but in stages. The land was once part of the Old Joost Van Brunt farm. Mr. Van Brunt sold the farm to Hendrick Suydam in 1772, who passed it on to his son Cornelius. Several acres were sold to Dr. Adrian Vanderveer. A group of speculators bought a number of acres and planned a village within the town of Flatbush. The financial crisis of 1837 put an end to that plan. A gentleman named John Gill took over the land from the speculators. During the 1840's a Brooklyn coffee and spice merchant, James Duffey, paid Mr. Gill $2,700 for land where he intended to build a mansion and a spice-mill. Mr. Duffey changed his mind and sold the land to Father McDonough. The purchase was made in June 1849 and consisted of seventeen acres three rods. Another acre was bought from a Samuel Young for $500.00. Mr. Young's house had burned and he did not want to rebuild it. Dr. Vanderveer would not sell his land to the Church. After his death his heirs sold the property to the Church. Nineteen acres three rods were purchased for $500 per acre. In 1869, another twenty-two acres were bought from Leffert Cornell for $18,000. Before the turn of the century, the final boundaries of Holy Cross cemetery would be established.

The Town of Flatbush was settled by Dutch farmers in the 17th century. In 1849, the descendants of those Dutch settlers were still in control of the town government and in many other aspects of daily life. Many Americans who were descended from earlier European immigrants were not happy with the large influx of Irish- Catholics. There were people in Flatbush who agreed with their fellow Americans. The first burial at Holy Cross took place July 12, 1849. The funeral did not go off smoothly. The deceased was Michael Moran, a cholera victim from Flatbush. Fuelled by references made by some Protestant ministers as to "countless hordes of semi-barbarous immigrants", several Flatbush farmers stood across the road with weapons attempting to prevent the burial. The farmers finally moved and Mr. Moran was laid to rest in peace.

Michael Moran's death from cholera was not unusual at that time. Cholera epidemics or "The Cholera" as it was also known visited Brooklyn many times. In one week prior to 1883, Holy Cross had 278 burials. Cholera being the cause of death for a large portion of the deceased.

In 1855, John Loughlin, first Bishop of the Diocese of Brooklyn, dedicated the chapel which is still used. In 1926, a large scale renovation took place under the leadership of Bishop Thomas Molloy. The task was directed by the Rt. Rev. Msgr. John N. Gorman with Msgr. Edward J. Mullaney assisting.

Because burial space was running out, the Cloisters, a building for above ground burials was built. The building was completed sixty years ago in 1932. For the past three decades Monsignor George A. Mooney has been the director of Cemeteries of the Diocese of Brooklyn. Despite urban decline and the effect it has had on cemeteries, Holy Cross remains a well kept and serene final resting place.

(This is an abridged version of the history of Holy Cross Cemetery authored by Joseph M. Silinonte which originally appeared in Vol. 6, 1991-92 of the Journal of the New York Irish History Roundtable.)

THE BROOKLYN DAILY EAGLE

FIGHT AT EDGE OF GRAVE

The solemnity that usually attaches to an interment was disturbed late yesterday afternoon by a free-for-all fight between Italians and Polaks at the very edge of a grave in Holy Cross Cemetery. It was caused indirectly by the big storm which broke suddenly just as the body was lowered into the earth. Tony Elonzella of 8647 Twelfth avenue was burying a relative, and a large crowd attended the funeral. When the coffin had been placed in the grave Elonzella expressed a desire to throw in the first spadeful of earth. The rain was beginning, and the gravediggers objected, saying they had no time for elaborate ceremonials. A general riot resulted. The police came and bundled many of the participants off to the station, where it was claimed that Stanislaus Maronsky, 26 years old, of 653 Sackman street, had struck Elonzella with a shovel, and, that Joseph Audla, 23 years old, of 653 Sackman street, had struck Andrew Frank in the abdomen with a shovel. Audla had a stab wound in the left side and he was taken to the Kings County Hospital. He identified Frank as the man who stabbed him.

On charges of disorderly conduct the following were jailed: Michael Meo, 20 years old, of 167 Prospect street; Joseph Lopinski, 28 years old, of 314 Blake avenue; John Poroski, 23 years old, of 182 Osbzorn street, and Tony Elonzela.

Ambulance Surgeon Sage had to use yards and yards of sticking plaster in fixing up Meo, Lopinski and Elonzella, who were badly cut up.

The whole affair will be thrashed out in the Flatbush court this afternoon.

WILLS FILED TODAY.

MINNA BERGHAUSER, who died June 18, in her will dated June 5, 1912, cuts off her son, George, and her daughter, Minnie, with $5 each, and leaves the residue of her

www.ingramcontent.com/pod-product-compliance
Lightning Source LLC
Chambersburg PA
CBHW081257170426
43198CB00017B/2822